Pedagogy of Place

Studies in the
Postmodern Theory of Education

Joe L. Kincheloe and Shirley R. Steinberg
General Editors

Vol. 263

PETER LANG
New York • Washington, D.C./Baltimore • Bern
Frankfurt am Main • Berlin • Brussels • Vienna • Oxford

Pedagogy of Place

Seeing Space as Cultural Education

EDITED BY

David M. Callejo Pérez, Stephen M. Fain,
and Judith J. Slater

WITH A FOREWORD BY

William H. Schubert

PETER LANG
New York • Washington, D.C./Baltimore • Bern
Frankfurt am Main • Berlin • Brussels • Vienna • Oxford

Library of Congress Cataloging-in-Publication Data

Pedagogy of place: seeing space as cultural education /
edited by David M. Callejo Pérez, Stephen M. Fain, Judith J. Slater.
with a foreword by William H. Schubert.
p. cm. — (Counterpoints: studies in the postmodern theory of education; vol. 263)
Includes bibliographical references.
1. Educational sociology. 2. Geography—Philosophy.
3. Aesthetics—Philosophy. 4. Postmodernism and education.
I. Callejo Pérez, David M. II. Slater, Judith J. III. Fain, Stephen M.
IV. Counterpoints (New York, N.Y.); v. 263.
LC189.P39   370.11'5—dc21   2003011173
ISBN 0-8204-6910-6
ISSN 1058-1634

Bibliographic information published by **Die Deutsche Bibliothek**.
Die Deutsche Bibliothek lists this publication in the "Deutsche
Nationalbibliografie"; detailed bibliographic data is available
on the Internet at http://dnb.ddb.de/.

Cover design by Lisa Barfield

The paper in this book meets the guidelines for permanence and durability
of the Committee on Production Guidelines for Book Longevity
of the Council of Library Resources.

Printed in the United States of America

To the Readers

Contents

Contents

Foreword

Reflections on the Place of Curriculum

William H. Schubert

Pedagogy of Place magnifies the idea of *place* as a significant contributor to education, especially to curriculum and teaching. The editors and authors rightly focus criteria for good educational experience on the release and nurturance of potential and spirit in human beings. They help direct the attention of educators toward realizing such experience in schools. The book prompts inquiry into how such educational experience can be realized in non-school settings, as well. I want to elaborate how this book has caused me to reflect more deeply on these matters, urging readers to do the same for themselves.[1]

Reading the manuscript for *Pedagogy of Place* stimulated considerable reflection on my life in education, on my career in the curriculum field, on the *places* and *spaces* that have contributed to my life in curriculum. I see this book as a significant part of the expansion of curriculum studies[2]; thus, I want to couch my comments around literature of the curriculum field. A lot of ideas were initiated at association *places*, large and small.[3] Returning to these places over the years has been like attending class reunions, places to share memories and aspirations, places of pedagogy. It is curious to note that my colleagues in the field are individuals I confidently tell my doctoral students that I know well (I often hear myself say, "Why, yes, I've known _____ for twenty years!"). Yet, the time I have actually spent with most of these valued colleagues over many years would only total a few hours each. Nevertheless, I feel that I know them well. Why? From other *places*: pondering their books and articles, listening to them present at conferences, exchanging correspondence (letters, phone calls, and e-mails), and even listening to tapes of their presentations while driving in the car (and it really does keep me alert, rather than putting me to sleep at the wheel, as some have warned). With a few colleagues, I have engaged in projects (books or articles), wherein we came to communicate more fully, and occasionally visited one another. All of these connecting points continue to be valued pedagogical *places* for me. They are places of *transaction* as John Dewey and Arthur Bentley (1949) and Louise Rosenblatt (1978) have so admirably taught. It is, indeed, a worthy contribution to link ideas and places of origin. A whole study of place could be focused on the array of organizations attended by curriculum scholars. Such a study might examine how the curriculum field emerged from the broad scope of interests in educational foundations (history, philosophy, sociology, anthropology, and politics of education), became rather narrowly focused on the development and design of school curriculum for several decades, and during the past two or three decades has moved to concerns of larger political, cultural, philosophical, and historical matters—in a sense regaining its origins.

This potential sociology of curriculum scholars, however, only partially speaks to the contribution that *Pedagogy of Place* makes in the curriculum field. The authors insightfully show us that we need to move beyond places in which we live out our scholarly lives to reflect more fully on *places* that our scholarly ponderings influence and should influence. In Deweyan fashion we must address the consequences of our pondering. Why do we write, present, discuss, debate, deliberate, and teach doctoral students about curriculum? Why have we created a curriculum field? Why, who, and how does this field serve? As I studied this manuscript, I saw the emergence of a new countenance for curriculum studies. It helped me shape already emerging responses to these and related questions. More than anything it causes me to wonder about the *places* of curriculum studies. What are the places in which we ponder? What are the practices that our pondering informs—and I reiterate, perhaps more importantly, should inform? In a mere Foreword one cannot do justice to such questions; however, I want to respond to what the editors/authors say they hope to "inspire." In the last paragraph of their Introduction, they state, "The essays that comprise this text are intended to encourage new ways of thinking about the work of teachers and curriculum makers." And in the last sentence of the Epilogue, they again invite readers thusly: "[T]he purpose of this collection is to open conversations with persons interested in curriculum making and teaching and learning, which includes the issue of working at the act of creating the spaces and places which release human potential and nurture the human spirit."[4]

My own response to this wonderful call is both depressing and uplifting. It depresses me because it hurts to bring into question a big part of the very *raison d'etre* of curriculum studies. Namely, we want to influence schools. I have actively consulted with many schools for 30 years, and was an elementary school teacher before that. My father was a long-time school administrator and my mother was a high school teacher; my grandmother and two great aunts were teachers in rural elementary schools. My wife, Ann, was a teacher in the Chicago Public Schools and later a teacher educator. For me, family discussions often revolved around schooling, and these family members were wonderful, dedicated educators, often recognized for the good that they did through teaching. Sometimes, the good that they did as *educators* outside of schools was more powerful than what they could do within them due, perhaps, to the limits of organizational context. My worry, then, is whether schools should continue to be the main *places* of focus for the work of curriculum scholars.

Since watching a PBS special in 1979, I am still haunted by a question raised by physicist Gerald O'Neill of Princeton, which is said to have shocked theorists in his realm of inquiry. He challenged them to consider, "In the long run is a planetary surface, any planetary surface, really the right place for an expanding technological civilization?"[5] His challenge was to raise the possibility of smaller, human-constructed environments as more effective than large, unwieldy planets. This line of questioning made me raise an educational question that I am convinced must be addressed. Namely, are schools the right place, even a good place, to *release human potential and nurture the human spirit?*[6] I think the small schools movement (see Ayers, Klonsky, & Lyon, 2000; Meier, 1995) moves toward this goal. Simultaneously, I think we need to entertain the idea of non-school places for educational experiences to occur. Small, reformed, or democratic schools (e.g., Apple & Beane, 1995) are admirable places to ask *the what's worthwhile question*; yet, why are such places so rare? While this book makes me want to strive for *schools* that release potential, nurture spirit, and more, it also makes me want to seek other places where this can happen.

I think the expansion of the curriculum field in recent decades points in both of these directions. Proponents of both directions ask what I have found to be a constant theme that I have found behind the diversity of characters and events that constitute the curriculum field; namely, a simple yet profound asking of what is worth experiencing, knowing, being, doing, becoming, needing, sharing, overcoming, and contributing (see Schubert et al., 2002). More critical and postmodern than Herbert Spencer (1861), I do not argue that we should ask for a definitive answer about *the* knowledge that is most worthwhile. Instead, we must keep alive multiple narratives, continuously reconstructing them to fit different situations. When Michael Apple (1979/90) offered a new question (Whose knowledge, and who benefits?), he offered a clear alternative to the Spencerian end product (*the* most worthwhile) and his question enriches the question I raised above. So, from this book I am compelled to wonder more strongly about what constitutes *places* (in or out of school) that will be worthwhile by releasing potential and nurturing human spirit.

The big mistake that I see in the establishment of standards, definitive goals, tests for those goal, and standardized tests is assumption that the search can be concluded. Dewey warned about this throughout many of his works. In fact, the contemporary curriculum field can be seen to have begun with Dewey. Yet, his central ideas and ideals are too often crushed and distorted to fit an autocratic governance and corporate ethos of schools. I worry that school has become a place that crushes and distorts the progressive. Clearly, one kind of contribution should be to reconstruct the place of school itself to make it more progressive and democratic; however, another purpose should be to look elsewhere for fertile educational ground. As a curriculum scholar, should I not be more concerned about releasing human potential and nurturing the human spirit wherever it can be done, than I am with the perpetuation of the schooling institution for its own sake? In some of my more depressed moments I worry that we (education professors) advocate schools as seedbeds of democracy only because colleges of education (homes of our salaries, benefits packages, small-pond fame, and creative freedom) would not be funded without them. If we did not certify teachers and administrators for schools, would there be legislation or even public faith to fund scholars to imagine educational possibilities, because educational scholars are deemed central to human growth in cultural life at large, whether the sorting machines called schools exist or not?[7] Again, however, sparks of hope, of course, are kindled for me by efforts of small schools (e.g., Ayers et al., 2000; Meier, 1995) and democratic schools (e.g., Apple & Beane, 1995), wherein human potential is released and human spirit is nurtured.

Curriculum scholarship is often accused of having moved into more ethereal realms and away from being directly relevant to school improvement, curriculum development, and design. I argue that this move is not *away* from our original calling, but directly harkens back to origins in Dewey. He was far more education-oriented than school-oriented. He knew that a society (perhaps humanity as a whole) must be oriented to education, to the release of human potential and the nurturance of human spirit, or schools within that society cannot enable such release and nurturance (Dewey, 1933). Yet, the rise of curricular specialists along with a host of other administrators to facilitate universal schooling simply balkanized those who were once inspired to be educators to be managers of schools, confined to societal sidelines. Eventually, the space of school (its physical, temporal, emotional, psychological, and social milieu) became corporate, autocratic, and often militaristic—like the central threads that bind the surrounding context.

The panoply of what we have labeled *synoptic curriculum texts* (Schubert & Lopez-Schubert, 1980) is a microcosm that amplifies an important part of this story of what has happened to the curriculum field. The proliferation of curriculum books and articles during the first third of the twentieth century produced a body of literature too great to read, especially for busy curriculum leaders, so Caswell and Campbell (1935) created a text to summarize and present the literature to give busy practitioners a glimpse into its complexity. We named the term *synoptic text* after the theological reference to the *synoptic gospels* (Matthew, Mark, and Luke in the New Testament) that summarize the life of Jesus Christ. I suppose even that the analogy connects to the idea of word becoming flesh and dwelling among us—curriculum becoming embodied in students, but I don't think we had that in mind at the time—only a kind of encyclopedic summary. Synoptic curriculum texts dotted the curriculum landscape for the next three decades, some providing new conceptualizations of knowledge or lore in the field (e.g., Alberty, 1947; Gwynn, 1943; Saylor & Alexander, 1954; Smith, Stanley, & Shores, 1950; Taba, 1962; Tanner & Tanner, 1975; Zais, 1976) and I even tried my hand at a synoptic text (Schubert, 1986/1987).[8] A rapidly increasing variation on synoptic text provided background knowledge geared to a how-to manual of presenting curriculum knowledge. Ralph Tyler's (1949) tremendously influential *Basic Principles of Curriculum and Instruction* directly fits neither category, but is related to both. He succinctly summarized four key questions (purposes, learning experiences, organization, and evaluation), bases for purposes (society, learners, and subject matter), and posited the need for checking curriculum assumptions through philosophical and psychological *screens*. Almost 50 years later, a brand new kind of synoptic text appeared, *Understanding Curriculum*, written by Pinar, Reynolds, Slattery, and Taubman (1995). After an historical portrayal of the field and its varied array of associations, the authors presented a range of new discourses that characterize the curriculum field (e.g., politics, race, gender, phenomenology, postmodernism/deconstruction/autobiography/biography, aesthetics, theology, and international). They provide elaborate chapters on each of these topics, with immense bibliographies to illustrate the scholarship in each category. Separated from the aforementioned discourses is the *institutionalized* curriculum discourse, which includes a range of curriculum writings, wedded to the institution of schooling (focusing on curriculum development, teachers, and students). The emphasis on multiple discourses symbolizes the gradual expansion of curriculum studies into realms of literature and concern about an array of matters that speak to, support, and inhibit the release of human potential and nurture the human spirit.

While *Understanding Curriculum* (Pinar et al., 1995) was written almost ten years ago, its subject index has 21 citations to *place*, indicating that *place* has been emphasized in curriculum discourse for some time before that present volume. Moreover, Kincheloe and Pinar edited a volume in 1991 called *Curriculum as Social Psychoanalysis: Essays on the Significance of Place*, and one can find ample references to *public space* in the corpus of Maxine Greene's earlier writings (1965, 1973, 1978, 1988). This trend in the field is precisely why I argue for the significance and originality of *Pedagogy of Place*. Surely, it is partly due to the fact that it conceptually integrates a novel array of sources (Arendt, Freire, Bourdieu, Lefebvre, Soja, and others) as noted in the Introduction. But the reasons for significance run deeper, and from a personal perspective the book helps me address the questions of both worry and hope that I noted above. I illustrate by drawing on each of the chapters.

The three essays in the first section help me wonder about *place* in new ways, so I want to suggest to fellow readers a question I derive from each author. In Chapter 1, I share Stephen Fain's respect for the strivings of the curriculum field. Having entered the field at roughly the same time as he did, we share the hope that systematic curriculum construction could lead to Deweyan democratic engagement; further, that such engagement could bring the kind of public spaces that Maxine Greene has often advocated. When I question myself on the positive regard I feel for all those curriculum *development* advocates from the 1940s through the 1960s, I feel with Fain that they were constructing, not just critiquing. At the same time, I am convinced that the critics from the 1970s onward are not just critiquing. Their critiquing is constructing in a different *place*. The work of such critics has helped me critique schooling as education managed and separated from the flow of societal life. Fain offers original direction by drawing on principles of architecture to couple Freire and Dewey in a notion of public community that could enable new forms of individualized education. Here he reminds me of Dewey's conviction that the reciprocal relationship between individual and social good lies in continuous reconstruction (Dewey, 1920, Chapter 8). I ask readers to help me as I ask: Behind the facade of control, standardization, and surveillance that too often dominates schooling, how can we keep convictions of Dewey, Greene, and Fain alive in school and non-school *places*? This represents a seeking of education in the culture writ large.

Judith Slater helps me think about this dilemma as she turns to literary sources to depict erosion of public space. I resonate positively with the use of literature to study education and the *what's worthwhile* questions of curriculum. In graduate and undergraduate courses over the past several years I have used an array of novels, poems, plays, and films, which have helped me see and convey the integrated, nuanced patterns of a curriculum of life. Our curricular ancestors often wrote of life-long learning and growth as a worthy purpose of curriculum; yet, test scores in the present are increasingly the end-in-view. Critics, such as Slater (who draw on literary sources), often write of the whole culture as both educator and inhibitor to authentic education. We need such perspective. Literary sources reveal erosion of public space, as Slater helps us see in the likes of Elmer Gantry and Willie Loman. They represent more of experience than many want to admit. Coupling this with Slater's perceptive use of poststructural geography and Hannah Arendt's theory brings both doubt and hope. I want to believe the promise and hope with which Slater concludes, building on Dewey and Greene, but then I look at the world and am diminished. Yet, I look at friendship and loving relationships and am emboldened. I encourage readers to join me in asking: Wherein lies hope for places that release potential and nurture spirit?

Donna Adair draws on two groups in which I have known for over two decades (Professors of Curriculum and the Spring Conference) to build her case for the re-building of the public academic. Through these and other scholarly associations I have experienced release of potential and nurturing of spirit. However, such experiences have derived largely from one-to-one conversation, exchange of ideas, and encouragement of work, sometimes-collaborative action, and friendship. Thinking back on my participation in such groups, I do not think that the groups as wholes brought the inspiring spirit and the alleged community of the rural towns. Having grown up in a small, rural community, I see as much political intrigue there proportionally as I see anywhere else. In any setting I have known, it has been the one-to-one relationships that have made all the difference for me, personally and educationally. The one exception may be seminar groups; still, even these have greatest value because of networks of one-to-one relationships within them. Perhaps, however, the education of friendship that I experienced in scholarly associations over the years is due to the pedagogy of place more fully than I realize. So, my question to share with readers is: How can schools, universities, and scholarly groups foster inspiration for service, spirit of dance and fair play, and a sense of public that enhances the individual, as Adair sketches so well? Moreover, how can academics become more public-oriented to reach out widely and still maintain the ethos of the best one-to-one friendships?

When I teach about different dimensions of philosophy that pertain to education, one of the most difficult for students to comprehend is the practical relevance of aesthetics. I guess this may be due to the association of aesthetics with a limited notion of beauty rather than with the perception of and response to patterns that are in a state of continual flow. Perhaps, too, it is due to the homogeneous construction paper art projects that have been the tradition of the elementary schools, experience of too many individuals. Authors in the second section of *Pedagogy of Place* speak to the need of aesthetic sensibility as a basis for understanding place.

Margaret Macintyre Latta forges her aesthetic sensibility from traces of Kant, Schiller, Hegel, Dewey, and Gadamer, among others. As these thinkers had turned to the aesthetic to understand and express their fundamental encounter between subject and the world, so does Latta as she recalls her encounters in middle schools that strove to integrate the arts into classroom life. In the end Latta raises powerful questions of schools about how to move from current preoccupation with results to focus on acts of mind, from technical rationality and fixed sequence to fluid purposeful learning adventures, from planning all in advance to judgments in process, from monolithic curriculum to multivocal conversation, from covering curriculum topics to pleasurable dwelling in subject matter; and from focus on the disconnected and superficial to unities of meaning. It is heartening to read of Latta's evidence that this is largely accomplished in the places she studied. If it can occur in some places, then it could occur in more. Therefore, I encourage readers to scour their own experience with schools and to wonder as I am wondering: Why in so many schools is there an emphasis on results, technical rationality, planning in advance, monolithic curriculum, coverage, and disconnected experience? What attributes of place promote these debilitating values, and (more importantly) what dimensions of place (in school and non-school settings) empower focus on more positive counterparts: acts of mind, purposeful and fluid learning adventures, judgments in process, multivocal conversation, dwelling in subject matter, and unities of meaning? The latter clearly seem to be conditions that release human potential and nurture spirit.

If we want to nurture the spirit, why not turn to a scholar whose work is permeated with the spiritual? Bruce Uhrmacher's study of Rudolf Steiner's ideas clearly does this. Although Waldorf schools are accepted as a viable educational alternative, Steiner is still categorized as a practitioner of the occult in many sources. Uhrmacher does an excellent job of arguing for the benefits of employing Steiner's insights about connectedness of environment and education. The cosmic environment, the primacy of art and architecture, the connection between forms one creates and thoughts one is able to have, spiritual functionalism, and an overall aesthetic orientation to environment and development are powerful contributions that could be incorporated into the larger efforts of schooling. Or could they? I wondered as I read Uhrmacher's citation of Goethe, and sadly speculated that many schools might excommunicate a Goethe who called for education as a process of intuiting the creative purpose of the universe and entering the rhythm therein? Nevertheless, I ask readers: How schools and other places of learning and growing incorporate hallmarks of Waldorf education? What forces of place would inhibit and support such a move? For, as Uhrmacher implies, these are qualities that release potential and nurture the spirit.

If schools as they are usually known do not provide this, then where? Cheryl Craig gives a strong hint, intended or not, that parks might be such places through her creative, historical rendition of the landscaping of Central Park in New York City. As I pondered her call to create spaces that inspire autobiography, I wondered where such places can best be created. Craig's emphasis on autobiography invokes the method *currere* as developed by Pinar and Grumet (1976) (Grumet, 1980; Pinar, 1994) who called for a kind of educative interaction that encourages exploration of one's past and present for purposes of understanding oneself and context and for creating one's future. Analogously, I think of the transformation of Scrooge in Dickens's *Christmas Carol* as a metaphor for the conversions that education could be (Schubert, 2000). Again, I encourage readers to consider the best places (school and non-school) for such experience. And in doing so, we need to take a cue from Craig's depiction of landscape change at Cochrane Academy, noting how reflection on one's landscape can transform ways we see ourselves. With the reader I want to challenge myself by asking: What is an educational transformation I have known and can I imaginatively reconstruct the landscapes that helped create the transformation? I find that such reconstructions are valuable exercises for inventing invigorating educational settings.

The final three essays (by Michael Apple, David M. Callejo Pérez, and Corey Lesseig, respectively) are about forces of power that foster and reduce the possibility of public space. Apple comes down heavily on home schoolers, accusing them as wanting to do away with teachers. This is an extension of his well-known critiques of the conservative undermining of the public sphere through advocacy of vouchers and charter schools that serve those who already have more than those who have not. Apple has done more than anyone to add to or correct the what's worthwhile question, by asking: Whose knowledge? Whose conception of worth? And who benefits and who does not? (Apple, 1979/1990). While his critique holds for many who select home schooling, e.g., the religious right and those who simply want test score and college entrance advantages for their children, I suggest that there is also a small, promising dimension of the home schooling movement that builds public spaces apart from schools, and therefore needs separate consideration. Some who call it *unschooling* (Holt, 1981), as did our family, have reached into the larger polity to strive for democratic experience that they could not find in schools (see Lopez, 1993). Herein is an illustration of non-school places that enable release of potential and nurturance of spirit. To oppose out-of-school ventures on the grounds that to leave school is to leave behind a crucial site of democracy is problematic. Such grounds are couched in an assumption that public schooling is somehow a strong basis for democratic society. Perhaps this contention is that if the ideal place called school is based on sound democratic hopes (as universal schooling seems to have been), then practical applications flowing from the name of that place strengthen democracy. If striving for education by families is deemed inequitable because it is usually done by those with some level of privilege, where should blame be directed? Should it be mainly toward those families or toward *rulers* of a society that force the young into barricades of schooling? Is there nothing else to do with the young in a society where the families of lower, working, and middle classes are so close to poverty that they must spend most of their time in workplace servitude to a government of corporate structures that benefit the ultra-rich? This makes faith in schools, devised by oppressors, more akin to a children's crusade in the Middle Ages than to the last hopeful spark to rekindle democracy.

Yet, that is a severe scenario that I do not want to believe, although I am tempted to accept at times in today's world. Alternatively, I am buoyed by a conviction that schools are contested ground, and at least they symbolize a place that draws people together who have aspirations to release human potential and nurture the human spirit. Associating with teachers, school leaders, and professors of education over the years I have witnessed many persons who exhibit a hope for goodness and democracy. In them I see a love of children and a hope for the future.[9] Of course, in the ranks of teachers, school administrators, and education professors, too, I have seen petty autocrats and sadistic bullies of the young. I encourage readers to wonder with me: How can schools and families together be *places* that use societal and cultural resources to create public spaces? How can we more adamantly critique institutional structures created by those whose greed and imperial aspiration prevents families and schools from pursuing public spaces without institutions that perpetuate that greed and empire? Is it perhaps time to reopen our tattered copies of Ivan Illich's (1971) *Deschooling Society*? Perhaps we need to de-school schooling and in Deweyan fashion have good schooling and good deschooling coexist. Might this not lead to new kinds of public spaces, not defensibly accused of supporting privatization—an education that is principally about deriving meaning from life.

The novels of William Faulkner, Robert Penn Warren, Ralph Ellison, Richard Wright, and Alice Walker are all about education in the whole space of lived experience. I have used most of these authors in my courses on curriculum. David M. Callejo Pérez helps us see them as an evolving depiction of changing racial identity in America. I see them, too, as an ideologically and racially enlightened incarnation of the *bildungsroman* tradition that runs from Parcifal to Goethe's Wilhelm Meister novels and extends all the way to Hermann Hesse's novels of the twentieth century (see Swales, 1978). In both the original *bildungsroman* genre and the new incarnation if novels of identity beyond citizenship to one nation, I see education sketched thickly in the context of race, politics, history, aesthetics, gender, phenomenological experience, postmodern multi-narrative, autobiography, biography, theology, global perspective, institutions, and especially place. It seems to me that this is the breadth and depth of concern that curriculum studies must embrace, not only through both school and non-school places, but because it *is* life's curriculum that educates. Should that not be where our focus ought to be fixed?

Similarly, it is in the depiction of a single dimension of life (notably the automobile) as a microcosm of curriculum that Corey Lesseig helps us see this expanded *place* for curriculum studies.

Lesseig vividly shows the alteration of place and its educational consequences over time wrought by one technological item, the car, and its historical impact on emergent identity in a particular setting. This work symbolizes that educational history wrought by any example of technology could be a seedbed for understanding the shifting development of identity as education in and from life. Does this mean that the study of curriculum should continue on a trajectory to become a special instance of cultural studies? What about the doing, the influencing, that derives from education as a dimension of cultural studies? I encourage educators to consider together: How can hope for such reflective inquiry be realized? Assuming that schools should not be solely responsible, where and how should this kind of education occur in the non-school and school life of a society or culture?

Returning again to my theme from the next to last line of this book's Epilogue, this book has inspired me to more fully suggest that curriculum should be practiced wherever we can engage the young in "creating spaces and places which release human potential and nurture the human spirit." While I share hope that this can be done in reformed schools, and while I work toward that end, I am not sanguine that this alone can do the job. I find hope in human relationships outside of large bureaucratic structures—in the ordinary curriculum of life experience. Toward this end, I have begun to encourage the telling and gathering of stories about transformative experiences, journeys of individual lives that lead to profoundly held interests or values. Listening to these stories, I hear about curricula of powerful learning, and think that they should be a basis for curricula of mutual influence in both schools and the variegated milieu of living. The stories and analyses in this volume should enable readers to ponder deeply the pedagogy of place and the places of pedagogy as we reconstruct our ways through the worlds we inhabit.

I thank and congratulate the editors (David Callejo Pérez, Stephen M. Fain, and Judith J. Slater) and the authors for giving such provocative food for thought, and I encourage others to partake in the feast of this book.

Endnotes

[1] I thank Youngjoo Kim for enhancing ideas and writing expressed here by asking questions and making insightful clarifying comments on a draft of this Foreword.

[2] The idea that the *place* of curriculum was expanding came to me even after two AERA sessions that I organized for the 1980 Annual Meeting in Boston, and I argued that it needed to move from move back to origins as the study of curriculum in culture (i.e., the substance of learning and growth in life itself), not just curriculum for schooling alone. I wrote about this in *Curriculum Inquiry* (Schubert, 1982), and drew heavily upon inspiration from Lawrence Cremin (1976), who argued for education as a large societal concern, not merely a concern of schooling. I suggested implications of this perspective for curriculum, and called for curriculum inquiry to investigate the educational impact of homes, families, peer groups, communities, mass media, non-school organizations, jobs, hobbies, and more. I am still convinced that all of these are *places* where we recognize that curriculum exists and should be studied and reflectively practiced (Schubert, 1981, 1986/1987).

[3] Among them are AERA, ASCD, SSCH, AATC, JCT, SPE, JDS, P of C, AESA, Bergamo, Spring Conference, various SIGs in AERA, all of which could be spelled out and described, but to list the acronyms or shortened versions emphasizes curriculum talk and the challenge to name and characterize each could be used as a kind of curricular trivial pursuit, or should I say significant pursuit!?

[4] I see this phrase as so central to the essence of *Pedagogy of Place* that I will return to it frequently, in an effort to emphasize that a significant criterion of whether a place is educational is the extent to which it releases human potential and nurtures human spirit.

[5] Nova television special called *The Final Frontier*, first aired about 1979.

[6] Influences within the field of education on my recommendations that out-of-school realms of education be considered seriously derive from the work of Bailyn (1960), Cremin (1961, 1976), and Tyler (1977).

[7] See Joel Spring's *The Sorting Machine Revisited* (1989) for a pertinent discussion.

[8] This, of course, is not a comprehensive list and here I list only the first edition of some long-running synoptic texts in several editions (sometimes with new co-authors). For a much longer rendition, along with a presentation of many other kinds of curriculum books, see Schubert, Lopez-Schubert, Thomas, and Carroll (2002).

[9] I thank Ann Lopez-Schubert for discussion that inspires these wonderings, especially the hope that infuses critique.

References

Alberty, H. (1947). *Reorganizing the high school curriculum*. NY: Macmillan.

Apple, M.W. (1979/1990). *Ideology and curriculum*. NY: Routledge.

————— & Beane, J. A. (Eds.). (1995). *Democratic schools*. Washington, DC: Association for Supervision and Curriculum Development.

Ayers, W. C., Klonsky, M., & Lyon, G. (Eds.). (2000). *A simple justice: The challenge of small schools*. New York: Teachers College Press.

Bailyn, B. (1960). *Education and the forming of American society*. Chapel Hill: University of North Carolina Press.

Caswell, H. L., & Campbell, D. S. (1935). *Curriculum development*. NY: American Book.

Cremin, L. (1961). *The transformation of the school*. NY: Knopf.

————— (1976). *Public education*. NY: Basic Books.

Dewey, J. (1920). *Reconstruction in philosophy*. Boston: Beacon.

————— (1933, April 23). Dewey outlines utopian schools. *New York Times*, 7.

————— & Bentley, A. F. (1949). *Knowing and the known*. Boston: Beacon.

Greene, M. (1965). *The public school and the private vision*. NY: Random House.

————— (1973). *Teacher as stranger*. NY: Wadsworth.

————— (1978). *Landscapes of learning*. NY: Teachers College Press.

————— (1988). *The dialectic of freedom*. New York: Teachers College Press.

Grumet, M. (1980). Autobiography and reconceptualization. *JCT*, 2(2), 155-158.

Gwynn, J. M. (1943). *Curriculum principles and social trends*. NY: Macmillan.

Holt, J. (1981). *Teach your own*. NY: Dell.

Illich, I. (1971). *De-schooling society*. NY: Harper & Row.

Kincheloe, J., & Pinar, W. F. (Eds.). (1991). *Curriculum as social psychoanalysis: Essays on the significance of place*. Albany, NY: State University of New York Press.

Lopez, A. L. (1993). *Exploring possibilities for progressive curriculum and teaching in three urban contexts*. Unpublished Ph.D. Dissertation, University of Illinois at Chicago.

Meier, D. (1995). *The power of their ideas: Lessons for America from a small school in Harlem*. New York: Beacon Press.

Pinar, W. F. (1994). *Autobiography, politics and sexuality*. NY: Peter Lang.

————— & Grumet, M. R. (1976). *Toward a poor curriculum*. Dubuque: Kendall/Hunt.

—————, Reynolds, W. M., Slattery, P., & Taubman, P. M. (1995). *Understanding curriculum: An introduction to the study of historical and contemporary curriculum discourses*. New York: Peter Lang.

Rosenblatt, L. (1978). *The reader, the text, and the poem: The transactional theory of the literary work*. Carbondale, IL: Southern Illinois University Press.

Saylor, J. G., & Alexander, W. M. (1954). *Curriculum planning for better teaching and learning*. NY: Holt, Rinehart, and Winston.

Schubert, W. H. (1981). Knowledge about out-of-school curriculum. *Educational Forum*, 45(2), 185-99.

—— (1982). The return of curriculum inquiry from schooling to education. *Curriculum Inquiry, 12*(2), 221-232.

—— (1986/1997). *Curriculum: Perspective, paradigm, and possibility.* NY: Macmillan.

—— (2000). Curriculum inspired by Scrooge or a 'curriculum carol.' In G. Willis & W. H. Schubert (Eds.), *Reflections from the heart of educational inquiry: Understanding curriculum and teaching through the arts.* Troy, NY: Educator's International Press.

—— & Lopez-Schubert, A. L. (1980). *Curriculum books: The first eighty years.* Lanham, MD: University Press of America.

——, Lopez-Schubert, A. L., Thomas, T. P., & Carroll, W. M. (2002). *Curriculum books: The first hundred years.* NY: Peter Lang.

Smith, B. O., Stanley, W. O, & Shores, J. H. (1950). *Fundamentals of curriculum development.* Yonkers-on-the-Hudson, NY: World Book.

Spencer, H. (1861). *Education: Intellectual, moral, and political.* NY: Appleton.

Spring, J. (1989). *The sorting machine revisited.* NY: Longman.

Swales, M. (1978). *The German bildungsroman from Wieland to Hesse.* Princeton, NJ: Princeton University Press.

Taba, H. (1962). *Curriculum development: Theory and practice.* NY: Harcourt, Brace, and World.

Tanner, D., & Tanner, L. (1975). *Curriculum development: Theory into practice.* NY: Macmillan.

Tyler, R. W. (1949). *Basic principles of curriculum and instruction.* Chicago: University of Chicago Press.

—— (1977). Desirable content for a curriculum syllabus today. In A. Molnar & J. Zahorik, *Curriculum theory.* Alexandria, VA: Association for Supervision and Curriculum Development.

Zais, R. (1976). *Curriculum: Principles and foundations.* NY: Thomas Y. Crowell.

ACKNOWLEDGMENTS

This volume has been two years in the making. The initial idea for this project surfaced as a conversation in Denver at the American Association for Teaching and Curriculum. We left that meeting with an idea to bring together an eclectic collection of scholars who saw the importance of place and identity in education. In the following years, we were able to flesh out the conversation into the volume that follows. Like many projects of this nature there are many people to thank.

First, we wish to thank the authors for believing in the idea that a volume with such diversity of topics and essays about place would come together and be published. Second, we would like to thank Peter Lang, Shirley Steinberg, Joe Kincheloe, and the Counterpoints Series for their vision in seeing the value of such a work for the educational market. Also, we would like to express gratitude to the editorial staff at the University of Nebraska-Lincoln, especially Cindy DeRyke for her selflessness and "enlightened eye" in seeing and copyediting our words; Mike Jackson and the Design Center at Teachers College, Nebraska for their work with the wonderful photographs on the cover and within the book; and benvu and Anna Latta for their artwork and photographs.

This project has benefited and gained immensely from the insights and criticisms offered by colleagues and friends. David Callejo Pérez is grateful to his parents Jose and Barbara, Margaret Macintyre Latta, Karl Hostetler, Steve Swidler, Nancy Wyner, Shawn Elliott, Tom Kolbe, Mike Nelson, Kelsi Swanson, Keri Matoush, Tim Mock, Matt Fohlmeister, Tony Wells, and Leah Reedy for their advocacy and support of this project. Stephen Fain would like to thank his family and teachers for their lifelong support and dedication in his career. Judith Slater would like to thank Maxine Greene and her Center for the Imagination for the inspiration for this collection about new ways to think about public spaces.

Finally, we wish to thank William Schubert for his reading and passionate foreword, which has elicited and given language to our hopes for alternative curricula and notions of education beyond *No Child Left Behind*.

Introduction

Understanding Place as a Social Aspect of Education

David M. Callejo Pérez, Stephen M. Fain, Judith J. Slater

Dispositions do not lead in a determinate way to a determinate action: they are revealed and fulfilled only in appropriate circumstances and in the relationship with a situation. They may therefore always remain in a virtual state, like a soldier's courage in the absence of war. Each of them can manifest itself in different, even opposite, practices, depending on the situation. (Bourdieu, 1997, p. 149)

The focus of this work is about place, the embodiment of a purposefully created space that is a creation and enactment of the cultural and social conditions of participants. It is also about education, the purposeful creation of spaces that comprise learning environments, and the aesthetic dimensions of the created space called school. Our concerns are the forces that shape the space we call school and the ability of that public space to represent the needs and desires of the constituents it serves. The public space of education is much like an object; it can purposely be created since it is a potential with the possibility of being filled. This space becomes place when life is entered by those who understand that place is defined by boundaries and understandings or as dispositions of potential ready to be occupied and possibly used situationally by the participants and authorities that run them.

The contributors to this collection understand that the nature of the space in which teaching and learning occur is an important factor in shaping the educational experience. The chapters present the concept of space as the place where learning happens and where the lives of student and teacher can thrive or wither—a place rich in human potential. The space called school is also rich in political potential and, as is the case with Bourdieu's (1997) dispositions, has the potential to manifest itself in different, even opposite, practices, depending upon the situation.

In an attempt to expand place beyond the geographical, we hope to begin this essay by intentionally tampering with the standard visions of time, to rethink the linearity of time and text to allow for the reinterpretation of what counts as place. First, using Edward Soja (1989) to experiment with time and place by breaking the "linearity of geography," we exchanged the sequentiality of edited works to a narrow focus for a delineation that allows the reader to see text as a map. This creates spaces or realms of meanings, a pedagogy of place. Second, using Lefebvre's classic *The Production of Space* (1997), we have collected and organized chapters to address issues around place and identity in three segments: 1) as a philosophical tool, a way to begin a conversation as individuals and groups or communities; 2) as aesthetic, using space to redefine what counts as knowledge and teaching and to restructure classrooms and inner-city schools; and 3) as political and historical examinations of identity in light of home schooling, literature and curriculum, and school consolidation. Engaged by Stephen Fain's essay on architecture in this book and Margaret Macintyre Latta's (2001) book on aesthetics and learning, we chose the concept of segments in the organization. Each segment or part can stand alone or as a part, a movement within a larger collage, as we attempt to meet Lefrebve's call for space as identity. The breadth and uniqueness of each chapter open doors to new questions and address lingering issues around identity and place, causing the reader to question ideas of meaning.

In the first section of the text three essays cast place as a philosophical tool. Stephen M. Fain examines curriculum building as an attempt to create individual spaces for each learner. Using Paulo Freire's (1970) concept of authentic dialogue and principles of architectural design, he re-addresses John Dewey's concept of individualized curricula. While Fain looks at difference, he reminds the reader that the goal of public space is community. In a thought-provoking essay, Judith J. Slater brings readers on a literary quest through the eyes of Elmer Gantry as she tells us that the erosion of public spaces leads to alienation of the populace. Using the concepts of poststructural geography, she explores public spaces as psychological and warns that it can create public spaces of control and submission. Her twist on this notion comes in the form of a re-examination of Hannah Arendt's (1958) concept of natality. Donna L. Adair considers the growth of the curriculum field since the 1970s. She examines the new spaces for curriculum workers and considers the implications growing from the lack of communal spaces for the sharing of their philosophies. Using John Dewey's concept of community, she fosters the argument that even as we create personal spaces for those who agree with us, we exclude ourselves from the larger community that provides meaning and identity.

A set of three essays then ground the reader in reality-based analysis of the aesthetics and environment of place. Margaret Macintyre Latta takes the reader on a journey through a school in her essay as she (re)collects experiences from a variety of classrooms visited in which students and teachers wrestled with living out aesthetic teaching/learning. Her data represent two years of inquiry at a middle school that was charged with infusing the arts into its curriculum. Bruce Uhrmacher examines Rudolph Steiner's holistic approach to the environment in an essay grounded in Waldorf education. For Steiner, environments were not merely inert shells, but instead they stimulated thinking and shaped moral possibilities. The author posits that an understanding of Steiner's perspective on the environment offers much to inform our thinking about education and the educational environment in particular. Uhrmacher connects the experiences of the Waldorf to the classroom in an attempt to foster spaces for learning in schools. This section concludes with an exciting piece by Cheryl J. Craig that is built on the work of Jean Clandinin and Patrick Diamond. The author challenges us to re-consider schooling as a parkland. She draws on the landscaping of a barren area in New York City to create Central Park. She provokes the reader, through a project of narrative inquiry, to create spaces for the reclamation of autobiography by children. In her case study of an African American school and community, the author explores children's attempts to learn about the self by learning about their spaces, thereby, re-creating their identity.

The final segment of this text presents three essays that reflect the power of forces that shape the public space and ultimately engage individuals in the creation of their understanding of place. In an eye-catching piece, Michael W. Apple asks the readers to re-examine the idea of home schooling and forces us to deal with the concept of public responsibility of education. The author seeks to critically examine the idea of home schooling as detrimental to our public schools. Apple argues that, although lacking in many areas, public schools are the space where learners can explore living. David M. Callejo Pérez uses the work of five Southern writers as metaphor for identity and curriculum. William Faulkner, Robert Penn Warren, Ralph Ellison, Richard Wright, and Alice Walker are seen as developmental stages in the literature of identity as it pertains to race. The author takes the challenge of racialized curriculum to create a space where we can explore our racial identity and still remain organically connected. Finally, in an in-depth historical piece, Corey Lesseig traces the relationship between the social changes and the automobile in Mississippi in the 1920s, describing the re-definition of public space. One such concern was literacy, which the author masterfully weaves into the discussion of the automobile and its effects on local society. One such effect was the loss of local control as the automobile made it feasible to consolidate schools. Along with school consolidation came the loss of control by local schools and the rise of segregation.

The essays that comprise this text are intended to encourage new ways of thinking about the work of teachers and curriculum makers. We welcome reactions to the diverse and thoughtful pieces in this book, which attempt to tackle learning and space as important and controversial issues in education and identity. Although there is no universal agreement among the contributors on all educational issues, there is agreement that the space (physical, temporal, emotional, and/or psychological) in which one finds ones self is always a significant element in the equation linking learners and teachers. We invite the reader to consider this basic proposition when reflecting on questions of learning and teaching.

References

Arendt, H. (1958). *The Human Condition*. Chicago: The University of Chicago.

Bourdieu, P. (1997). *Pascalian meditations* (Trans., Richard Nice). Stanford, CA: Stanford University.

Freire, P. (1970). *Pedagogy of the oppressed*. New York: Seabury.

Lefebvre, H. (1997). *The production of space*. Oxford, UK: Blackwell.

Macintyre Latta, M. (2001). *The possibilities of play in the classroom*. NY: Peter Lang.

Soja, E. (1989). *Postmodern geographies: The reassertion of space in critical social theory*. New York: Verso.

Part I

Place as a Social Tool

Photograph by Anna Latta

Chapter 1

The Construction of Public Space

Stephen M. Fain

Understanding what happens in public spaces is important if curriculum workers are to respond to the challenges posed by this powerful concept. This chapter connects the intentional act of curriculum design and the concept of public space in a way that invites those who toil in the curriculum field to reconsider their positions on curriculum development. This work examines questions which define both public space, *the space of possibility* (Bourdieu, 1993) and curriculum in terms of intentional design and forges a connection linking curriculum development and the creation of public space. Architectural theory and work products are utilized to buttress the fundamental premise of this chapter as both architecture and curriculum are cooperative arts (see Adler, 1982, pp. 60–61; Neutra, 1969, p. v) as each field's primary purpose is designing structures within which human activity is expected and human potentials are to be nurtured.

For some time now I have understood that curriculum work is really related to the construction of space. Being grounded in curriculum, I have always believed that what distinguishes curriculum work from the work of colleagues in other related educational endeavors is that curriculum work is much like the building of structures which, among other things, connect theory with practice. As a student of curricular history and one interested in contemporary education in the United States, I am concerned about a shift away from the construction of liberating public spaces to the construction of controlling spaces that, by design, reduce the environment to sets of minimum standards and narrow opportunities for choices.

My belief that curriculum work is ultimately the construction of spaces has led me to explore the potential of a relationship between the design of educational spaces and the design of spaces intended for human living, more precisely the relationship between curriculum work and architecture. You are invited to consider a set of perceptions and possibilities link curriculum designers and architects. I hope this piece will challenge readers to open their minds to new possibilities that have the potential for intentionally opening up public space in schools by considering the curriculum as an architectural plan, a blueprint if you will, for a designed dynamic environment. Further, I hope this effort will advance the notion that curriculum work can be much more than a technical response to policy—it can be an enterprise which has a "social basis as an art of expression" (Sullivan, 1918/1947, p. 15).

The School as Public Space

At least three facts should be understood as basic to the concept of public space. First, what happens in public space "can be seen and heard by everybody and has the widest possible publicity" (Arendt, 1958, p. 45). For this reason, what happens in public space defines reality. Second, public space is always dynamic as happenings in this domain involve more than one person and result in multiple simultaneous individual experiences. These experiences combine as the collective defines and redefines the space in which it finds itself. This power to shape space is, as Hannah Arendt explains in *The Human Condition* (1958), generated "only where men [meaning all people] live so close together that the potentialities of action are always present..." (p. 180). The fact that power is generated by the collective is one explanation for the potential danger of political oppression and the subsequent eventual destruction of public space. Arendt goes on to inform us that the only limitation on the source of power generation is other people. This limit, she points out, is not accidental "because human power corresponds to the condition of plurality to begin with" (p. 180). Slater (2002) informs us that public spaces are free, open and accessible, and, buttressed with this awareness, we can come to a better understanding of public space.

Finally, we must realize that public space is not without structure nor is it open to all just because it is public. These spaces are free and open, but access is governed by convention. We are told that

> there are a great many things which cannot withstand the implacable, bright light of the constant presence of others on the public scene; there, only what is considered to be relevant, worthy of being seen or heard, can be tolerated, so that the irrelevant becomes automatically a private matter. (Arendt, 1958, p. 47)

Choice is one emancipating dimension of the spaces we think of as free. Individuals are free to think and act as they choose. However, when considering free space, we must also consider the structural dimensions that create the limits, or boundaries, of the spaces in which the masses find themselves. "Crucial is the recognition that conditions must be deliberately created to enable the mass of people to act on their power to choose " (Greene, 1988, p. 18). When we think of the spaces in which students and teachers meet we think of school. And, when we think of school as a space that should be a free and open public space, we realize that school is constructed space as opposed to some form of "natural" or "automatic" space. That is, when free space exists in schools, we understand that this free space exists intentionally rather than accidentally or by chance. Knowing that the constructed space called school has the potential of being either emancipating (free) or controlling (oppressive), those who make the space must choose what kind of space they want to create and then they must act accordingly. As Greene (1988) points out, free space must be "deliberately created" (p. 18).

Form and Function

In an imagined conversation between a young architect and a master, Louis Sullivan (1918/1947) introduces a most enlightening and invigorating concept. He explains "that which exists in spirit ever seeks and finds its physical counterpart in form, its visible image; an uncouth thought, and uncouth form; a monstrous thought a monstrous form...a living thought, a living form" (p. 44). We join the conversation as the master is trying to lead the student to an understanding. We begin with a series of responses from the student:

student: I suppose if we call a building a form, then there should be a function, a purpose, a reason for each building, a definite explainable relation between the form, the development of each building, and the causes that bring it into that particular shape; and that the building...must, first of all, clearly correspond with its function, must be its image, as you would say...

And that, if a building is properly designed, one should be able with a little attention to read *through* that building to the *reason* for that building...

Well, then, I suppose if the law is true of the building as a whole, it must hold true for its parts.

master: That's right.

student: Consequently each part must so clearly express its function that the function can be read thought the part.

master: Very good. But you might add that if the work is to be organic the function of the part must have the same *quality* as the function of the whole; and the parts, of themselves and by themselves, must have the quality of the mass; must partake of its identity. (Sullivan, 1918/1947, pp. 46–47)

As the conversation continues, the master directs the discourse to the concept of the *organic,* carefully differentiating between the *organic quality,* which is described in terms of generative themes (Sullivan, 1918/1947, pp. 47–49), and *organic thinking,* which is described in terms of thoughts grounded in issues of the present as opposed to the past or the future (see Sullivan, 1918/1947, pp. 47, 50–52). The master informs his student that the concept *organic* is manifest in the buildings as a result of the conscious act of design on the part of the architects. Further he explains that the source of this *organic quality* in design is the result of the *organic thinking* of the designer. It is in this logical context that the axiom *form follows function* is generated.

This axiom is most applicable when we think of the construction of spaces called school. John Dewey, a contemporary of Sullivan, also demonstrates his commitment to the organic in most of his writings and in the creation of the renowned Laboratory School in 1896. The organic quality of his work is evidenced in writings such as "My Pedagogic Creed" (Dewey, 1897), where he states his belief that "all education proceeds by the participation of the individual in the social consciousness of the race" (in Dworkin, 1959, p. 19), and a chapter in Kilpatrick's *The Educational Frontier* (1933) where, joined by his colleague John Childs, he observes that "organisms, selves, characters, minds are so intimately connected with their environments that they can be understood only in relation to them" (as cited in Tanner and Tanner, 1975, p. 306). Dewey's (1902) organic thinking is evident in his appreciation for experience as demonstrated in such works as *The Child and the Curriculum* where, in a criticism of traditional education, he points out "the lack of any organic connection with what the child has already seen and felt and loved makes the material [the curriculum] purely formal and symbolic" (Dewey in Dworkin, 1959, p. 106)—not organic. It is the combining of organic qualities and organic thinking that provides the compelling foundation for the educational programs which grow from Dewey's philosophy.

Both Sullivan and Dewey sought an alignment of philosophy and practice. Each recognized that the product of their work was less if this alignment was not achieved. For Sullivan, the product of his work appeared to be a building, while for Dewey, it seemed to be a school. Yet, upon reflection, each was focused on more—each sought to create an experience that both educated and emancipated. Obviously, the architect and the philosopher had much more in common than a belief in the organic. Each was a teacher, and the work of their students tells us as much about them as do their words. It is noteworthy that Sullivan's student Frank Lloyd Wright and Dewey's students William H. Kilpatrick and Boyd H. Bode advanced the beliefs of their mentors and played active and important roles in shaping an architecture and a school that were reflective of the American experience. In transcending the physical, their work reflected a spirit which has been called American (Rugg, 1947). Each understood that the construction of public space, a free public space, was the ultimate expression of their philosophies. Each understood the power of the concept form follows function.

The Form and Function of Curriculum Work: A Continuing Struggle

"The life which happens in a building, or a town is not merely anchored in the space but made up from the space itself" (Alexander, 1979, p. 74). Space is multidimensional. When considering questions related to the construction of public space, it is important that we differentiate between the linear and the multidimensional. The modern curriculum, grounded in principles of modern science, has been a closed linear process according to Doll (1993, pp. 47–55). Central to this argument is the influence of Ralph Tyler and his popular Tyler Rationale (1947), which is embodied in the following four fundamental questions:

1. What educational purpose should the school seek to attain?
2. What educational experiences can be provided that are likely to attain these purposes?
3. How can these educational experiences be effectively organized?
4. How can we determine whether these purpose are being attained? (p. 1)

Doll (1993) was not the first to point out the power of Tyler's influence. For instance, Tanner and Tanner (1975) argued for the interdependence of the basic elements of the Tyler Rationale and pointed out that the "...linear sequence of questions appears faulty because it fails to show this necessary interdependence" (p. 57). In spite of this apparent flaw, it is significant to note that Tyler's work did, in fact, permeate the curriculum field by providing a foundation for what we have come to call the synoptic curriculum texts. Schwab (1970) argued that the curriculum field was in crisis mainly because of its dull routine. Schubert (1997) supports this argument when he points out that many textbooks and teachers' manuals claim to be grounded in the Rationale. And, Pinar, Reynolds, Slattery, and Taubman (1995) sum up this criticism with the following brief critique: "The Tyler Rationale, conceived first as a rational scheme for curriculum development, [has] become a rationale for narrow, behavioristic conceptions which [reduce] curriculum to objectives and outcomes" (p. 177).

Hilda Taba's 1962 text *Curriculum Development: Theory and Practice* aimed at connecting Tyler with more Deweyan thinking. Considered as the "true swan song for the disappearing field of curriculum development" (Marshall, Sears, & Schubert, 2000, p. 57), this text simultaneously marked the demise of the synoptic texts in curriculum development and the emergence of what would become the critical theory and postmodern movements in the field of curriculum. Although there are basic texts being published that are reminiscent of what the synoptic texts (e.g., see Oliva, 2000, or Henson, 1995), it appears that the current curriculum field has disregarded the linear structure associated with Ralph Tyler and has moved beyond design to critique. For me, the problem with critique is that it, in and of itself, adds little to the curriculum development process.

Whereas curriculum work was initially guided by theory and values toward a plan for practice (praxis), the new directions have focused on social, political, and philosophical criticism at the point of praxis. The crisis that Joseph Schwab described in *The Practical: A Language for Curriculum* (1970) has not yet been resolved. Clearly the newer texts, which represent cutting edges of the contemporary curriculum work, signal a "flight from the subject of the field" (Goodson, 1994, pp. 32–39; Schwab, 1970, p. 17). Currently there are three distinct, well-meaning contemporary curriculum movements (the critical theorists, the postmodernists, and the reformers) and none of them speaks to the question of curriculum construction.

Consider the critical theorists. This movement stands on a platform grounded in questions of social justice and equity. Marxist in orientation, this politically based ideology is focused more on relationships than it is on process. Michel Apple, in *Cultural Politics and Education* (1996), once again examines power relationships in the cultural, political, and economic context in which schooling takes place. Realizing that his analysis may fall short of a practical connection, the author directs the reader to *Democratic Schools* (Beane & Apple, 1995) for case studies demonstrating the principles that Apple discusses. However, the case studies, as well as the theoretical and ideological insights advanced in these texts, speak to process and not to curriculum construction. The contribution of the critical theorists has been most helpful in shaping the contemporary field. However, the shift to the political and ideological and away from curriculum construction has led to a "translocation" (Schwab, 1970, p. 17) of problems from site-level policies and procedure that provide structure to (albeit vital) questions of social justice, equity, and power. Schwab sees this behavior as indicative of a crisis and names it a "flight from the field" (p. 17).

The second movement, postmodernism, addresses the experiences of the learner and sometimes the teacher (Slattery, 1995). Although this school speaks clearly to the relationship between student, teacher, and the environment, it offers only criticism. In fact Aronowitz and Giroux (1991) call for a redefinition of curriculum and suggest that teachers learn to "take student voices seriously" (p. 104). The postmodern view speaks directly to pedagogy rather than to curriculum. The postmodernists engage in "discourse about discourse," and Schwab refers to this action as "flight upward" (1970, p. 17). Again, although they are helpful in terms of the awareness levels their discourse raised, the fact remains that curriculum construction is not the focus of postmodernists. As vitally important as the encounter is for the learner, the teacher, and the school system, this needs to be bolstered by structure if the creation of the public space is central to schools and if it is to result in an environment where students and teachers can access freedom. The postmodernists' existential critique is helpful, but the critique, grounded in deconstruction, fails to facilitate the "construction" of dynamic public space.

The most powerful movement shaping the spaces we call schools in America today is school reform. The widespread use of standardized statewide assessment tests is reflective of the power of these reformers. Academics and social critics who have come together in this movement offer structural guidelines that ensure that the curriculum of the schools within their domain operates within a structure defined by policy. Most notable are the performance standards that speak directly to questions of content, skills, and time. Perhaps no force has done more to shape current curriculum than this movement. The debate regarding these standards has continually and systematically excluded both the critical theorists and the postmodernists. There is an absence of these two forces in the debate on questions of applied policy or the "formal" level of curriculum decision-making (Klein, 1991, p. 28). Teachers and school administrators who comply with school policies can be seen as being co-opted by their employers, or they can be presented as champions of a cause. Either way, by returning to the "subject matter in a state of innocence" (Schwab, 1970, p. 17) without critical reflection, they represent a flight "downward." It is important to note that, dispositions aside, this is an example of the power of constructed space. In this case, the form is represented by the standards and the tests, and the function is to control rather than provide an emancipating environment.

Of the three schools of thought presented above, the reform movement easily accepts curriculum as linear in character. The critical theorists do not reject the linear as a valid curriculum construct outright because their focus on social justice and equity does not invite a discussion of this issue. However, because this is of no concern to them, we are forced to conclude that structure, beyond the point of the interaction between student, teacher, and text, is unimportant. The postmodernists reject linear curriculum structures as inappropriate. It may be that Ralph Tyler's (1947) work has led to a behaviorist model that has dominated the curriculum field for more than half a century. Or, it may be that the organization of curriculum automatically takes on a linear character at the point of praxis and that one significant challenge facing the curriculum designer is managing this reality.

When we construct linear models, we place elements in a precise order, with one specific element necessarily placed before another in a form that is best described as *static*. When we construct multidimensional models, we create many possibilities, and the form of the model is *dynamic*. The linear models are fixed; the multidimensional ones are flexible. The former are controlling; the latter are, at best, directing. The former are precise and predictable; the latter are loose and unpredictable. Finally, the linear creates no opportunity for the multidimensional, but the multidimensional easily accommodates the linear. Recognizing that one important dimension of life is linear, the designers of spaces cannot overlook the importance of incorporating this element into their multidimensional designs. To ignore the linear is to act indifferently toward those who will not just pass through the constructed space but will live in it. because the fundamental element of the argument has to do with the linear dimension of living in school, that is where I will begin to forge my analysis.

When the child enters school in the fall knowing that summer vacation is only about ten months away, she provides evidence of the linear nature of living in school. Similarly, when parents talk to their children about progress in school in terms of getting grades and building a grade point average or how many years before college, they bring a linear view to the questions of living in school. And, when teachers think in terms of nine-week blocks, semesters, and minutes before the bell rings, they, too, invoke linear thinking. The fact is that time is a linear force, and time is perhaps the single most powerful force shaping life in schools because it is the prominent force in controlling access to public space. The clock and the calendar force the shape of schooling as virtually all schools respond to their pressures. Prerequisites in various forms add to the linear character of schools. For instance, grade-level placement related to age and required knowledge or experiences is a common linear condition in curriculum construction. Prerequisites add strength to the form of schools. In some cases, the reason may be tied to developmental stage theory (Piaget & Inhelder, 1964) or to a learning theory such as chaining (Gagné, 1977). In such cases the form (graded schools and sequenced courses) may be directly related to a learning system. On the other hand, grade-level placements and sequenced curriculum can be used as controlling structural elements. The rationale for the use of these elements will be better understood if the analysis considers the entire construct rather than eliminating potential by considering linear as something negative.

Those who criticize the curriculum because of its linear character are missing the point. The linear nature of the curriculum represents the tension that supports the building. The tension is the source of the building's strength, and this strength has the potential of "unlimited performance" (Fuller, 1963, p. 212). Linear form has the potential to define space so that it is dynamic as well. For example, we are well advised that linear offers the architect a set of dynamic possibilities (Ching, 1996), or as Bruno Zevi puts it in a discussion on internal wall partitions, "this creates the possibility of...passing from the static plan of the traditional...to the free, open and elastic plan of modern building" (1993, p. 141). For example, a wall may support a building and block easy movement from one place to another but at the same time provide visual access with a window or direct access to a specific point with a door. Looking through the window or walking through the door will create specific experiences that should be, from a design perspective, purposeful. The choice of a window that opens rather than one of fixed glass limits possibilities in the same way the size, the lock, and the width of the door limit access. Each possibility represents a choice made by the designer and either suffered or enjoyed by the inhabitants of the structure.

Building with and from the linear, curriculum makers have the opportunity to re-engage with the fundamental questions of scope and sequence and create free spaces where others have created spaces that only control. For example, the information provided to a student prior to the lesson may well shape the view of the landscape on the next lesson in much the same way as a tinted window changes the color and intensity of the view. Similarly, the skills mastered prior to a lesson may facilitate or prohibit access to a new set of skills or concepts in ways similar to a door that is easily opened or one which is selective and restrictive. Although linear constructs may not be easily seen as free spaces, the linear principle has emancipatory potential when deliberately applied in the construction of spaces in which students and teachers will be enabled to act on their power to make choices. They can stop and stand in front of the window, lingering to take in a little more of the view, or they can choose to pass it by with hardly a glance; they can walk through the door and enter new space, and they can choose to close the door on the space behind or leave it open and connected to the new space. In reality, these moves create new dynamic structures within form of the dominant structure. This dynamic, this ability to shape, is the possibility provided by free and open public space, and it is important to recognize that without the initial linear form, the dynamic could not be generated as the condition (opportunities for change) is the result of the construction (the form).

Linear and Dimensional Space

It is important to reiterate that the construction of space is an intentional act. In order to achieve access to space through design, we must try to understand the structure of the space itself (Alexander, 1979). Our first impulse may be to perceive space as an empty void without structure. From this perspective, we are faced with the task of filling the void with structural elements in order to create the desired environment. However, Bill Hillier suggests that we look at the question of space from a different perspective. He makes the point that:

> in its raw state, space already contains all spatial structures that could ever exist in that space. It is in this sense that space is the opposite of "things." Things only have their own properties. Space has all possible properties. When we intervene in a space by the placing of physical objects we do not create spatial structure, but eliminate it. (Hillier, 1996, p. 345)

This view of space makes it clear that free space, purposefully created to allow people to exercise choice, cannot be so narrowed as to minimize the opportunity to choose. Yet, at the same time it is clear that purposefully constructed space requires that some things are eliminated and some things are minimized as form is given to the space. Thus, it becomes clear that the construction of free space is not so much what we add to the space we are creating but rather what we take from the realm of possibility of choice. Because in the universe there is so much to experience and so much to know, curriculum construction requires that some things be removed from the purposefully structured space called school (Phenix, 1958) without removing them from the free space into which the individual may choose to enter. The power of this position is found in the arguments supporting the teaching of reading and the teaching of thinking which make the point that these are access skills—skills which bring the individual to choice points or opportunities for personal growth.

We know from reading Freire (1970/1997) that liberation comes to those who liberate themselves, and we understand this to be a critical choice point for each individual as she stands on the edge of public space. Schools can lead to this point, and schools can facilitate entry into this public space—but schools cannot liberate, structures cannot emancipate, and public space cannot accommodate individuals who refuse to free themselves. The best structures make choice obvious and accessible, inviting actualization of human potential, but only the individual can free herself. Schools present opportunities in the form of literacies that can be acquired through other means but which are required for access to public space. Believing that access paths are understood, curriculum developers traditionally select paths to be followed by teachers and students rather than design spaces in which all parties grow. Often these paths prove to be good ones as most who succeed have traveled them rather faithfully—but the anomalies persist. Individuals who have traveled both paths often choose to enter public space and contribute while many others linger in secure private spaces defined by culture, status, and profession. Here is where the question arises that separates linear space from dimensional space.

Linear space, not the concept of linear, requires forward movement from point to point, whereas dimensional space is created by the opportunity resulting from the alignment of something in the linear with something from outside. Consider for example two texts, Peter Oliva's *Developing the Curriculum* (2000) and Maxine Greene's *The Dialect of Freedom* (1988). In the first case we have a carefully structured and well-supported text presented in a linear fashion. The text is clear and on point; practical real-world examples are provided for support and clarity, and, when the book is read in its entirety, the reader comes away understanding principles that are accepted by the curriculum field as basic. The reader closes the text and says, "I understand." In the second case, the reader is confronted with a series of personal ideas, beliefs, and values which challenge the broader social system. The challenges represent observations, questions, and points of view that are supported, in the main, by texts authored by others who bring observations, questions, and points of view to issues. The dynamic is evident, but the underlying differences can easily be missed. In the first, linear, case, the knowledge the reader is expected to acquire is clearly spelled out. In the second case, the obvious hope of the author is to challenge the reader to sharpen, adjust, or even relinquish a point of view after encountering new ways of thinking. Oliva invites the reader into the professional sphere; Greene encourages the reader to enter public space. Each provides access to a unique literacy.

School is a form rather than an amorphous mass of unstructured possibilities. Just as a building is an intentionally imposed, planned structure on the landscape with which it becomes a part, school is a designed social/cultural imposition upon the learner, who is, while still becoming, a part of the social/cultural landscape in which he or she grows and lives. Each structure places limits upon the space created, and each structure has the potential of being a liberating space. Each structure places limits on those who move within them, and each structure has a liberating potential growing from the possibilities it offers. To access the liberating potential of the structure, the structure itself (its form) must be clearly defined, for in this definition, opportunity becomes event and possibilities begin to come to life. The key elements shaping the school are related to its linear form and the opportunity the elements provide for multidimensional experiences within the constructed space.

The Construction Public Space

In an effort to open up the discussion on how to construct public space, I look first at two contemporary structures: the glass and steel pyramid designed by I. M. Pei for the renovation of the Louvre museum in Paris and Maya Lin's Vietnam Veterans Memorial in Washington, D.C. These constructions and their architect/designer have been selected for consideration for several reasons. First, each project required the blending of an intrusion into an already occupied and clearly defined space (as does most contemporary curriculum work); second, each designer had to accommodate the intent and interests of different parties with specific practical and political agendas as they created their designs (as is required in most curriculum work); third, upon completion, each architect/designer understood that the structure would be defined by its use and, as such, would be subject to many interpretations (as it is with the development of curriculum). Consideration of the question of the construction of public space will follow after a brief discussion of each design project.

In the early 1980s architect I. M. Pei accepted a commission to transform the Louvre from a traditional place that contained magnificent works of art into a modern museum. The task can be explained as an effort to convert the private space of kings into a public space. This required detailed design work on two fronts. First, there was the problem of creating a modern infrastructure within a centuries-old edifice to facilitate the work of a modern art museum. Much of this work might go unnoticed as one enters the museum today as one of the construction feats required in this revitalization project was a major excavation in the Cour Napoleon and the Cour Carree. This delicate project took more than a year to complete and, once completed, was only obvious to those who were quite familiar with the Louvre prior to the renovation. The most notable and obvious structural adjustment to the physical landscape was the addition of the aboveground and underground glass pyramid which now simultaneously defines the entry to the museum and stands as its symbol. Centered above the three pavilions of the museum, the glass pyramid confronts the visitor and evokes conversation, adding to the museum experience without distracting from it. Pei explained his choice of form by stating that the pyramid is most compatible with the architecture of the original buildings, that it is one of the most structurally stable forms available to the architect, and that the form "assures its transparency, a major design objective "(von Boehm, 2000, p. 84). Pei goes on to differentiate between his glass pyramid and the stone pyramids of the ancient Egyptians by explaining that "one is for the dead and the other for the living""(von Boehm, 2000, p. 85). During a discussion on the intent of the design itself, Pei points out that "the scale and nature of such a pyramid concerned us from the very beginning. It needed to be prominent enough to be the focus of this complex without compromising its authenticity as a national monument" (von Boehm, 2000, p. 84). Finally, when looking back on the project he observes that "as it is constructed of glass and steel, it signifies a break with the architectural traditions of the past. It is a work of our time" (von Boehm, 2000, p. 84).

Unlike I. M. Pei, an established architect known the world over, Maya Lin was completing her studies in architecture at Yale when she submitted her design for the Vietnam Veterans Memorial to the Vietnam Veterans Memorial Fund. Working amid the politics of Washington, D.C., and the many factions associated with the veterans and the war itself, Lin responded to the published design program creatively. At no time in her essay (Lin, 2000, p. 4:08–4:17) on the creation of this project does she express any resistance to the requirements set down by those funding the project. Rather, she describes the process of accommodating to the requirements while inserting her personal feelings and beliefs into her creation.

The memorial, completed in 1982, is unique among the monuments on the mall. In response to the criteria established, Lin created a simple design. Its form reveals its function in ways which invite engagement rather than awe. The key elements in the simple design are the names of those who died or were missing (57,000 of them), two polished black granite walls positioned so that one points to the Lincoln Memorial and the other points to the Washington Monument, and the site on the mall into which the construct is inserted. The space is truly public as demonstrated by the varied behaviors associated with the Memorial—some simply touch a name; some just stand or sit; some protest in support of those missing in action; some come by and leave a token for personal reasons, but all who come make a public statement even in their privacy.

The only design requirements for this monument were that it be "apolitical, harmonious with the site and conciliatory" and that all 57,000 names of those killed or missing in action would be a part of the memorial (Lin, 2000, p. 4:10). Prior to visualizing a form, Lin asked and answered the question of why these names were important: "What then would bring back the memory of a person? A specific object or image would be limiting. A realistic sculpture would be only one interpretation of that time. I wanted something that all people could relate to on a personal level" (Lin, 2000, pp. 4–10). Lin goes on to point out that she had no form or specific artistic image in mind initially; she did know what she wanted in terms of function or purpose.

The names of the memorialized are chiseled in the polished black granite in chronological rather than alphabetical order, starting at the apex where the granite walls meet. This design requires that veterans and visitors search for names, each aware of "his or her own time frame" (Lin, 2000, p. 4:16), while encountering names for which they were not searching. In the process all visitors must face a reflection of themselves in the polished surface—there is no escaping the result of war. People are encouraged to touch the walls and the names; it is not uncommon for someone to place a sheet of paper over a particular name and rub the paper with a pencil, transferring the permanent engraving onto a transportable sheet of memory. For many, private acts become public statements—dialogue with other visitors such as mourners, veterans, activists—and bring new possibilities to all in a place where some find only an ending.

Today, as a result of a political compromise, two statues stand by the polished black granite walls, one of infantrymen, the other of a woman. These definite forms define precisely those who served and, in so doing, limit the universality of the original design. Maya Lin sadly observes, "These statues leave only the false reading that the wall is for the dead and they are for the living, when the design I made was for returning veterans and equally for the names of all who served regardless of race, creed, or sex" (Lin, 2000, pp. 4–17).

Both I. M. Pei's Louvre and Maya Lin's Vietnam Veterans Memorial are highly acclaimed and carefully designed public spaces. Each is different enough from the mainstream to provoke discussions on many levels. Intellectuals and the general populace continue to publicly react to these intrusions on established landscapes, thus affecting the public space they are a part of and adding to the human dynamic. Whereas each designer's intention was to communicate with both individuals and the masses, each gave up control of the design at the completion of the projects—the point at which the work became a public space. Both the pyramid at the Louvre and the chiseled black granite walls on the Mall in Washington, D.C., demonstrate the power of design in the creation of public structures.

But in the latter case we also see an example of the dynamics of public space as control of the design is taken from the designer.

Years after the creation of the glass pyramid at the Louvre, I. M. Pei finds pleasure in noting that the project has resulted in the acceptance of Le Grand Louvre (von Boehm, 2000, p. 80). On the other hand, looking back at the Vietnam Veterans Memorial, Maya Lin expresses sadness at the adjustment made to her design by the authorities in response to politics within the public space. While other voices have been heard clearly, she feels as though hers has been compromised (Lin, 2000, pp. 4–17). However, once space is made public, control is no longer an individual matter. Those who design/ construct public space would do well to find satisfaction in the fact that what they have created now belongs to the public.

The Power of Public Space

Public space is a space of possibility (Bourdieu, 1993). The power of public space is directly related to the degrees of freedom, openness, and accessibility associated with the space. The power of Le Grand Louvre and the Vietnam Veterans Memorial is generated by a combination of politics, bureaucracy, and design. Both are fully accessible to locals and tourists (who can afford the journey) as there is no admission charge. While Le Grand Louvre stands as designed, the Vietnam Veterans Memorial was modified by politics and bureaucracy. But, because each stands free and in the open, each invites the creation of new possibilities. Encountered by vast numbers who have no idea of the creator of the space, and with respect to those who control and maintain each space, the meaning(s) of each particular space now acts as an aesthetic catalyst for the creation and re-creation of social, political, and artistic interpretation.

The public space has a higher status than the private space. This creates great class distinctions. The established culture of the public space has a specific reference point as it supports its own brand of truth, exploits those events which are congruent, and suppresses ideas, actions, and people who are outside. What occurs is a "banal consensus" (Slater, 2002) by the public. The onus is on the holders of the public space to make the audience believe. They can do this truthfully, building up structures that support the common good, or they can do this by advancing their own hidden agenda of power and position (Slater, 2002).

Public space has the power to sustain, and it has the power to transcend. While supporting the established culture, the holder of public space has the potential to advance the common good by transcending the past and creating new futures. In this way the work of the architect has transformed public space, and, by virtue of the acclaim their designs have achieved, they have stimulated transition in art, architecture, and other related design fields. In the case of the Vietnam Veterans Memorial, a new culture has been established, and a new public space has been created. This new public space has transcended the physical and resulted in a new life form. In each case the public space created by the respective designers has produced the intended result. This fact speaks directly to the power of the axiom form follows function.

Architecture: Curriculum Making and Public Space

Unlike architecture, one of the most public forms of art, curriculum making is generally unseen by the very people who experience it. When we come upon a building, we may ask who was the architect, but we rarely ask about the skilled tradesmen who implemented the plan of the architect—the carpenter, the mason, and so on. When we come upon a school, we almost never ask who designed the curriculum—the assumption is that all that goes on is the result of the force we call tradition or culture, or, in some special cases, we may recognize the actions of one person—a specific administrator or teacher. Dominated for almost half a century by reformers, critical theorists, and social critics, the curriculum field appears to have lost sight of its core element—the subjects to be taught. Ivor Goodson describes the curriculum as the result of a "process of social construction" (1994, p. 16) and then goes on to point out that

> what is most important to stress is that the written curriculum, notably the convention of the school subjects, has, in this instance not only symbolic but also practical significance: symbolic in that certain intentions for schooling are thereby publicly signified and legitimated; practical in that these written conventions are rewarded with finance and resource allocation and with the associated work and career benefits. (Goodson, 1994, p. 19)

The separation of the symbolic and the practical represents two important considerations. First the symbolic relates to the function or in this case the purpose for which the curriculum is intended, while the practical speaks to the form (the curriculum). Today the public space (as related to schools and schooling) is dominated with discourse about the failure of our schools. Diane Ravitch's *Left Back: A Century of Failed School Reforms* (2000) is widely read and Berliner and Biddle's *The Manufactured Crisis: Myths, Fraud, and Attack on America's Public Schools* (1995), never a best seller, has faded from the scene. Reform dominates the public space as seen in the accountability movement and calls for alternatives to public schools, alternative teacher certification, and vouchers. The postmodernists and critical theorists are not generally heard by the public, and, therefore, they fail to stimulate a social construction that generates alternatives associated with possibilities.

In the realm of curriculum, as with architecture, the power of the symbolic function ultimately becomes subsumed by the obvious and dominant force of the structure (form) at the practical level, demonstrating that the greatest power lies in the dynamic interactions brought to the encounter by the structure rather than the conception. Both in architecture and curriculum, the designer's intent is central to the creation of the symbolic form. Those who build monuments can choose to build a dynamic Vietnam Veterans Memorial or a static formal grave marker such as the Tomb of the Unknown Soldier. In the former case, visitors bring life to the memorial as they interact, while in the case of the latter, the only life on the site is that of the solemn military honor guard. Curriculum can be dull and formal, and teachers will face the difficult task of breathing life into it, or curriculum can be dynamic and invite interaction, involvement, and possibilities. Structural decisions must be made when designing the curriculum, and, if an interactive curriculum is the desired goal, then care must be taken to ensure that structural integrity is maintained while the opportunity for choices and possibility of new visions are provided to all who participate in the curriculum encounter. Those seeking to create curriculum that has the power and possibilities associated with public space are challenged to create interactive curricula that responds to those demanding educational account-ability while at the same time proving opportunities for dynamic interaction among and between all participants.

The architect must direct his/her attention to questions of structure and design. Structural questions consider issues related to engineering and design focus on "surface, form, proportion, space, and light—the traditional palette of the architect" (Wigley, 2000, p. 17). The curriculum designer also deals with questions of structure and design. The traditional questions of scope and sequence remain central to the design process with sequence providing the basic structural form and scope addressing questions of tone and texture. The organization of content by grade level and associated formal objectives presents the structure of the curriculum, whereas the selected texts, teaching and evaluation methods, and activities provide the design elements. The range of choices provided the deliverer of the curriculum (teacher or tradesman) varies and reflects the need to control (reduce possibilities) or liberate (open possibili-ties). The greater the control over the process of curriculum delivery, the greater the chances of achieving the intent of the design.

In a few carefully constructed paragraphs Ivor Goodson (1994) brings us to understand the importance of the written (formal) curriculum as a structural extension of the policies that govern and support the school (pp. 17–20). The most enlightening aspect of the discussion turns on the distinctions Goodson makes between the "high ground" and the lower levels of curriculum where "renegotiation" naturally occurs (p. 18). This "renegotiation" is reminiscent of the now-classical curriculum approaches associated with Smith, Stanley and Shores (1957), Taba (1962), and Goodlad (1966), as well as being aligned with more contemporary understandings of curriculum as articulated by Apple (1996), Aronowitz and Giroux (1991), Slattery (1995), Doll (1993), and Barone (2001). In all cases we are reminded that there is a significant distinction between the written or formal curriculum (the "high ground") and the dynamic lower level of the classroom. In each case the teacher is recognized as a force shaping the environment that ultimately becomes the experiences we call the curriculum. Goodson (1994) demonstrates this point in the closing chapter of his text by recounting the experiences of a team of teachers (as reported by Shipman, Bolam, & Jenkins, 1974) working on a particular curriculum project where they developed curriculum "in the field" with "nothing on the drawing board" (Shipman et al., 1974, p. 118). His analysis is that the teachers used what worked but that "only what is prepared on the drawing board [ultimately] goes into the school and therefore *has a chance* (sic) to be interpreted and to survive" [in the curriculum] (Shipman et al., 1974, p. 119). Another way to look at this situation is to understand that the construction of the space this particular team of teachers created for their students cannot be considered as an action leading to the construction of public space as we know not its form or purpose, nor do we understand the possibilities associated with the work of the team in relation to the intent of the school. If this construction was an act of resistance (Pinar et al., 1995, p. 24), it may be heralded by critical theorists as liberating and rejected out of hand by conservatives who see it as rooted in countercultural politics in the same way as critical theorists reject the traditional "linear" curriculum. What is missing is the unity of actions (teaching) that connect the "high ground" with the common ground (the classroom). What is needed is an organic connection linking structural reality with vast possibilities. Whereas resistance, as with control, limits rather than opens possibilities, a synergy of intent and actions will force "the irrelevant to become a private matter" (Arendt, 1958, p. 47) that can open the public space.

The Vietnam Veterans Memorial and the glass pyramid at the Louvre are examples of innovative structures created in response to specific design criteria. Each reflects the spirit of its creator while serving a public purpose; each has been constructed as designed; each has become a part of the landscape upon which it sits; and now each waits silently for human interactions to release its potential as it is understood that structure is only a catalyst for the release of the dynamic possibilities simulated by the structure. And so it is with curriculum. A curriculum design created for a specific purpose can meet the specifications of control criteria that may be measured in desired behavioral outcomes while providing an array of endless possibilities for those who bring the design into the public space of school. The success of each design may be measured in terms of the aesthetic or structural character of the work (form), or the designs may be appreciated for their potential to engage and open possibilities (function).

Finally, just as the architect must understand that once the project is completed, she or he must relinquish control of the finished work, the curriculum worker must recognize that, although the basic structure remains fundamentally intact, those who control life within the structure may make choices contrary to the intent of the designer. The acid test of the quality of the architectural design or the curriculum design may well be the interactive behaviors demonstrated by those who live and work with the design product after its creator has completed her work. That is the potential of praxis. That is the potential of open public space.

References

Adler, M. J. (1982). *The paideia proposal: An educational manifesto*. New York: Macmillan.

Alexander, C. (1979). *The timeless way of building*. New York: Oxford University Press.

Apple, M. W. (1996). *Cultural politics and education*. New York: Teachers College Press.

Arendt, H. (1958). *The human condition*. Chicago: University of Chicago Press.

Aronowitz, S., & Giroux, H. A. (1991). *Postmodern education: Politics, culture, & social criticism*. Minneapolis: University of Minnesota Press.

Barone, T. (2001). *Touching eternity: The enduring outcomes of teaching*. New York: Teachers College Press.

Beane, J. A., & Apple, M. W. (1995). *Democratic schools*. Alexandria, VA: Association for Supervision and Curriculum Development.

Berliner, D. C., & Biddle, B. J. (1995). *The manufactured crisis: Myths, fraud, and attack on America's public schools*. Reading, MA: Addison-Wesley.

Bobbitt, F. (1941). *The curriculum of modern education*. New York: McGraw-Hill.

Bourdieu, P. (1993). *The field of cultural production*. New York: Columbia University Press.

Ching, F. D. K. (1996). *Architecture: Form, space, and order*. New York: Wiley.

Dewey, J. (1897, January). My pedagogic creed. *The school journal* (Vol. LIV, No. 3) (pp. 77–80). In M. Dworkin, *Dewey on Education: Selections*. New York: Teachers College Press.

——— (1902). *The child and the curriculum*. Chicago: University of Illinois Press.

Doll, W. E. Jr. (1993). *A post-modern perspective on curriculum*. New York: Teachers College Press.

Dworkin, M. (1959). *Dewey on education*. New York: Teachers College Press.

Freire, P. (1970/1997). *Pedagogy of the oppressed*. New revised 20th–Anniversary Edition. New York: Continuum.

Fuller, R. B. (1963). *Ideas and integrities*. Toronto, ON: Collier-Macmillan.

Gagné, R. M. (1977). *The conditions of learning* (3rd ed.). New York: Holt, Rinehart and Winston.

Goodlad, J. I. (1966). *School, curriculum, and the individual*. Waltham, MA: Blaisdell.

Goodson, I. F. (1994). *Studying curriculum: Cases and methods*. New York: Teachers College Press.

Greene, M. (1988). *The dialect of freedom*. New York: Teachers College Press.

Henson, K. T. (1995). *Curriculum development for educational reform*. New York: HarperCollins.

Hillier, B. (1996). *Space is the machine*. Cambridge, UK: Cambridge University Press.

Kilpatrick, W. H. (1933). *The educational frontier*. New York: Century.

——— (1936). *Remaking the curriculum*. New York: Newson & Company.

Klein, F. (Ed.). (1991). *The politics of curriculum decision-making: Issues in centralizing the curriculum*. Albany, NY: State University of New York Press.

Lin, M. (2000). *Boundaries*. New York: Simon & Schuster.

Marshall, J. D., Sears, J. T., & Schubert, W. H. (2000). *Turning points in curriculum: A contemporary American memoir*. Upper Saddle River, NJ: Merrill/Prentice Hall.

Neutra, R. (1969). *Survival through design*. New York: Oxford University Press.

Oliva, P. F. (2000). *Developing the curriculum* (5th ed.). New York: Longman.

Phenix, P. H. (1958). *Philosophy of education*. New York: Holt, Rinehart and Winston.

Piaget, J., & Inhelder, B. (1964). *The early growth of logic in the child*. New York: Harper & Row.

Pinar, W. F., Reynolds, W. M., Slattery, P., & Taubman, P. M. (1995). *Understanding curriculum: An introduction to the study of historical and contemporary curriculum discourses*. New York: Peter Lang.

Ravitch, D. (2000). *Left back: A century of failed school reforms*. New York: Simon & Schuster.

Rugg, H. (1947). *Foundations for American education*. Yonkers-on-Hudson, NY: World Book.

Schubert, W. H. (1997). *Curriculum: Perspective, paradigm, and possibility*. Upper Saddle River, NJ: Prentice-Hall.

Schwab, J. J. (1970). *The practical: A language for curriculum*. Washington, DC: National Educational Association.

Shipman, M. D., Bolam, D., & Jenkins, D. R. (1974). *Inside a curriculum project: A case study in the process of curriculum change*. London: Methuen.

Slater, J. J. (2002). Limitations of the public space: Habitus and worldlessness. In J. J. Slater, S. M. Fain, & C. A. Rossatto (Eds.), *The Freirean legacy: Educating for social justice.* New York: Peter Lang.

Slattery, P. (1995). *Curriculum development in the postmodern era.* New York: Garland.

Smith, B. O., Stanley, W. O., & Shores, J. H. (1957). *Fundamentals of curriculum development* (rev. ed.). New York: Harcourt, Brace & World.

Sullivan, L. H. (1918/1947). *Kindergarten chats and other .writings.* New York: George Wittenborn.

Taba, H. (1962). *Curriculum development: Theory and practice.* New York: Harcourt Brace and World.

Tanner, D., & Tanner, L. N. (1975). *Curriculum development: Theory into practice.* New York: Macmillan.

Tyler, R. W. (1947). *Basic principles of curriculum development and instruction.* Chicago: University of Chicago Press.

von Boehm, G. (2000). *Conversations with I. M. Pei: Light is the key.* Munich: Prestel.

Wigley, M. (2000). Inside the inside. In J. Casebre & G. Seator (2000). *The architectural unconscious.* Andover, MA: Addison Gallery of Art, Phillips Academy.

Zevi , B. (1993). *Architecture as space: How to look at architecture.* New York: Horizon.

Chapter 2

The Erosion of the Public Space

Judith J. Slater

Elmer Gantry (Lewis, 1960) stands before the potential converts, prospects for redemption. The revival tent is open to the elements but warm inside. The crowd waits, skeptical. Elmer stands before them. He will sell the Lord to them. The traveling salesman opens his suitcase for the client. He convinces them he has something that they not only want but also desperately need. A vacuum cleaner, a Fuller brush, an elixir, the Lord. Sinclair Lewis creates an Elmer devoid of substance but glib enough to take in all who hear him. He has wormed his way onto the stage and holds the potential converts in rapt attention. He uses words that shame them and cajole them into submission. They are the unschooled (Gardner, 1991) minds that are childlike and receptive. They scare easily. They learn to believe even if the messenger only bears false witness. Elmer knows something they do not, they surmise, and the "truth" becomes what he delivers, what they come to believe.

What makes for their childlike faith in his message? The 1920s was a time of doubt and superstition, of science that held out a new way of working and farming for these people—middle Americans in the throes of social Darwinism, vulnerable to the measurement of a person's ability by some inherited obsession of superiority promulgated by Thorndike and the eugenics movement (Selden, 1999). They were shown scientifically what they were worth, what to expect from their genetic heritage that limited their outlook and belief in themselves, in their future, and in their children. Elmer's audience members are the unsophisticated who stand up and proclaim that they believe in heaven, hell, love, hate, sin, and corruption, all delivered by a mountebank who has little belief in anything but who commands the stage and holds them in rapt attention and fear of not paying attention. His message must be simple for these folks. He has the power of the audience and a command of the stage as a platform that holds him aloft. He has such power that for a moment he even convinces himself as does the despot who is able to justify to himself his own evil. He delivers his message and commands them to accept his position on faith.

The undoing of Elmer Gantry is the intelligence of the press, particularly a newspaper reporter named Jim. He exposes Elmer, stating "Every circus needs a clown." He questions the qualifications and training of the person on the stage. "Why do these people need a revival meeting?" Jim asks, "What gives you the right to speak for god?" Jim knows Gantry stands on the shoulders of rhetoric and persuasion, not core beliefs that people hold in common about their community. He generates fear as a motive, and once that fear is assuaged, there is compliance. Revivals need to be resuscitated continually. Beliefs become fragile when they are not constantly reaffirmed. In a world of scientific proof, this becomes a tall order. The Bible is not scientific fact. There are no artifacts of belief to prove it. Elmer says of the Bible, "You don't debate the existence of god, you proceed from the premise, and build a structure around it—doubt is not heresy."

Elmer is the salesman, but salesmen fade, like Willy Loman in *Death of a Salesman*, and they easily lose their audience. Their one skill becomes obsolete as the public changes and becomes more sophisticated. Beliefs in simple truths give rise to a more complicated vision that fits in with a changing worldview. The salesman who loses his audience loses his identity. He can exist no more, and he moves on to the next object to be pitched, to the next unschooled audience. For this movement to occur, the salesman must be exposed; he must be undone, and his message must be replaced with a more compelling vision. You can't keep the tent atmosphere going when there are more compelling competing forces gaining the attention of the public. Once the support is gone from the public space, the space can and should be changed.

What does it mean to revive a community and to bring the people out of the shadows of the unlit audience and provide them with an avenue to participate in the performance on the stage? Novak (2002) provides an historical analysis of the humanization of democracy and its relevance to common democratic life. He describes the problem of democracy as one of a public that is unquestioning of its processes and artifacts. To participate fully in a democracy means for the public to make something of it, to actively work the institutions and procedures that are built around it. Those structures, and the people who control them in the public space, have dehumanized what could be a great potential for the public private space. The public school system is an example of such a structure that seems to have lost its ability to live up to a potential and instead is mired in concrete structures, rules, and regulations. Novak (2002) cites Matthew Arnold's (p. 595) communitarian view of democracy as one that envisions an education system that is focused on standards of "high-minded individuality, a deliberative sensibility, and a social spirit." Arnold questioned whether the structural arrangements created to protect individuals against the powerful wielders of the public institutions and the public spaces they inhabit pose a danger of a tyranny over those who separate themselves from and do not participate in public life. Etzioni (1999) has written about the spirit of communitarianism that would provide a milieu in which the voice of the public could be heard. He, too, describes the limitations to public participation created through the very structures and artifacts that have been established as a result of pursuing and serving the common good. These, Etzioni theorizes, have limited the public's right to private reflection and decision making. In deference to privacy, the common good is being neglected, and a balance needs to be restored between the public and private positions, one that privileges neither over the other. It is the responsibility of good rulers, policy makers, and those who hold the rapt attention of the audience to make an effort to balance individual rights with the common good. If this is not attended to, there is autocracy of thought and action that is not translated into sustainable and responsive community. But, if those in power balance their position with that of the public, there is equity in the process, and everyone's voice has an opportunity to be heard. But often the community and those in power mislead.

Standards and rules should be established that are collectively agreed upon so that the charlatans cannot wrest control. Then society can stand on the shoulders of facts and core beliefs. Wise decisions require understanding by the voice heard on the public stage. That spokesperson cannot be an outsider. This is the flaw of Elmer Gantry—and the vehicle for his exposure is Lulu, the preacher's daughter he has undone in the past. She knows him as a grifter, and she seeks revenge. It takes an exposé to get the person off the stage. Such figures do not go willingly once they seize power and experience the adulation of the public. The guardians of the stage cut off the voice of the audience, and they limit their participation. The speaker exists on a higher level that is untouchable. He remains there with the consent of the audience and is protected by his peers since his exposure could be theirs. Mountebanks must imbibe their own elixir. Charlatans must be defamed, exposed, vilified, and embarrassed—they must themselves be undone to allow a new authority to take the stage. There cannot be a void; that would be unthinkable for the unschooled who crave to be led because they do not know how to participate. They repent; Elmer repents, and once more he is allowed to take the spotlight. But Jim, the reporter, says, "Mobs don't like their gods to be human." Elmer needs the people; he needs the audience. Faith must vilify the existing order to maintain him in the public space. "Faith is the strongest voice in the world," Elmer says, but even Sharon, the true embodiment of goodness, was duped by him, and Sinclair Lewis's message is clear; even the faithful must be wary of those who take the public stage and do not have firm convictions of what is right and wrong. There cannot just be blind acceptance that everyone seeks to do right, even by others who share the stage. Elmer needs the testimony—a deaf man asks for help, "Heal me," he says. "Pray with me," Elmer answers. "I need your faith (of the group) to heal, reward us for our faith."

In the end, it is fire and damnation, a confirmation, perhaps, that the stage holder is fragile and can be undone. He is undone just when he, too, gets close to conversion and redemption. He is undone perhaps by god, but more likely he is undone because the public needs to move on to other truths, other stage holders, other public spaces that comfort them more. The tents cannot rise again, but there are so many others that go up too quickly, that provide a quick fix to a public that is impatient with problems of right and wrong. People flock to those who offer quick solutions to problems that do not address their underlying causes. Public speech about poverty does not meliorate the fact of living. Public speech about literacy does little to teach the adult and child how to sound out the words. Public speech about equity and vouchers does not deliver competitive programs that level playing fields with elite schools. The public must be schooled so that they understand how to transform that public space into one that hears their voice and lets them participate fully in the public discourse.

Limitations of the Public Space

The public space is a product of the mind. It is a fabrication that exists in people's heads, containing the form and practice of the theory of social life within it. There are no limits to this mental space, except those that are set by the occupants. Every public space needs an audience filled with people to legitimize the activities that go on as a public performance. People come to occupy each of the spaces through conditions of participation. In the United States, democracy was seen to be a means to make the public space a reflection of the wants and needs of the people. In practice, democracy has become a dehumanizing force, where individual control has been given over to a public space that has become more and more powerful and less and less responsive to the needs of the public it serves. Novak (2002) questions citizens who are made dependent upon those that they choose to represent them through elections. Blindly following those elected and being dependent upon a central authority far removed from the everyday life of the citizens result in a loss of humanity for one's fellow men and for the common ties that bind people together. Novak posits a withdrawal from fellow men and a loss of native country, a loss through the promise of "collective prosperity" with what goes into the makeup of a common people (p. 597). People become directed by the power rather than participating as thinking collaborators. Novak cites education as an instrument in this scenario and calls the result a "collective fantasy." He posits the idea that schools and teachers normalize, manage, and disseminate a model of schooling that is being duplicated all over the world. This normalization stops participation in shaping the future or in thinking independently from those in power or engaging with others in dialogue about possible futures. Our culture is rife with instances of this. We are told what we want, what clothes to wear, what car to buy, as we are subjugated into a "fantasy" that we helped create and sustain by acquiescence. New ways to participate are thwarted in the face of the rising social power of the public space.

Although democracy encourages utilitarian thinking, the people realign their personal interest to that of the supposed interest of the public space. A democratic tyranny of the majority is intentionally created and justified as the status quo of operation (Novak, 2002, p. 599). The public is made weak because they comply and follow the leader blindly. Matthew Arnold (cited in Novak, 2002, p. 600) believed that freedom was cultivated by being actively involved and that educational institutions could serve as the vehicle to naturally "humanize" the public and make a personal form of communitarianism that would allow people to participate fully in the evolution of democratic participation. Novak says (p. 602) that "our system has conquered the world and that each of us has some significant measure of independence, [but] we cannot help despising ourselves and the institutions that produce such great outward wealth and such great inward poverty."

What is there about the public space that so limits the possibilities of such participation? One view is that of Lefebvre (1997), a French Marxist theorist who linked the production of space to the rise of capitalism. The social space was created as a political positioning of the players who grabbed the arena as the observers watched and waited, hoping that they would be taken care of and be heard. It has turned into a public space of domination and control, the users passively accepting what is provided for them, but in the using or observing think they have contributed. This occurs when the observer accepts the speech of the actor on the stage, is taught to follow and obey, and is blinded by the dazzle and sparkles of promised protection. They exist in what Greene (1995) calls the opaqueness of life, which does not let them see clearly how they could more fully participate in the public arena and participate in their fate. On the stage are the vocal, political perpetuators for the bureaucracy. Dewey (1927) noted that the

> public is a fiction, a mask for private desires for power and position...[the] state is conceived either as sheer oppression born of arbitrary power and sustained in fraud or as a pooling of single men into a massive force which single persons are unwilling to resist. (pp. 21–22)

The public is a political state, and it is the guardian of customs, laws, and judgments; it cares for special interests by regulating the actions of individuals and groups (p. 35).

The creation of public space is a process that is a transformed and surreal representation of the people's wants, needs, and desires. Space becomes consecrated (Bourdieu, 1993) as it grows and becomes more complex as it sustains itself with surrounding structures. Different social spaces impose themselves on each other and support each other's existence. School bureaucracies help perpetuate all sorts of structures that occupy spaces around them, making the surrounding structures stronger and more difficult to change practices within. Evidence of this is found in those supporting structures such as the diplomas, titles, bureaucratic structures, ordered uses of time, etc., which create restrictions and imbedded social relationships that solidify the public space of schools. The private space of needs of subgroups representing community uniqueness has little ability to permeate the public space defenses which perpetuate its social practices.

Communities are distinguished by the style in which they are imagined, not by their genuineness (Anderson, 1991). Therefore, the status conferred on the public space and those who subscribe to its tenets is conveyed by those who hold the space and those who aspire to enter. Those who dominate promulgate their ideas onto the private space, where the participants hold less status, creating great class distinctions. The inclusion or exclusion of specific points of view within the public space is limited, and the perception of what is possible in the arena becomes distorted by the imposed sanctions and limitations. What occurs is a "banal consensus" to the space by the public, for who out there takes issue with the truth. Elmer's audience will not dissent once the truth is preached in the public arena and repeated over and over in the public space. The audience comes to know and believe the same truth as those who command the circus. But with Elmer, there are illusions of truth, lies, all appearance and no substance because he does not truly believe what he spouts and only acts out his part on the stage. What you see is what you get, and what you see is all you get. It takes a public, an audience, for the person to remain on the stage. Once the audience becomes disillusioned with the status of the speaker, his use of the public space as a forum for dissemination of his ideas is in jeopardy. It is then that observers in their private space move onto others who offer a less flawed ideation for them to believe in. The onus is on the holders of the public space to make the audience believe. They can do this truthfully, building up structures that support the common good, or they can do this by advancing their own hidden agenda of power and position.

The stage, the public space, is a hegemony of class, a dictatorship held over the community, the culture, and the particular audience. It exercises power over knowledge and practices ingrained in the production of the public space, and it limits the ability of the audience to know it for what it is. The hegemony uses closely kept knowledge to keep the public on the periphery of participation. The semiotic or personal interpretation of the social space is reduced to a message that is read literally by the observers, and they act in ways consistent with the signs and symbols they receive. The function of this is to flatten the cultural and social participation in the public space. The public accepts social practices performed in that public space; they accept political power and restrictions; they enshrine the everyday practice of speaking up about the issues; and they give themselves over to actors who hold the spotlight on themselves.

Elmer Gantry's truth seeks to convert the observer rather than modify itself to be of the people. The public space includes only positions that are indistinguishable from the knowledge it promotes as truth and excludes the observer's ideology unless it is compatible. But, the public space is a theater of the absurd, because it may have no basis in reality. Community participation in the public space is eroded and deferred to those in control—to politicians and bureaucrats, to knowledge makers, and scientists who tender their own versions of truth. It does this to solidify its own existence, to remain closed and mysterious to the public for whom the space was designed in the first place. Violence keeps people away from the stage; violence to the minds of the public, the unschooled, keeps them thinking and speaking about only what is preached. It is hard for our pulpit holders to keep the flock with them through the use of speeches. It is harder still to bridge the gap between the stage and the audience and to incorporate a position that more truly represents the observers' ideology if it is different from that of the exalted ones. It would require a continuing disjuncture between the stage and the audience that presented a very compelling need of the larger community to reform and motivate a change in orientation for the public space. It takes, perhaps, money, a commercial exchange of knowledge, and democratic participation of persons willing to step forward and assert themselves and establish an audience. It also requires an open system free from bureaucratic concerns of control and perpetuation of the structure and placement of props on the stage.

Elmer Gantry enters an established space, one that may have been the voice of the people, devised in an egalitarian way, but he takes center stage, and he is a false prophet in the field. The followers line up behind the leader, reproducing the status quo along with the limitations of opportunities for action within that space. As long as the transactions between stage holder and audience are satisfactory, there is little opportunity for a transformation to occur. Elmer's falsity is an erosion of the public space that astute observers must look for. Erosion implies a wearing away of the barriers for the observer to gain entrée in order to participate in the evolution of that space.

Schools play a role in the perpetuation of the inaccessible public space by transmitting the social space; they consecrate certain actions over others that are part of the transmission of the habitus of the culture that prepares students for adulthood. Among those habits are the consecration of abeyance to authority, the scientific proof of test scores and standards, and legally imposed attempts at equality to produce an equitable playing field for the public to participate and compete. The public has faith in the predictions of success and failure, and they recapitulate the explanations given by the speaker on the stage that the solution to the crises lie in this voucher, that charter, this or that new program, or a return to the tried and true solutions of the past. Bourdieu's (1993) habitus is reinforced by doubt in their own private ability to solve the problems of a more just, democratic community of caring through means other than those preached on the stage. Learned societal expectations are reproduced and expounded (Lefebvre, 1997, p. 36). Participation is limited as knowledge is secreted and restricted to that which is spoken, and teachers, parents, and the community espouse the expectations without critical commentary.

Schools are designed to create a mode of thought and serve as a mediator between the stage and the audience. Anything hidden or dissimilar is a danger to the status quo; therefore, these dangers must be eliminated as a threat to those in power. An understanding of the space can facilitate a transparency into the operations of the producer. This requires the overcoming of the cemented written words which codify, like the Bible, action within the space. The written rules overshadow the spoken word, and the latter is the voice of the people. Speech and voice provide clarity of communication that creates the opportunity for the unschooled to participate, but voice often is stilled as it is seen to be subversive and a threat to the organization. The public must create the transparency, obliterate the opacity of naturalized structure and operation, and advance the common good of the community by being aware of the possibilities for personal and collective action.

Erosion of the Public Space

The purpose of opening up the public space is to advance the common good. To accomplish this, Lefebvre (1997) says that the space must be read and also constructed and reconstructed by the audience, not just those who hold the power. Freire's (1970) idea of praxis can only occur if the contradictions of various space needs are experienced and understood by those who pass through them. Deciphering the rules of each space should be the result of some binding forces and understandings that permeate all public spaces so that the observers recognize the potential to involve themselves in meaningful ways within each while keeping their core of beliefs and enacted positions intact as confirmation of their worldview. As the separate common worldviews come together, the public space becomes transformed by the actions and understanding of the collective.

In order to open spaces, making them more transparent and dialogic for collective action, there needs to be active involvement. The conditions are reminiscent of Freire's (1970) praxis or, as Arendt (1958) calls it, a new beginning, a natality, the unique voice potential which is an embodiment of our social world. This is not a conscious representation in either student or teacher, but it exists outside of the awareness of the ritualistic behaviors that compel everyday actions (Greene, 1995). The freedom created from the erosion of the rigidity of the operation in the public space comes about through collaboration. Only with others is there the opportunity for the free possibility of choice. There is risk involved, and there must be a conscious awareness of how the rules govern and how to work them for the benefit of the community. Freire's vision of praxis requires the interpretation of the public space as a potential. When the individual enters the stage, when they participate in a common project with others, they lose the designation of someone defined by the system. Greene (1995) suggests that the public space actualizes the person through the struggle of discovering the ability to act and the choice to comply or to invent for themselves and with others that which could be. This requires knowing what the obstacles and boundaries are that limit freedom of participation and opportunities for action. The coming together of diverse groups to share their points of view can create a public space that facilitates an alternative vision (Sibley, 1995). Then people can position themselves in roles that are not circumscribed by class and status but by common ends and common goals.

Activist reform movements are part of the history of this country, and they have an underlying dynamic that generates the possibility for transformational change (Euchner, 1996). In local public spaces, participants can come together and share their efforts for action. A requirement for this is a primary trust in others, which is not a natural human condition according to Arendt (1958). These actions require the creation of a collective public space that is all encompassing and tolerant of diversity and respect for each other's points of view. The public space needs to be opened to dialogue from all, not just as a pulpit to disseminate the views of the few who have taken over the stage.

Such freedom of thought and action has of necessity an understanding of what Greene (1995) calls the ambiguities, but the reporter in *Elmer Gantry*, Jim, would say the charlatans and false gods need to be purposefully exposed. The audience must challenge the stage actors. The audience must name them and the structures which block the way and purposefully dismantle them so that the space is more inclusive. The public space does not cause freedom because it normalizes operations (Schutz, 1999, p. 83). The public space should constantly be challenged in order to be renewed. Complacency of teachers, students, parents, and university researchers as observers rather than participants creates rigidity, repetition, and acting about the space and about the issues. The community must be aware of the possibilities for its own advancement through the active opening up of the public spaces so that they are responsive to change.

Creation of a New Public Space

In 1927, Dewey wrote

> The same forces which have brought about the forms of democratic government, general suffrage, executives and legislators chosen by majority vote, have also brought about conditions which halt the social and humane ideals that demand the utilization of government as the genuine instrumentality of an inclusive and fraternally associated public. "The new age of human relationships" has no political agencies worthy of it. The democratic public is still largely inchoate and unorganized. (p. 109)

A Great Community, according to Dewey, has not resulted from the democratically organized public, primarily because

[t]here is too much public, a public too diffused and scattered and too intricate in composition. And there are too many publics, for conjoint actions which have indirect, serious and enduring consequences...each one of them crosses the others and generates its own group of persons especially affected with little to hold these different publics together in an integrated whole. (p. 137)

The prime difficulty...is that of discovering the means by which a scattered, mobile and manifold public may so recognize itself as to define and express its interests. (p. 146)

The question persists today as to how to create humane public spaces. Novak (2002) notes that there is a preoccupation with winning liberty for oneself or for a subgroup, for equity or equality, creating the situation where there is little concern about how to use liberty. This results in a tyranny of the majority, winners or losers in the competition for recognition, rather than a corrective spirit of liberty that is utilitarian. Novak (p. 607) cites Mill, who suggested that education that is focused on what we would now call the basics of science, mathematics, etc., was thought to guarantee progress in democratic participation. Mill recognized that this was inadequate in reducing the gap between the public and the private spaces. What is needed is a teaching class to enfranchise rather than segregate knowledge that could provide a social value to people rather than things. Teaching the individual in relationship to others in the world needs to be cultivated.

We can turn again to Matthew Arnold to help define what is meant by humane environments that are responsive to private space needs. Arnold (cited in Novak, 2002) recognized the need to direct people to join together in "the common pursuit of happiness," and the vehicle for this would be education that focused on higher thought and feeling (p. 611). In trying to create a high tone for the nation, Arnold advocated that the activity of freedom in the service of an ideal is greater than the individual. Education could create a social environment and deliver courses of study that would humanize people so they could come to see themselves and others in a mutuality of caring. Arnold called this the "social spirit" of common betterment (p. 612). This conjoining of education with the concept of a humane democracy provides a possibility for change by forging opportunities for greater personal contact between individuals and groups. It creates a broad citizenry that is actively engaged in a moral ideal of democracy that is above that of the marketplace of material interests (p. 619). Boundary breaking provides the opportunity for a public discourse about the kind of public space education should serve, making the public space "our agent, not master" (p. 617).

Specifically, public spaces should be small enough to permit participation, and school reform should focus on individual schools or communities of feeder patterns of schools that can form their own identity and methods of problem posing and solution finding. Individuals can then be schooled and make decisions for themselves about their own choices and the way to live and interact with others in the interests of others. This is not uncontrolled, because an uncontrolled space splinters and falls apart, as seen in some protest movements. Public action must instead mediate between individual voice and the public mission (Schutz, 1999, p. 78). True participation is the goal here—participation of the teachers, parents, students, and community.

Students represent an opportunity as they acculturate into the social space. They threaten the stability of the public space because they are a potential for democratic participation (Schutz, 1999). Therefore, structures that restrict student participation are the norm in schools. First, there are rules that restrict their opportunity to participate in or affect the ritualized day-to-day operations of the school. They are subjected to a school curriculum that segregates subject matter so as to dilute transferability of knowledge, have courses delivered in restricted environments, and suffer limited opportunity to provide input; this is also true for teachers (Sibley, 1995). New ideas and knowledge are suppressed or ignored if they are seen as a threat to organizational goals. Teachers remain isolated and do not participate in important curricular decision making. Innovation and research from the university are alienated from the public space of school reform and policy making. Parents are told by the press and the popularly disseminated political rhetoric what knowledge is most valued, and this perpetuates the public space and the control of those in power. Teachers can play a role in changing this. They can instruct children about the potential of the stage so that they are future-oriented. Children passively learn the hidden curriculum of assumptions about culture, positions of truth, and appropriate acceptable behavior in the public space. There could be power for children who are taught to recognize that choice is the freedom of participation in the community, but students have no narratives to form a public space that meets their needs. They are subservient to the dominant discourse unless their education and their teachers present them with possibilities. The audience is taught to be passive from an early age, and only those who conform have an opportunity to become the elite on the public stage.

Curricular focus needs to be directed toward civic learning that can provide the skills and desire to form public spaces (Greene, cited in Schutz, 1999). Civic learning includes health issues, social awareness issues, drugs, alcohol, political awareness, and technology issues. The teacher becomes the collaborator in the process of liberation (Freire, 1970) by providing students with the abilities, capabilities, and the beliefs and values to reflect who they are in relationship to the collective group. The boundaries between the public stage and the private needs can be made ready for action when the teacher engenders in students the situationally appropriate opportunities for problem solving and action on issues that concern their current and future participation in the community.

In 1927, Dewey wrote, "Associated or joint activity is a condition of the creation of a community. But association itself is physical and organic, while communal life is moral, that is emotionally, intellectually, and consciously sustained" (p. 151). At least four elements are needed to create responsive public spaces—leadership, discourse, nurturance of the public, and imagination. Leadership should represent not just the best interests of the public but should morally understand the elixir of leadership and how easily the vision of those in power can stray from that of the followers. Leadership must include the private space positions, which are learned by contact with the common man in direct discourse and dialogue.

Second, a new discourse must be participatory and future oriented. Public questions must be raised as to the morality of the greater group vs. the individual voice. Voice needs an audience, and the public space should be re-created so that it engenders authentic dialogue concerning relevant issues. It must raise the issues in public forums concerning the objectiveness of the world and the consumerism of desires and be replaced by dialogue about sustainability, global connectiveness, and the role the individual plays in that redirection of purpose.

Third, the public space players must actively nurture community. Arendt (1958) calls this the "in between," the renewal of the common world. Dewey (1927) refers to the need for a committed public community. The community of voices must inform the closed ideas and end the dominion and supremacy over the weak, the children, the disempowered, and the disengaged so that there is opportunity for them to participate. This requires the understanding of the conditions of the communities of the past that were responsive to the individual voice.

Fourth, Greene (1995, p. 5) suggests that there must be a restoration of imagination as to possibilities, of "social imagination: the capacity to invent visions of what should be and what might be in our deficient society, on the streets where we live, in our schools." This rebirth of community includes a rebirth of calmness, of images and actions, that create a worldview and understanding that each person tries to live up to and communicate to others. It requires the destruction of the consecrated tokens of behavior that are followed mindlessly (Bourdieu, 1993; Langer, 1997). It requires that the public understand the meaning of emerging discourse that is future oriented. It requires authentic soul, vision, and actions (Freire, 1970). Finally, public displays and artifacts must require the merging of actor and audience. Open dialogue for authentic public discourse is the arena for educative forums about change, about the public space itself, and how each person can contribute to the continuous evolution of a better society.

Public spaces, if they are truly authentic, create changes in lives and changes in democratic society. Social and physical space needs reform into mental space that opens opportunities for citizen action. Then the public space will respond to private needs. At a dialogue about public space at the Center for the Imagination, Teachers College (December 1998), William Ayers suggested the creation of public spaces through the building of movements for people to come together in the real world by connecting with allies, attending to the interests of the poor and disenfranchised for whom the system is not working, being committed to small changes that can lead to larger structural change, being willing to rethink and be open to new narratives for education and for society. Michelle Fine talked about creating linkages between threads of small changes that connect one innovation to another, so that there is finally the possibility of a redefinition of public discourse that is collaborative and collective and democratically "high-minded."

This is the opportunity to change the focus of current public space restrictions and regulations on educational practice, for a changing of the guard, and for the programs, initiatives, and standardized testing to be reflected upon and possibilities to emerge that embody a fabric of interconnectedness within the educational space. The educational space is a public space that needs to be for the common good. In order for it to be responsive to private space needs, there must be participation by the audience. Authenticity must always be tested, just as government and testing companies that hold power over the student's future do.

Our society should sustain community building and be responsive to the environment which gives it a reason to be; otherwise we face a tyranny of democracy in which selected persons speak for you, but are not true to the needs of the community and the common good. Breaking up a public space when it no longer serves the purpose for which it was created leaves a void that can cause a contradiction of the space. But this is one characteristic of the democratic tradition, that it should always exist in a process of transformation. Social criticism is a success if it creates what Greene (1995, p. 61) refers to as an "effort to overcome false consciousness by rejecting an absolute and static view of reality and its resulting subject-object separation." A new space is a transformation of a worldview. Questions of value, worth, and usefulness to the community are part and parcel of the creation of an alternative space, but the product can be an alternative society that engenders public involvement in its own evolution. This is the promise of education in a democracy. This is the common good goal that Dewey (1927) foresaw as the great opportunity of change.

References

Anderson, B. (1991). *Imagined communities: Reflections on the origin and spread of nationalism*. London: Verso.

Arendt, H. (1958). *The human condition*. Chicago: The University of Chicago Press.

Bourdieu, P. (1993). *The field of cultural production*. New York: Columbia University Press.

Dewey, J. (1927). *The public and its problems*. Denver: Alan Swallow.

Etzioni, A. (1999). *The limits of privacy*. New York: Basic Books.

Euchner, C. C. (1996). *Extraordinary politics: How protest and dissent are changing American democracy*. Boulder, CO: Westview.

Freire, P. (1970). *Pedagogy of the oppressed*. New York: Seabury.

Gardner, H. (1991). *The unschooled mind: How children think and how schools should teach*. Basic Books.

Greene, M. (1995). *Releasing the imagination: Essays on education, the arts, and social change*. San Francisco: Jossey-Bass.

Langer, E. J. (1997). *The power of mindful learning*. Reading, MA: Addison Wesley.

Lefebvre, H. (1997). *The production of space*. Oxford, UK: Blackwell.

Lewis, S. (1960). *Elmer Gantry*. New York: Dell.

Novak, B. (2002, Fall). Humanizing democracy: Matthew Arnold's nineteenth-century call for a common, higher, educative pursuit of happiness and its relevance to twenty-first-century democratic life. *American Educational Research Journal, 39*(3), 593–637.

Schutz, A. (1999, Spring). Creating local "public spaces" in schools: Insights from Hannah Arendt and Maxine Greene. *Curriculum Inquiry, 29*(1), 77–98.

Selden, S. (1999). *Inheriting shame: The story of eugenics and racism in America*. New York: Teachers College Press.

Sibley, D. (1995). *Geographies of exclusion*. London: Routledge.

Chapter 3

The Fall of the Public Academic

Donna L. Adair Breault

To Build a Community

The decade of the 1970s brought a fascination with the condition of curriculum as a field. Schwab (1969) sparked the fascination with his pronouncement that the field was "moribund." His declaration was followed by Huebner's (1976) statement about the field, saying, "for all practical purposes it is dead." Pinar (1975) followed shortly after with his comment that the field was in an arrested condition, and consideration should be given to the potential heirs. Jackson (1980) responded to these pronouncements with his critique about mixed metaphors and their implications. Since that time, others have stated strong positions about the field and about specific factions within it (Hlebowitsh, 1993; Pinar, 1975; Wraga, 1999). Opinions may vary regarding curriculum theory and practice, but I think we could all agree that this is the season of our curricular discontent, and it has become a fairly long and unproductive season.

So, what of it? Is this yet another lament about the state of curriculum for curriculum professors? No. The purpose here is to examine the trail of discontent throughout our professional associations and to seek means through which we can revive our field by building a vibrant intellectual community.

Currently, we have a wealth of associations but no true communities. Association is natural. As Dewey notes, nothing exists in isolation. Sands shift on a beach when the wind blows. Their movement is an association, but it is causal; it is not deliberate. What distinguishes natural associations such as those found in shifting sands from community is "the function of communication in which emotions and ideas are shared as well as joint undertakings engaged in" (Dewey, 1916–1917).

How do we create a community? First, it is important to note that Dewey (1954) equates the term "community" with democracy itself. He states, "Regarded as an idea, democracy is not an alternative to other principles of associated life. It is the idea of community life itself." Therefore, the qualifications he ascribes to democracy apply to communities in general and thus apply to potential communities for professors of curriculum specifically:

- A variety of opportunities
- Free exchange of ideas and experiences
- Realization of the purposes that hold members of the field together
- Common intellectual and emotional traits.

Regarding these qualities, Dewey (1916–1917) notes that a social democracy is a moral democracy. I would extend that argument to state that creating a community for curriculum professors is a moral act, for the work we do in curriculum will impact the lives of teachers, and the work teachers do will impact the lives of children. Dewey also contends that the traits that constitute a democracy "do not grow spontaneously on bushes" (p. 139). Perhaps that is why a community of curriculum professors has not spontaneously emerged. It will take work and a lot of it.

When exploring the possibilities for building communities, however, it is necessary to examine the context in which we operate as curriculum professors. Not only have we not experienced spontaneous community building within our field, but we have also operated within a social psychological state that impedes such efforts. We have lost any sense of publicness as curriculum professors, and this state of privatization parallels a similar malaise evident within our society.

In his book, *The Fall of Public Man: On the Social Psychology of Capitalism*, Sennett (1974) offers an astute analysis of the privatization of man since industrialization, and his analysis offers a number of parallels for curriculum professors today. Close examination of professional curriculum organizations clearly points to the fact that we lack a public life, and without a public life, our field will remain stagnant at best.

The Fall of Public Man

According to Sennett (1974), public life has eroded since industrialization, and parallels of this social psychological phenomenon are evident within Roman society during the Augustan regime. Romans during that period viewed their public roles as formal obligations, and they performed their duties with a passive spirit. Their energy shifted from a public to a spiritual arena as they refocused their energy internally on spiritual transcendence. Sennett offers parallels to current conditions within our society. He argues that postindustrial society has likewise become more and more private. However, rather than seeking spiritual transcendence, we seek a reflection of ourselves—our psyches.

According to Sennett (1974), we do not make a conscious connection between our psyches and society. Rather, we see them as mutually independent phenomena. This is problematic because knowing one's self becomes an end in itself rather than a means to better know the world. The irony, of course, is that the more isolated our psyche, the more difficult it is to really know ourselves because we are social beings. Hence, privatization isolates our psyche by removing social stimulation. He warns:

> The obsession with persons at the expense of more impersonal social relations is like a filter which discolors our rational understanding of society; it obscures the continuing importance of class in advanced industrial society; it leads us to believe community is an act of mutual self-disclosure.... (Sennett, 1974, p. 4)

Sennett (1974) goes on to create a theory of expression in public life. He looks at concrete changes in behavior, speech, dress, and belief since industrialization as evidence of privatization. From his historical examination, Sennett generates a number of themes regarding the social psychological shift toward privatization, and these themes offer curriculum professors vivid anecdotes for their professional associations. Three themes offered as metaphorical public arenas provide a substantive ideological screen through which we can filter our professional interaction: the public square, the stage, and the coffeehouse. To clarify the connection between Sennett's critique of social life and the quality of our collective professional lives in curriculum, we first need to examine the history and structure of specific organizations. For the purposes of this chapter, the Professors of Curriculum and the Spring Conference are examined.

Professors of Curriculum

The Professors of Curriculum is a small, invited group of noted and esteemed professors. The organization itself was formed in the mid- to late 1940s when its first members came together in a room at Teachers College, Columbia University. During the early meetings, topics would be suggested, and discussions would ensue. One of the earliest members, Arthur Wells Foshay, recounts the experience,

> I remember attending the first meeting in a room at Teachers College, and I was very awe-struck by all these people I'd been reading. All these big names. I was sort of floored by their presence.[1]

At the end of the meetings, the group would pass a hat to collect money to pay for the room. Over time, the group began meeting, first at the annual meetings for the Association of Supervision and Curriculum Development (ASCD) and eventually at both the ASCD and the American Educational Research Association (AERA) annual conferences. According to one long-standing member, William Van Til, the close relationship maintained between ASCD and the Professors of Curriculum in the early years led to a number of the professors becoming president of ASCD. He notes,

> The Professors of Curriculum started out with a very close relationship with ASCD. One thing that some historian would be interested in is that the Professors of Curriculum was, for quite a few, a springboard into the presidency of ASCD. I am an illustration. When I was nominated for president of ASCD it was, "Oh yes, Van Til, he's Professors of Curriculum."[2]

Not only have some of the members of Professors of Curriculum served as president of ASCD, but several have also served as officers and presidents of other professional organizations including AERA, the American Association of Teaching and Curriculum (AATC), and the John Dewey Society.

As with any organization, members of the Professors of Curriculum have dealt with a variety of tensions as the membership and the ideals of its members have changed over the years. Two primary tensions evident within the group's history involve the structure of the organization and the collective identity of its members. The organization began as an informal group, and for a number of years they maintained that informal nature. Van Til describes the early meetings:

> I came to the Professors of Curriculum at a time when the great emphasis was on group process and group dynamics. In other words, having the sessions in which people express their ideas, trade opinions, and interact with each other, argue amicably with each other, with an emphasis on everybody in the group being around a circle and being co-equal and everybody having the opportunity to talk and so forth.[3]

The informal structure of the organization was sustained for the first 20 years. The group appointed a factotum each year to plan the meetings and maintain the treasury when they began to collect dues. During this time formal records were not kept. The group progressed from passing the hat to charging annual dues of two, three, and finally five dollars.[4] The few rules established by the organization involved its membership. Because so many were interested in the organization and because the members wanted to keep the group small, they established member guidelines and set up a procedure for member nomination and selection.[5]

Over time, however, the structure changed. More of the meetings included formal papers given by members of the organization as well as guest speakers. By the late seventies, tensions erupted over the publication of papers presented at one of their meetings.[6] Van Til describes the changes he noticed following his time as president of ASCD. He notes that the meetings of the mid- to late sixties were meetings in which "experts" within the organization would give presentations, and as Van Til describes them, "the more esoteric the presentation, the greater the respect of the audience for the person."[7] According to Van Til, the organization had lost what he had prized from its inception—the interaction of its members as equals to try to make a difference in the field.[8]

Through the years, the organization has attempted to address its structural issues. In 1977, the group debated the format of the next annual meeting, and many argued against speakers from outside the organization. Instead, they advocated a renewed emphasis on social interaction and a limited number of formal papers presented by members in the group.[9] In 1989, the factotum, Gerald Ponder, conducted another survey regarding the format of the meetings. Overwhelmingly, members indicated that they preferred member-led discussions to formal presentation of papers. Many of the members responding to the survey indicated that they wanted to return to the original nature of the group.[10]

Issues of identity have also emerged within the Professors of Curriculum. Beginning in the late sixties, the academic foci of the newer members stood in stark contrast to that of the longer-standing members. Many of the new members' research agendas dealt with curriculum theory and social issues rather than curriculum development and school operations. The differences were so significant that the organization was, in many ways, divided along ideological and physical lines.

Ideological differences are most evident within the record of conference discussions and presentations beginning in the early seventies. In 1972, several members were asked to critique the *Seventieth Yearbook of the National Society for the Study of Education* (NSSE). The yearbook focused largely on curriculum development, and it was influenced by a number of the more traditional members of the Professors of Curriculum. During the 1972 meetings, several members attacked the yearbook. Paul Klohr (1972) argued that it did not generate a language with which to think about curriculum outside of technical constraints. He also criticized the yearbook for ignoring the political dimensions of the field.[11] John Mann (1972) argued that the yearbook had "none of the internal movement or organization or development that might have made the whole greater than the sum of its parts." He also argued that it showed a weakness in the curriculum professor's perspective upon itself, and it ignored the sense of historicity that Huebner and others had argued characterized the field.[12]

In addition to the attacks on the NSSE Yearbook, presentations of the late seventies reflected more and more of the newer "reconceptualist" ideas.[13] The group began to reflect upon the field and make predictions about its future. By the 1980s, the meetings addressed curriculum theory and social criticism as much as they addressed practice and research. A number of the members began to look at the social implications involved in curriculum and question whether the problems in the field could be solved. By 1984, the group responded to national reports on education and began to question the role curriculum should play in school improvement. It was also during 1984 that the group began to question the original purpose of the Professors of Curriculum and discuss whether the original purposes were still appropriate. By the mid-80s, reconceptualist notions of curriculum were discussed to a greater degree than more traditional concerns and included issues of feminism, teacher empowerment, and multiculturalism.[14] By the mid-eighties, tensions emerged regarding the topics discussed at the conferences. In a 1985 survey, Harold Drummond made the following comments about the group:

> (Professors of Curriculum) had served marvelously through the years to maintain professional friendships, provide opportunities for sharing concerns, directions, dreams, etc. Perhaps it's just my aging, but it doesn't seem to me that we have had as many real, significant discussions of educational issues in recent years.[15]

Physical shifts accompanied ideological shifts, and the group began meeting in conjunction with the ASCD and the AERA. The more traditional, longer-standing members of the organization continued to meet at the ASCD annual meeting while the newer, more theoretical members met primarily in conjunction with the annual meeting of AERA. Although some professors met at both, others chose to gather at only one of these meetings, and their choice of meeting reflected their curricular perspectives. In a survey regarding the location of the organization's meetings, one member, O. L. Davis, Jr., stated the following:

> I believe that this small group never intended to be large and always related to ASCD. It would change profoundly if it were to meet at other places and without the conversational nature it has fostered. I am not against a different group, but I am for this group, as it is. It has served me and my purposes well. I would not be served well with a group that met as suggested. What may well be needed is another group to meet at AERA. I could support that idea. . . . My purpose in saying this is to affirm my interest in fostering dialogue, friendship, and collegial relationships in as many forms as people find useful. I don't have to/need to be a member of each one...and am not.[16]

The Professors of Curriculum began debating the location of their meetings because of changes in ASCD. According to Van Til, ASCD changed significantly in the seventies and eighties when, under the leadership of Gordon Kawelti, its membership increased significantly. In the process, the nature of the membership also changed drastically. Although professors and curriculum developers made up the majority of ASCD's membership in the early years, over half of its current members are principals and graduate students of education. In addition, while the initial focus of the organization was to create a dynamic forum for professional interaction, its current focus has shifted to increasing its membership and to developing professional materials to be distributed for profit.

At the Professors of Curriculum 1993 meeting held in conjunction with ASCD, the issue took on significant form. In response to complaints voiced earlier by members of the Professors of Curriculum, ASCD organized a Review Council to address the issue and to report its findings to the group. The report focused on statistics regarding involvement of professors in the organization and concluded that the arguments posed by the Professors of Curriculum were based upon misconceptions. The Review Board recommended that ASCD add more sessions appealing to professors at their annual meetings and that the organization should also host a reception each year for the Professors of Curriculum.

The findings of the Review Council were not well received by the Professors of Curriculum. Members of the group argued that ASCD had become too large and too commercialized, and as a result, it had lost its progressive heritage. The Professors argued that the Review Council's focus on quantitative concerns of membership and operations ignored and undermined the heart of the issue. In a response to the Review Council, former and acting factotums, George Stansbury, Gerald Firth, and J. Dan Marshall responded with the following:

> In short, our concerns have to do with the professional "soul" of ASCD, a soul breathed to early life by many members of both that organization and the Professors of Curriculum. Ours are not so much concerns about how many higher education faculty play an active role in committee work and convention presentations as they are issues related to the quality of ASCD's life—and our association with that life.[17]

Thus, within this small professional organization, a variety of issues have emerged. The most prominent issues in recent years involve the group's collective identity and the tenuous negotiations of personal identity and professional association of its members.

The Spring Conference

The Spring Conference is an organization that was formed in 1935. The group began with 30 members and later grew to 70. Members of the Conference held a variety of positions including university presidents, teacher educators, school superintendents, community activists, philosophers, economists, union leaders, elected officials, and classroom teachers. Regardless of the status of their positions, members of the Conference came together as equals. As Harap (1984) notes in his report about the organization, "In the Spring Conference all were equals, all were important."

Throughout the history of the organization, the members have worked to keep the membership varied. The group was always open to African American members, but decades passed before women were allowed to participate. Van Til[18] describes his efforts to include women in the organization. He notes that his "fellow liberals" in the group argued that they would not feel comfortable with women in the group because members occasionally used profanity. To this argument Van Til replied that he knew "a great many profane women," and by 1973, the organization finally allowed women to participate.[18]

The general nature of the Spring Conference has changed little over the years. The annual meeting consists of two days during which the members engage in a "free trade of ideas."[19] Just as in the early years, Saturdays of their annual meetings begin with members sitting in an open square or circle formation. Members take turns sharing what they are doing and decide what problems or issues they would like to discuss during the weekend. Selected members record ideas shared during the Saturday morning discussions, and these same members use the information to determine the discussions that will take place during the weekend. Members are then assigned to different groups, and, within those groups, they help lead the discussions. According to Henry Harap (1984), records of the discussions were kept during four of the meetings between 1937 and 1967, and in those notes, a number of topics discussed were noted for each of the years.

In 1937, the group discussed whether the teacher union movement, particularly the affiliation with the American Federation of Labor, was a healthy professional relationship. They also discussed whether elementary and secondary education should be continuous without failure. They questioned whether "America's plunge into peasantry" could be stopped. In addition, they addressed the status of teacher education and identified significant innovations in education. In 1947, the group examined the conflict between liberals and UNESCO. They looked at the role of leadership within school program development. In addition, they talked about teacher shortages as well as the effect of teacher strikes on the position of teachers. In 1967, the group looked at national organizations and leadership in education. They explored promising educational changes and directions. In addition, they discussed the disadvantaged in slums and suburbs, new strategies in desegregation, and the dynamics of society. As indicated by the list kept by Harap (1984), discussions at the Spring Conference spanned broad and timely social and educational issues. That tradition continues today.

In addition to the discussion groups, members of the Conference interact socially throughout the weekend. According to Van Til (1975), it was important to have the conference in a location where no one in attendance would be tempted to return to their offices during the weekend, instead they would spend time with the other members in a variety of contexts. Harap (1984) also notes the importance of social interaction within the Spring Conference. In a 1961 letter to his wife, he describes his activities during the conference. He recalls having lunch with a number of the members, joining a group of members in one member's hotel room for cocktails following the afternoon sessions, and having dinner with others from the Conference. Harap remarks to his wife, "After the evening meeting I was thoroughly tired because I had been going continuously without rest and relaxation from the moment I arose." In recent years, conference members often walk together to Powell's Used Book Store (Chicago), and later in the evening they join the factotum in his suite for wine and conversation before going to dinner together.

To borrow a phrase from Voltaire, the Spring Conference appears to be the "best of all possible worlds." Created in our country's most stressful period of social and economic disarray and forged by noted liberals and radicals, the membership has a history of fearlessly addressing important issues head on. This group lived out its egalitarian beliefs by each member setting aside his title, however awe inspiring, when entering the conference. Members also equalized the expense of conference attendance. In a process that was called "put-and-take," conference members who received financial compensation for travel and members who did not have significant travel expenses because they lived in or around Chicago would offer money to those who had incurred more personal expenses in order to attend the meeting.

So what happened to the Spring Conference? Its membership has changed dramatically in recent years—both in size and in composition. The activists and well-known academics from education and elsewhere no longer attend. In recent years, the number of members present has fluctuated significantly. Often there are between 20 and 30 persons, but there have been as few as five in attendance. The members at the meetings fluctuate as well. According to Van Til, each factotum often brings groups of friends and associates to the conference during his term, but these individuals do not always commit to the Conference for future years.[18]

In addition, the organization struggles to find diversity among its members. Most of the members live in or around the Chicago area. Those members in other parts of the country often find it difficult to personally or institutionally justify the expense of the trip because the conference is no longer held in conjunction with another professional conference. Geography is not the only force for homogeneity. In recent years, very few individuals with diverse ethnic and racial backgrounds have joined the organization, and the few such members of the organization have not attended the meetings. Few, if any, women are joining the group, and in 1999, only one woman attended the conference.

Van Til and Gilchrist (early 1980s) warned of the Spring Conference's demise in the early eighties. They mused,

> The greatest danger to the Spring Conference is ourselves; Pogo once said, "We have met the enemy and he is us." For, rather than consciously seeking out mavericks for invitation to membership, we understandably, yet shortsightedly, too often bring into the fold like-minded associates. We need more irreverence and less respectability, more young and old prophets crying in the current educational, political, and social wilderness. If we can recruit creative and provocative members from labor, government, organizations, publishing, industry, et cetera, as well as stimulating educators, someone other than Bob and Bill will be writing the latest chapter in the Spring Conference history as the twentieth century becomes history. If not, the Spring Conference might wither away. Even worse, it might—God forbid—become a group that publishes its proceedings after lovefests characterized by mutual admiration and bland self-adoration.[20]

The Public Square

The public square of pre-industrial times was an arena for congregation. People within a community gathered there for specific purposes. The square was the focal point for interaction among members of a community. Those members might or might not have known one another. They might have been friends, relatives, or co-workers, but this was not a prerequisite. The mere fact that they were all members of a specific community provided reason enough for them to associate and interact with one another in a public square. Regular transactions, such as buying and selling, took place in such arenas. For good or for ill, the public square was a vibrant manifestation of one's community, one's culture.

Sennett (1974) contrasts the pre-industrial public square with what he refers to as "dead public space" that became prevalent in architecture following World War II. He offers as an example Gordon Bunshaft's Lever House in New York. This post-World War II architectural structure has an open-air square on its first floor, but Sennett notes that the square is designed for passage, not for congregation or community. He states,

> The form of this International-type skyscraper is at odds with its function, for a miniature public square revivified is declared in form, but the function destroys the nature of a public space, which is to intermix persons with diverse activities. (Sennett, 1994, p. 12)

Sennett (1974) continues that most architecture developed since World War II has been designed with the same thought in mind: open spaces for movement. He adds that many new structures also incorporate glass to remove distinctions between the buildings and their surroundings. In this design concept, Sennett argues, "the aesthetics of visibility and social isolation merge" (p. 13).

Do we find parallel "dead public space" within our curriculum organizations today? One merely has to stand back in a lobby of a Hilton or Marriott during AERA or ASCD to see the similarities. The nature of our professional conferences typically promotes movement—moving from one session to another, moving from one publisher's booth to another. Occasionally you may see a couple or a small group sitting at a bar between sessions, but the predominant scene is one of movement. We lack a sustained space for purposeful interaction among "others." There are occasional get-togethers—the John Dewey happy hour, different universities' social gatherings; but these functions bring together people with official associations, and the time together is very temporary. The social functions do provide opportunities to mingle, but they do not offer opportunities to create community.

What fate befalls a community lacking a public space? Sennett (1974) offers three consequences. First, individuals within a dead public space do not form relationships with those around them. How can you build relationships with others when you are merely passing through? While the Spring Conference offers the appearance of a community, its open forum is much like that of a facade of modern architecture. A few members are committed and come year after year, but many of the newer members come upon the advice of a friend and attend only as long as it is convenient. They do not establish relationships with other members that motivate them to return year after year.

Second, because movement also indicates freedom to move, individuals believe they have no connection to their surroundings unless those surroundings are a means to their destination. Institutional pressures to publish and the professional prestige that accompanies publishing and holding offices in professional organizations create, to varying degrees, a "What's in it for me?" attitude among professors. Therefore, organizations such as the Professors of Curriculum resort to offering invited papers from members. Likewise, organizations like the Spring Conference lose attendees because those professors find it difficult to justify attending professional meetings that do not afford opportunities to add lines to their vitas.

Third, Sennett (1974) argues that isolation is actually created by one's visibility to others. Like the glass windows of modern architecture, we are all very visible to one another when we come together for professional conferences. We see and are seen as we present papers or lead roundtables. Yet do we ever feel that we are building relationships with those around us as we participate?

Passive conference formats and ideological arrogance form the foundation of our glass walls in curriculum organizations. With presenters, as Van Til describes, offering esoteric papers and "occasionally speaking in the foreign tongue," Professors of Curriculum shift their focus from a dynamic and democratic community to linguistically and ideologically exclusive enclaves.[18]

If we believe in the democratic ideal, and if we wish to nurture that ideal within our professional organization, then we must create and sustain deliberate public spaces for purposeful interaction. The "public square," whatever form it may take in our professional organization, should be a vivid manifestation of our professional community.

The Stage

All the world's a stage, And all the men and women merely players.
                                        —William Shakespeare

According to Sennett (1974), we play roles within our public lives, and the world around us is our stage. He argues, however, that our efforts as actors have become less expressive and less artistic because we are unable to embrace external images of ourselves. We cannot use our imaginations to solve social problems because we do not accept our public roles. He states,

> As the imbalance between public and intimate life has grown greater, people have become less expressive. With an emphasis on psychological authenticity, people become inartistic in daily life because they are unable to tap the fundamental creative strength of the actor, the ability to play with and invest feeling in external images of self. Thus we arrive at the hypothesis that theatricality has a special, hostile relation to intimacy; theatricality has an equally special, friendly relation to a strong public life. (p. 37)

To counteract this social psychological dilemma in our public lives, we must create and sustain a public geography. We must create a social state in which the world around us and our relationships with others are consciously defined, so we are better able to negotiate our public interactions. Sennett (1974) offers conventions as a means through which we can create and sustain a public geography. He argues that conventions are the single most expressive element within society, but he adds that we reject conventions because they prevent us from revealing ourselves to each other. When we reject conventions, we reject the public possibilities found in role-playing.

For over 60 years, the Spring Conference has used conventions to create and sustain a public geography. First, roles within the meetings are clearly defined. Individuals are chosen to record the concerns and generate discussion groups, and the factotum organizes the meeting and takes care of all the necessary details for the weekend. In addition, individual members recognize their responsibilities within the group. They begin each annual meeting by sharing their concerns, or in the words of an early member, "Tell us what's on your mind these days as to school and culture—and don't take too long to do it."[20]

In contrast, the Professors of Curriculum have historically struggled with conventions within their organization. For nearly half a century, the group has debated the format of its meetings. They have repeatedly struggled with a balance between delivering formal papers and offering open forums for discussion. As a result, time and energy are spent on procedural issues at the expense of more opportunities to creatively explore and address curricular issues.

While conventions may help sustain a public geography, shared narratives are needed first to create the context through which we play out our roles. Unfortunately, postmodern angst and solitary retreats into theory often prevent us from forging these shared narratives. Philosophy is useful to the degree it links professors of curriculum and supports our moral responsibilities toward schooling. To this end, we should strive to live as *philosophes* rather than philosophers.

According to Postman (1999), *philosophes*, while guided by theory, were interested in practical matters and social issues. He identifies Jefferson, Franklin, Paine, and a number of other individuals from America's early history as *philosophes*. These men did not hold identical beliefs, and we could question some of their personal practices, but they did achieve a "transcendent narrative." They found common beliefs that, while held tentatively, led them to action. In order to form a community, professors of curriculum need a transcendent narrative. As Postman argues, "Without one (transcendent narrative), we can have no sense of purpose. Without a sense of purpose, we are left with only power as the source of authority."

The Coffeehouse

> *It is the folly of too many, to mistake the echo of a London coffee-house for the voice of the kingdom.*
> — Jonathan Swift

Coffeehouses were the "prime information centers" (Sennett, 1974) in London and Paris during the late seventeenth and early eighteenth centuries. When a man entered a coffeehouse, he would pay his penny at the bar, and if a newcomer, he would be directed as to the rules of the house. The conversations that flourished in the coffeehouses were guided by a cardinal principle. All distinctions of social rank were suspended within the house. Everyone was equal. Everyone at the coffeehouse had the right to speak, and everyone had the right to join conversations whether they knew the participants or not. Coffeehouses provided a temporary state of existence where social rank did not matter, and they accomplished this during a period of history when social rank outside the coffeehouse was of paramount importance.

Suspending rank and status among participants of a professional organization encourages richer interaction within the group. The Spring Conference has maintained the same rule throughout its existence. As Harap (1984) notes, everyone at the Conference is equal. It could be argued, however, that the degree to which the organization has maintained its absence of rank among members may also be a result of the absence of ranking status among individual members themselves. Van Til observes that current membership of the Spring Conference no longer includes the noted and notorious. Thus, one could argue that rank is not an issue within the Spring Conference because it is not an issue within its members in general.[20]

Arthur Wells Foshay was a member of the Professors of Curriculum who often dismissed issues of rank. While his colleagues would visit with each other before a presentation, Foshay would sit with graduate students and ask them about their research interests. Foshay also provided thoughtful and eloquent responses to a number of graduate students' inquiries on AERA's electronic research subscriber lines.

By creating a safe environment in which individuals of varying ranks could speak freely on public matters, London and Paris's coffeehouses offered refuge to a disappearing phenomenon. During this period of early industrialization, European society began to retreat from their public lives as the public display of status grew in popularity. Similarly, a curriculum organization dedicated to creating and maintaining a public life could offer a refuge at a time when the field itself is in such disarray.

According to Sennett (1974), the popularity of coffeehouses declined by the middle of the nineteenth century because European society became interested in the promenade. During this time, the number of public parks and outdoor cafes increased significantly, and members of the middle and upper classes frequented these areas to see and be seen. He notes, "At the café for the first time, there were large numbers of people massed together, relaxing, drinking, reading, but divided by invisible walls" (p. 217). This image offers a disturbing analogy to curriculum organizations. We have more and more opportunities to see and be seen, but within these opportunities we find ourselves also separated by invisible walls.

Recommendations for Building a Community

Choose a God to Serve

In his book, *The End of Education*, Postman (1995) discusses the existence of and the need for "gods" within schooling. However irreverent it may appear on the surface, Postman argues that schooling must serve a purpose or perhaps even several purposes. He contends, "There is no surer way to bring about an end in schooling than for it to have no end." I would offer the same argument for curriculum communities. In order to create a vibrant public space, we must esteem something greater than ourselves. We must clearly identify and articulate a sense of purpose for our collective existence. Postman adds, "Our genius lies in our capacity to make meaning through the creation of narratives that give point to our labors, exalt our history, elucidate the present, and give direction to our future" (p. 7).

It is important to caution, however, that choosing gods puts us in the position that we could choose poorly and thus create greater problems. As Dewey (1933) notes, the power to think frees us from being servants to instinct or routine; it does, however, afford the opportunity to make a mistake. Nevertheless, we should feel compelled to seek a common purpose in order to advance our collective relationships as well as our field. If no other sense of common purpose prevails, at the very least we should hold a common faith in what is possible:

> The artist, the scientist, citizen, parent, as far as they are actuated by the spirit of their callings, are controlled by the unseen. For all endeavor for the better is moved by faith in what is possible, not by adherence to the actual. (Dewey, 1934)

Dance

Why do people dance? Ignore those couples in ornate costumes with numbers on their backs. While you are at it, ignore the man in the bar offering the line that begins with, "Hey, baby...." Barring competitions and social aberrations, why do people dance? For many, dancing is an intrinsically rewarding practice. It falls into a category MacIntyre (1981) identifies as a social practice. According to MacIntyre, social practices are activities with rules that we pursue for their own sake. Contrast the professional baseball player with the children playing stickball in the field. Although professional baseball players may have an equally strong love of the game, they obviously have extrinsic motivations for going out on the field. The children in the field, however, play according to the same rules but do so for the sheer enjoyment of playing. They do not get money or recognition for playing a game of stickball. Their reward is purely intrinsic.

How can curriculum professors dance? You'd have to admit, taken literally, this image could be quite frightening. Curriculum professors can "dance" by forgetting status, vitas, titles, ranks, endowments, and publication records in order to inquire, to question, and to speculate, and they can do this for one purpose: to reach greater levels of understanding. As Dewey (1933) notes,

> It does not pay to tether one's thoughts to the post of use with too short a rope. Power in action requires some largeness and imaginativeness of vision. Men must at least have enough interest in thinking for the sake of thinking to escape the limits of routine and custom. (p. 139)

In order to consider our intellectual pursuits "dancing," however, we need rules or conventions. Just as the coffeehouses had rules of the house, forums within our professional associations that encourage inquiry for its own sake should also have established and clearly articulated rules for interaction.

Play Well with Others

Bellah and his colleagues (1985) contrast community with "lifestyle enclave." According to the authors, within a lifestyle enclave, a segment of a population comes together because of common personal traits. Two significant issues emerge from lifestyle enclaves. First, that which brings the members of an enclave together involves something about their personal lives. There is no public link within an enclave. Second, enclaves are by their very nature exclusionary. They do not include anyone who does not share the common personal traits.

I would argue that curriculum professors excel in creating and sustaining ideological enclaves. We tend to participate in conferences or subsets within conferences that contain like-thinkers. We do not make a conscious effort to build relationships with individuals whose perspectives differ from our own. When we do find ourselves in contact with ideological challenges, we fall into defensive, obtuse modes where we pride ourselves on the degree to which we can successfully levy theoretical attacks or the astute manner in which we can split theoretical hairs. At what point do we accept the advice of Dewey (1944) and enter into an opportunity for inquiry in such a manner that we are willing to have our own views modified? To what degree in our professional lives do we accept the notion that our ideas are, in fact, "working ideas" to be tested?

The Individual Within the Public Domain

Where does the individual fit within this proposed public life? After all, we have grown quite fond of our psyches, and we need to know their "place" within this conceptual scheme. Aha. This is the tricky part. In order to create a public life within curriculum, we must first reject the notion of the *individual* as a *given*. As Dewey (1954) notes, while our arrangements, rules, procedures, and even the organizations themselves are made for individuals, they are actually made for individuals insofar as those individuals exist within a social context. Professional organizations do not exist in order to cater to our narcissistic whims. Rather, "they are means of *creating* individuals." He continues, "Individuality in a social and moral sense is something to be wrought out. It means initiative, inventiveness, varied resourcefulness, assumption of responsibility in choice of belief and conduct. These are not gifts, but achievements" (p. 194).

Notions of the *individual as given* undermine our sense of community by misrepresenting our collective identity. According to Sennett (1974), collective identities formed outside of public life are based upon fantasy because they are shaped by appearances rather than shared action. He warns, "Just as personality itself has become an antisocial idea, collective personality becomes a group identity in society hostile to, difficult to translate into, group activity" (p. 223).

With this notion of *the individual achieved*, we come full circle. We began with ourselves, and we end with ourselves, only in the end we see ourselves as an achievement rather than a given right. Thus, we experience the promise of community. To the degree that we collectively achieve our ideals, we provide an ideal context in which each of us can live.

Final Thoughts

Let me tell you about a small city in the eastern corner of Atlanta. If you were just passing through and didn't know any better, you might think it is just part of the city, but it isn't; it's Decatur. In the heart of Decatur, right behind the old courthouse, you will find a large open area filled with beautiful trees and a tremendous gazebo. This is Decatur's square, and it is a square in the truest sense, defying Sennett's theories and modernity's stereotypes.

If you visit on a number of weekends throughout the year, you will see community bands playing and families gathering around on blankets with their picnic baskets. Parents are playing jacks and pick-up-sticks with their kids, and conversations abound between families, friends, neighbors, even strangers. When the music really gets going, you will see dancing. Parents and children, rich and poor, gay and straight, they dance. Their whirling and twirling around the gazebo displays a celebration of relationships and an unquenchable zest for a life well lived.

Stop by early on Sunday morning. On the steps of that same gazebo, you will see a group of homeless men holding their Sunday school lesson. During the week, visit one of the coffee shops and sit outside for a while. You can read the poetry someone has written in chalk on the sidewalk or start up a conversation with the person sitting at the next table. It's o.k. They do that sort of thing there.

In other words, Decatur is a community—a vibrant and remarkable municipality—where people don't just belong, they belong together. I spent a lot of time in that square this summer—taking it all in because I knew I had to leave. I had to move to Illinois to become a curriculum professor. Often when I sat at the coffee shop, I thought about what a community of curriculum professors might look like. I often thought, "Wouldn't it be wonderful if we could create a true community?" Regardless of our differences, how powerful it would be if we came together and esteemed something greater than ourselves. Our professional organizations offer the power of possibility for such a community. Let's use our organizations to create deliberate and vibrant public spaces. Let's work together, talk, play, and, yes, dance together; by all means, let us dance.

Endnotes

[1]Arthur Wells Foshay, interviewed over the phone by Donna Adair, 19 October 1994.

[2]William Van Til, interviewed by Donna Adair, Terre Haute, Indiana, 22 September, 2000.

[3]William Van Til, interviewed by Donna Adair, Terre Haute, Indiana, 22 September 2000.

[4]Letter to Craig Kridel from Hugh Wood, 9 April 1987. *Professors of Curriculum Collection* at the University of South Carolina's Teachers Museum, Columbia, South Carolina (Box 1, File 18).

[5]*Professors of Curriculum Collection* (Box 1, File 1).

[6]In 1979, a member of the organization published a collection of papers presented at their annual meeting. The following year the same member attempted to publish a second volume, but he was stopped in a heated debate by a number of the group's members. For more information, see *A History of the Professors of Curriculum: Reflections of the Field*, paper presented by author at the annual meeting of the American Educational Research Association, New York, New York, April 1994.

[7]William Van Til, interviewed by Donna Adair, Terre Haute, Indiana, 22 September 2000.

[8]William Van Til, interviewed by Donna Adair, Terre Haute, Indiana, 22 September 2000.

[9]*Professors of Curriculum Collection*, 1977 surveys (Box 2, File 3).

[10]*Professors of Curriculum Collection*, 1989 survey results (Box 2, File 3).

[11]Paul Klohr, "A Reaction to Section III, National Society for the Study of Education's Seventieth Yearbook," paper presented to the Professors of Curriculum, 1972 Annual Meeting (Box 2, File 1).

[12]John Mann, "The Curriculum: Retrospect and Prospect," a paper presented to the Professors of Curriculum, 1972 Annual Meeting (Box 2, File 1).

[13]The term "reconceptualist" was coined by William Pinar in his book *Curriculum Theorizing* (Berkeley: McCutchon Publishing, 1975), and it has often been used to identify curriculum theorists concerned with social, existential, and aesthetic issues within the field.

[14]*Professors of Curriculum Collection*, Trends in content of meetings can be found in the records of meeting agendas (Box 2, Files 1–29).

[15]Harold Drummond's 1985 survey to William Schubert (Box 2, File 18).

[16]O. L. Davis, Jr.'s survey to William Schubert (Box 2, File 18).

[17]Letter to Review Council from Gerald Firth, J. Dan Marshall, and George W. Stansbury, 16 August 1993.

[18]Van Til interview.

[19]Years ago, William Van Til borrowed this description from Chief Justice Holmes to describe the Spring Conference, and it has been associated with the group ever since.

[20]William Van Til and Bob Gilchrist. "Spring Conference: A Brief History (Continued)." Paper written for the Spring Conference in the early eighties.

References

Bellah, R. N., Madsen, R., Sullivan, W. M., Swidler, A., & Tipton, S. M. (1985). *Habits of the heart: Individualism and commitment in American life*. Berkeley, CA: University of California Press.

Dewey, J. (1916–1917). The need of an industrial education in an industrial democracy. *Middle Works, 10,* 139.

———— (1933). *How we think*. Boston: Heath.

———— (1934). *A common faith*. New Haven, CT: Yale University Press.

———— (1944). *The sources of science of education*. New York: Liveright.

———— (1954). *The public and its problems*. Athens, OH: Ohio University Press.

Harap, H. (1984). Spring conference: A brief history. Paper presented to the Spring Conference.

Hlebowitsh, P. S. (1993). *Radical curriculum theory reconsidered: A historical approach*. New York: Teachers College Press.

Huebner, D. (1976). The moribund curriculum field: Its wake and our work. *Curriculum Inquiry, 6*(2).

Jackson, P. (1980). Curriculum and its discontents. *Curriculum Inquiry, 1*(1).

MacIntyre, A. (1981). *After virtue: A study of moral theory* (1st ed.). Notre Dame, IN: University of Notre Dame Press.

Pinar, W. (1975). The reconceptualization of curriculum studies. *Journal of Curriculum Studies, 10*(3).

Postman, N. (1995). *The end of education: Redefining the value of school*. New York: Alfred A. Knopf.

———— (1999). *Building a bridge to the eighteenth century*. New York: Knopf.

Schwab, J. A. (1969). The practical: A language for curriculum. *School Review, 78,* 1–24.

Sennett, R. (1974). *The fall of public man: On the social psychology of capitalism*. New York: Random House.

Van Til, W. (1975). One way of looking at it: Start your own Spring Conference. *Phi Delta Kappan*.

———— (1983). *My way of looking at it: An autobiography*. Terre Haute, IN: Lake Lure.

Wraga, W. (1999). Extracting sun-beams out of cucumbers: The retreat from practice in reconceptualized curriculum studies. *Educational Researcher, 28*(1), 4–13.

Part II

The Aesthetics and Environment of Place

Photograph by Anna Latta

Chapter 4

Traces, Patterns, Texture: In Search of Aesthetic Teaching/Learning Encounters

Margaret Macintyre Latta

Art rooms in schools are often found in far-removed basement corners, tucked away at the nexus of numerous hallways. I have taken many such ventures on my way to visit student teachers in art classrooms in my capacity as a teacher educator. Today was not too different. The art room was tucked away in the basement, but students and teachers had temporarily relocated to a nearby room to accommodate some maintenance in the art room. I was particularly struck today by the nature of aesthetic teaching/learning encounters. Its visible presence was not immediately apparent. I found myself in a makeshift room with little visual appeal. But, as 25 grade 4 students entered and got involved in artistic learning, the makeshift classroom transformed into a dynamic learning space, a space that felt productive and energized. I dwelt in this wonder, conversed with it, and found myself reluctant to leave. What was it that I found so attractive and compelling? Was it the same fundamental encounter that many others have identified as the aesthetic?

Notions of the aesthetic have a long, venerable tradition. There, Kant (1790/1952), Schiller (1795/1954), Hegel (1835/1964), Gadamer (1960/1992), and Dewey (1934; 1938), to name but a few, address the human worth of the aesthetic. The location, purpose, and lived world of the knowing subject are addressed from differing perspectives by these thinkers, but all turn to the aesthetic as giving expression to that fundamental encounter between subject and world. It is particularly intriguing to me that these thinkers turn to the aesthetic as a medium that bridges theory and practice and to the arts as exemplary forms that embody these qualities. Kant redirects attention from the objects of experience to the experiencing subjects. Schiller and Hegel continue this search. Gadamer and Dewey remind me that the relationship between subject and world is reciprocal, both changing in the interaction. While exploring how the aesthetic might be embodied in teachers' discourses and discursive patterns and how it might be embodied in students' approaches to learning and in their work, I turn to these traditions. I (re)collect concrete incidents from a variety of classrooms visited in which students and teachers are grappling with taking aesthetic teaching/learning considerations seriously.[1] I then juxtapose these with historical sediments. In so doing, traces, patterns, and texture surfaces that have shaped the identity and purpose of the aesthetic, yielding insights into the creation of aesthetic teaching/learning encounters.

Historical Sediments

Kantian Traces

Through exploring the relationships between subject and world, Kant (1790/1952) concerns himself with human response, the aesthetic experience, rather than with the art object. He struggles against the general notion that art and the aesthetic is unnatural and that the artist is a rare and eccentric individual, having little or nothing in common with others. Kant's use of the word *genius* may at first glance appear to suggest quite the contrary. But he carefully describes genius not as a noun, but as a verb referring to the etymological origin *genie*, meaning *peculiar guardian* and *guiding spirit*. His portrayal brings to my mind a creative attitude, an invitation to free thinking, exploration, and growth. Kant asks us to concentrate on acts of mind rather than on already created objects.

I have observed concentrating upon acts of mind and not end products to be absorbing for some students and teachers. For example, a grade 8 student, Will, explains his thinking for a humanities class project:

> I lost all track of time. I could not believe it was time to pick up for the next class. We were drawing from a still life arrangement of personal objects. The objects chosen are supposed to recall strong memories for us. I have always been very attached to the stuff I brought so it did not take me long to decide what to bring from home for this project. I spent today drawing my composition. I am trying to represent the different textures accurately; like the basketball has a slightly tired look…missing parts of the logo, well used, but still okay; the rock my dad and I found at the top of a mountain is cold, flat, and heavy, with interesting markings. I have really had to examine each piece. Actually, I have probably never paid each piece so much attention. (Interview #2, Jan. 19, 1999)

Will's voice and body language represent the process as pleasurable. A language for describing the objects is fostered from the close observation drawing exercise, and this, in turn, feeds back into the visual portrayal as Will purposely adapts and changes his work and thinking. Will's teacher, Lorraine, comments:

> I do not know how to reconcile this kind of richness and complexity with outcome-based objectives except to say that in doing things this way we have explored the writing objectives that were the curriculum goals, but also made it possible to cover a lot of other territory as well. I find it fascinating to see how students loop back to previous literary or art encounters and link them with new ideas that are emerging.…Emerging is perhaps, the keyword here. The interactions seem to result in ideas moving to more complexity. This grappling in-between seems to be a way for individuals to discover meaning, a way to make sense of things that integrate mind and body. The interface is interesting. (Artifact #16, April 8,1999)

Lorraine's attentiveness as a teacher tells her students make learning connections that really matter to them through such involvement. Her use of the words "loop back" and "emerging" places value on unpredictable patterns of thought. Lorraine searches for ways to foster learning encounters that allow all students to come to appreciate, acknowledge, and utilize such patterns of thought. Lorraine struggles to make room for this way of thinking. An imaginary space needs to be created in students' understandings and a physical space needs to be created that is supportive and complementary. Marcuse (1978) talks of the aesthetic being such a location:

> A designated imaginative space where the experience of freedom is recreated. At times it is a physical entity, a site—a painting on the wall, an installation on the floor, an event chiseled in space and or time, a performance, a dance, a video, or film. But it is also a psychic location, a place in the mind where one allows for a recombination of experiences, a suspension of the established rules that govern daily life, a denial of gravity. It challenges the monopoly of the established reality by creating. Fictitious worlds in which one can see mirrored that range of human emotion and experience that does not find an outlet in the present reality....It is the reminder of what a truly integrated experience of oneself in society might be. (p. 41)

But, this sense of the aesthetic as an internal/external location seems difficult to create and sustain in classrooms. Lorraine explains:

> It is exhaustive at times and at other times exhilarating. There are so many tensions that interrupt and disrupt the flow in my classroom. Sometimes it's the pressures of grading and report card periods. Sometimes it's the kids themselves—I get frustrated with them, as some just want me to provide the easy way or right answer. Sometimes it's the classroom itself—the lack of supplies, the lack of storage, the lack of physical space for so many bodies to be creative. (Interview #4, Feb. 16, 1999)

Students also confront the difficulty of the aesthetic as an internal/external creation. Bruce, a grade 7 student, comments:

> At times I find the projects overwhelming—a lot to think about and keep organized in my mind. That is when I miss a tighter structure. It was definitely easier not to think as hard. In this classroom you must be willing to take risks and do things differently. Most of the time I like that the learning is not so unpredictable. And most of the time I like that the teacher asks me what I think. (Interview #1, Oct. 21, 1998)

The possibility of concentrating on acts of mind is often in tension with the desire for certainty and ease. Lorraine struggles to create learning encounters requiring students to discover a formula, not to follow one. Bruce begins to feel the demands of such learning encounters. Those without this sense fail to understand the purposefulness behind the learning encounters. Students and the teacher have to enter into learning as a problem to be explored or a new adventure as Will's and Lorraine's earlier words relay. This attitude coupled with commitment seems critical. Maureen, a grade 8 student, echoes this thinking, talking enthusiastically about her sculpture piece in progress after attending an art exhibit of local works:

> My first impression of this art gallery thing was that it would probably interrupt everything I was doing, and it did! But, really, I think that it is pretty neat because I like art. My favorite piece was the one with Winkin, Blinkin, and Nod in their so-called wooden shoe. The thing I liked most about it was that they were all girls instead of boys. It was also surprisingly colorful and bright. The sculpture I am working on is a shoe form too. Though my idea is different, this sculpture made me go back to my work with some thoughts about ways to really capture attention and make a statement. I need to think more about this, but it will change my work. (Interview #1, Oct. 21, 1998)

Maureen's words suggest that in the very process of perception and in the interconnected process of expression, a tendency to form is elicited. Kant's (1790/1952) event termed *delight* (p. 41), its presence, its possibilities, is given expression by Maureen. Kant claims this event arises from a mental state present in the free play of the imagination and understanding. Imagination is the activation of the senses, and understanding relates to the faculty of cognition in general. When they are freely interacting, delight emerges of its own volition. There is a feeling of "concert" in the play of mental powers (p. 71). A certain randomness, an unpredictability, is assumed in Kant's discussion. Within Maureen's forming experience of her sculpture, delight emerges through the insights gained. Kant (1790/1952) speaks of these insights as "aesthetic ideas" (p. 175) evidenced in the union of imagination and understanding acting together as catalysts within process.

Maureen experiences an allegiance to learning through manipulation of ideas, materials, and the demands of continual judgments in her creative process. I see this evoked in a fluid action rather than a rigid sequence. This fluidity of thought is evidenced again in an excerpt from a written reflection on some philosophical readings for a humanities class by Andrea, a grade 8 student:

I find Horace Walpole's statement, "This world is a comedy to those who think, a tragedy to those who feel, a solution to why Democritus laughed and Heraclitus wept" truly intriguing. I read somewhere else that Democritus is often called the laughing philosopher because he believed that we all have an individual conscience that can decipher right from wrong. I have met people who think very deeply about what has been said or done and seem to be able to make anything funny. But, I also know there are people who feel everything strongly, which is good when they are happy but they are often sad. I think it is easier not to feel, for feeling makes you vulnerable. Being vulnerable is considered weak. But, perhaps it shouldn't be. For sure, if you only ever think and never feel others get hurt without your knowledge. I now wonder if it is possible to separate thinking from feeling? Are they really different? (Artifact #61, May 25, 1999)

Fluidity of thought is not necessarily smooth and linear, rather an acceptance of living with doubts and uncertainties seems essential to respond to newly discovered relationships, determine ways of working and acting, attend to modifications derived from these discoveries, or trust intuitions. Kant (1790/1952) acknowledges these subjective responses to be the determining ground of the aesthetic. He roots these in immediate sensible particularities coining the term "disinterestedness" (p. 43). I do not confuse this with uninterest-edness. For Kant, disinterestedness assumes involvement, participation, and contemplation. I have come to see it as a paradoxical term, embracing impersonal objectivity with intense personal participation. Kant suggests that:

The cognitive powers brought into play by this representation are here engaged in free play, since no definite concept restricts them to a particular role of cognition. Hence, the mental state in this representation must be one of a feeling of the free play of the powers of representation. (p. 58)

It follows then that the outcome depends on the nature of the subject and the interaction taking place and is not held to a premeditated purpose with preestablished rules. Out of this awareness Kant identifies a respect for "the super-sensible substrate of phenomena" (p. 208), his central claim being that within aesthetic judgment, rules are created, concepts formed, and categories organized to fit the unique instance presented by works of art. For Kant aesthetic encounters are not mediated through existing rules but result in the creation of rules, forming the basis on which the work can subsequently be talked about (p. 168). I see expression of this in Maureen's and Andrea's descriptions of their thinking processes.

Schillerian Traces

Schiller (1795/1954) writes a series of letters, *On the Aesthetic Education of Man*, over a period of three years, documenting the evolution of his thinking on the aesthetic. The letters are poetic as Snell (1954) comments:

> As much a piece of feeling as of thinking; a passionate attempt, by gazing at the opposites of reason and sensuousness, freedom and caprice, mind and nature, duty and inclination, absolute and finite, activity and passivity...to grasp the unity lying behind there. (p. 14)

Schiller's (1795/1954) apprehension of this sense of unity monopolizes his thoughts throughout his letters. His pursuit of this unity throughout his letters comprises a doctrine of education embracing the aesthetic. Schiller understands an aesthetic education to be a meeting place of one's senses with the external world. This reciprocal relationship is taken up by Schiller as play. He is drawn to Kant's (1790/1952) use of the term *play* to characterize the cognitive meeting of *imagination* and *understanding* (p. 71). Fleshing out Kant's notions, he associates imagination with the sensuous impulse (p. 64) and understanding with the formal impulse (p. 65). Schiller sees these as two fundamental human impulses. The sensuous impulse impels experience of the changing world, and the formal impulse reflects *rational* and *absolute existence*, insisting on *changelessness* (p. 66). Schiller insists on the tendency of these impulses to conflict and encroach on each other, mediated by a *play impulse* (p. 74). This impulse is characterized by being a living form, "a free movement which is itself ends and means" (p. 134). He assumes reciprocity between the self and its determinations (p. 60). Schiller sees unity achieved through play, claiming "man plays only when he is in the full sense of the word a man, and he is only wholly man when he is playing" (p. 80). Thus, he refuses to compartmentalize human beings, insisting on an organic whole. In Schiller's words, the "cultivation of the whole of our sensuous and intellectual powers in the fullest possible harmony" becomes the educational imperative (p. 99).

The locus of Schiller's (1795/1954) sense of play is dependent on the other as much as self. A dialogical structure is suggested that is realized through an interdependent process. Jocelyn, a grade 7 student, reconstructs the relationship between self and other exploring this interdependence. She gradually becomes aware of the subtle complexities of such intertwining. She talks with me over a few weeks about the image she is creating in her humanities class to synthesize her thinking on a particular cultural concept that she feels needs to be addressed:

> My image is called "Story to Story." It depicts a story being passed along from generation to generation. A story gets changed just a little each time it is retold to someone new. Each of my purple circles represents a new telling of the story. If you look closely at them, you will see that each circle changes just a little from the last circle. They change slightly in size. The shapes in and around the circles change colors, shape, size, and in quantity. The circles evolve just like a story. I decide to use a geometric shape (circle) and a fibonacci sequence because we have been studying patterning in math and science. I can see that cultural stories have similar patterns. There are things that repeat themselves over and over again....But, as I was working on it, I also thought that it is not always the same—there are differences that make each story unique. That is why I chose clashing, dissimilar colors because they are like the stories of long ago; there are differences that make the story interesting to listen to. In the beginning, the story starts out as a small purple circle. It gets changed many, many times. It is a chaotic journey. But, in many ways it is still a small purple circle with little change. (Interview #2, March 9, 1999; Interview #3, March 16, 1999)

Jocelyn has become accustomed to addressing her schoolwork in this way. She expects that her ideas will change during process. Schiller (1795/1954) talks about this playful process being *energizing* or *melting* (p. 83). Similarly, Jocelyn's thoughts seem to be a catalyst to possibilities and precipitate reflection towards reassessment. A necessary relationship between self and other is assumed, informing how she approaches her work. Jocelyn brings selective resources from her past to bear on the present, linking her to her image, creating a belongingness. Thus, Jocelyn brings a way of thinking and being to her work by assuming these expectations.

Central within this relationship between Jocelyn and her image creation is a felt freedom. It exudes from Jocelyn throughout her creating/re-creating process. Schiller (1795/1954) talks of such freedom developing by inner necessities. Perhaps these are the pleasure and pride Jocelyn derives from decisions made and the course her learning takes. Increasingly, I see and hear in other student voices the anticipation of felt freedom within process. Participating students report deriving much pleasure from this felt freedom, and I see it acting as a catalyst toward establishing and sustaining relationships between self and other.

Akin to Schiller's (1795/1954) notion of freedom intimately associated with inner necessities is Greene's (1978) description of how discovery is taken out of learning in many teaching/learning situations: "The self as participant, as inquirer, as creator of meanings has been obliterated" (p. 12). Rather than conformity being rewarded in these classrooms, difference is not cause for alarm but celebration. These learning encounters attempted to build on personal uniqueness rather than dismiss or negate it altogether. Participating students were very much aware of this attempt. For example, Marjorie, a grade 8 student, comments:

> I did not realize until I came to this school that I had been missing something in my learning. I now feel very attached to some of my work, like it is a part of who I am. I have learned things about myself and who I am becoming. The class discussions of our work have really encouraged this because I get to see and hear so many ways to consider one question or project. (Interview #5, March 16, 1999)

In a later conversation I had with Marjorie, she explains she did not feel this same level of commitment in another classroom setting at the same school and felt it was important to discuss this with the school principal:

> I am not willing to just let this go. I feel let down. I am here to learn. And learning for me is questioning and being allowed to search for answers. I do not want the answers given to me; asking me to memorize them but not really know them. (Interview #6, May 18, 1999)

Marjorie has developed an appreciation for yearning, wonder, fear, and confusion throughout the learning process. She has also been listened to with great care by teachers and, in turn, classmates. In some learning situations Marjorie felt safe to convey her unique perspectives. Marjorie knows the difference. She likes the felt involvement in her learning and the sense of community participation. The alienation from learning she abruptly meets dulls and numbs her sense of herself as a learner, eroding her spirit of inquiry. It becomes risky for Marjorie to ask questions that matter to her. And yet, she is not necessarily searching for answers but rather, wanting simply to be heard.

The aesthetic becomes a medium in which a form emerges through engaged relationships between self and other. This was Schiller's (1795/1954) answer to human fragmentation—to follow the path of aesthetics leading to wholeness. Some students comment that they like the involvement they feel in their learning. I note a stronger sense of selfdeveloping in many students alongside a developing respect for and honoring of differences in each other.

Hegelian Traces

This revelation of self is explored by Hegel (1835/1964) as a transcendental quality existing as *Geist* or spirit. He conceives of spirit as a living and self-developing identity involving a relation between self and other. Through interactions with the other, one attains greater consciousness of oneself.

Lorraine initiates these interactions through valuing first impressions from her students. She deliberately asks students to note initial impressions as they confront new questions, projects, or mediums. Cindy, a grade 9 student, notes, "Strange, isn't it, how things in life can be two completely different emotions" (Artifact #20, Nov. 17, 1998). Megan, a grade 8 student, writes, "One piece that drew my attention was a drawing of just the trunks of trees. It was black and white and the artist used mainly vertical lines. Even though it was simple, it was striking" (Artifact #25, Nov. 17, 1998). These initial responses trigger further thinking. Lorraine terms these interactions "stretching exercises" deliberately positioning students to connect learnings across topics and disciplines. These stretching exercises take multiple forms, but students are meant to feel the pull between self and other. As they experience this pull, an animating or essential part of self is revealed in passion and commitment that intimately connects students to their learnings. Hegel's (1835/1964) sense of spirit comes alive, existing and thriving in a play of meanings between self and other.

Hegel (1835/1964) suggests the relation of self and other is best explored through a dialectical development. Instead of a dialectic taking a set course, as Hegel envisions, I see this play of meanings taking the form of conversations understood as Yinger's (1987) notion of a *conversation of practice*:

> One of the Latin roots of conversation is *conversari* meaning to dwell with. This suggests that conversation entails an entering into and living with a context and its participants. As such, conversation is not only a means of interaction and a way of thinking, but also a type of relationship with one's surroundings. (p. 311)

Most importantly, in my mind, it equates education with relation, content meaning little without contact.

Gadamerian Traces

Relationships between self and other established and nurtured seem to endure; a significance is retained. Lorraine's description of a teaching/learning incident reveals the need for this significance. Lorraine discusses the background of an assignment on the human body and disease that she has students working on:

> I mentioned to students that we were about to begin a unit of study on our bodies and the impact of disease. The class erupted with comments such as, "We have done that so many times; I am sick of looking up diseases in encyclopedias." The groans and moans were not something I could ignore. I did have something in mind, but the complete lack of enthusiasm was weighty and going to defeat my attempt. We had invited a playwright into the classroom last week to do some idea generating and writing activities with students. It just popped into my head that maybe students could write

about a disease in a science fiction play format. And, so, together we
invented "Ritchie," a fictitious person who was about to be invaded by
diseases of all types and intensities. (Interview #6, April 6, 1999)

Lorraine goes on to explain that she observed students' interest and
commitment to the assignment slowing growing as she let go of her
specific idea for the learning and let students author the learning.
Such authoring brings to life the reciprocal relationship between self
and other. This is Gadamer's (1960/1992) understanding of *play* as
distinct from self and the other. Play is its own experience, resisting
means and ends, reliant on the performance (p. 134). The reciprocal
interaction and modification generates meanings within the
relationship. Gadamer emphasizes that such play has a spirit of its
own to which participants must attend and take up. Anna, a grade 8
student in this class, finds this playful spirit. I relay an excerpt from
her written script, which gives further expression to this play:

> (Tour group makes its way through destructed tissue tubes)
> TOUR GUIDE: Welcome ladies and gentlemen to this section of the
> endocrine system. I will be your guide today. I will lead you through
> Ritchie's pancreas. I am ready to answer any questions. Please follow
> me and our tour can begin.
> (Group follows guide through area that looks like a ratty old dish cloth; torn,
> battered, lots of holes, thin, etc.)
> TOUR GUIDE: Now, as you can see the pancreatitis has eaten away at
> Ritchie's pancreas causing destruction of the tissues. This has been
> caused by Ritchie's excessive drinking, and as a result he has two
> choices: to die, or pray to God that he can get a transplant in time. Take
> a minute to look around, and I will be over here if you have any
> questions.
> WOMAN ONE (speaking to woman two): This is worse than I thought it
> would be. Think what bad shape the boy must be in! (motherly) The
> pancreas is very important. Normally it secretes digestive enzymes,
> insulin, and many more hormones, but that is only possible when the
> pancreas is healthy. On average the pancreas is about 1.3 to 2.5
> centimeters thick.
> WOMAN TWO (responding): Yes, I know. I thought this was going to be the
> calmest tour of them all. Look at the size of those holes and how thin
> and frail the tissue is. It looks like my old dishcloth I threw out last
> week! (Artifact #40, April 27, 1999)

Anna was positioned to find ways to relay meaningfully the information gathered on the pancreas for herself and others. Her search for visual images and descriptors transcends factual knowledge of the pancreas to a much wider sense of the ensuing impact and disruption of the disease. Thus, she appropriates and internalizes this thinking. The link between Anna and her thinking reflects a strong sense of belonging, and as Gadamer (1960/1992) claims, "(she) comes to belong to it more fully by recognizing (herself) more profoundly in it" (p. 133). It seems transformed subjectivities emerge from play, taking something away from the process. Thus, the centrality of the other is constitutive of the self. I hear in Anna's voice and in the voices of other participating students and teachers the impact of such involvement. Students and teachers invest themselves in their learning processes. Their comments hold an emotional commitment that intimately connects them to their work. They question, deliberate, and respond accordingly on an ongoing basis. A seriousness surrounds these learning encounters that is evidenced in care. Seemingly, such responsive care entails responsibility. The subject matter does matter to students and teachers.

Deweyan Pattern

I find Dewey's (1938) notion of *experience* to embrace the Kantian, Schillerian, Hegelian, and Gadamerian traces of the aesthetic identified above. Experience is a fully human activity, a way of being in the world that does not separate knowledge from interest or theory from practice but insists on a pervasive qualitative whole. Dewey (1934) explains:

> In such experiences, every successive part flows freely, without seam and without unfilled blanks, into what ensues. At the same time there is no sacrifice of the self-identity of the parts....In an experience, flow is from something to something. As one part leads into another and as one part carries on what went before, each gains distinctness in itself. The enduring whole is diversified by successive phases that are emphases of its varied colors. (p. 45)

The implied unity and movement are critical to understanding Dewey's notion of experience as a *moving force* (1938, p. 31) acknowledging past, present, and implications for the future. Simultaneously, all human experience is ultimately social, involving contact and communication. Thus, Dewey (1938) identifies the *principle of continuity* (p. 27) and the *principle of interaction* (p. 38). "An experience is always what it is because of a transaction taking place between an individual and what, at the time constitutes his environment.... They intercept and unite" (pp. 43-44). And it seems the determining ground, meeting place of situation and interaction, forms the necessary space for aesthetic encounters; such a space being always in the making, open to the play of possibilities.

It is Dewey (1934) who sees that experience comes to be "what it is because of the entire pattern to which it contributes and which it is absorbed" (p. 295). Thus experience involves participants actively structuring what is encountered. The voices included throughout this paper exemplify the active *undergoing* (open, vulnerable, receptive attitude) and *doing* (responding, organizing, discerning) entailed in Dewey's notion of experience. Their thinking grows, constructing and reconstructing, taking form through adapting, changing, and building meaning. The play between undergoing and doing is always evolving with beginnings and endings occurring throughout the learning encounters. Thus Dewey (1934) explains: "An experience has pattern and structure, because it is not just doing and undergoing in alternation, but consists of them in relationship" (pp. 50, 51).

Dewey (1934, 1938) emphasizes to me that identified traces sedimented in the writings of Kant (1790/1952), Schiller (1795/1954), Hegel (1835/1964), and Gadamer (1960/1992) are all linked and do not succeed one another but, rather, yield patterns. It is experienced as connected. These traces exist only within the creating, making play, attached to the learning encounter. It is impossible to separate each trace away from aesthetic experience. I see these traces as living parts and aspects in relation to the vital movement of the whole pattern or learning encounter. It seems they belong to the self and situation concerned in this movement.

Texture

I believe these traces and patterns draw attention to an awareness that the experience of creating precipitates. This attunement to the creating process is the nature of aesthetic encounters. Initiating, sustaining, and enhancing links between students and learning through aesthetic encounters is central in these classrooms. Thus, students and teachers take up learning as a constant process of reciprocal interaction and modification between self and subject matter. This entails teachers and students developing a sensitivity to the many nuances and possibilities present in learning situations and a willingness to play along with them. The catalyst for learning is generated within the teaching/learning experience rather than imposed. Curriculum in classrooms forms as it lives through aesthetic encounters. Thus, the curriculum is neither entirely foreseen nor preconceived, animated with movement and life. It is experienced differently for individuals and the class as a whole, and yet I am aware of a sameness in lived sensations that the aesthetic traces speak to. The patterning or interplay of these traces seems to involve teachers and students in a *mindfully embodied* way demanding that they be "in touch with self, others, and the character of the circumstances they find themselves in" (Field & Macintyre Latta, 2001). I believe this is an aesthetic encounter's philosophical significance in teaching and learning. The lostness and foundness self-inherent within such attunement to process are constituted within Dewey's (1934) metaphor of the *live creature*, "the live being recurrently loses and reestablishes equilibrium with his surroundings" (p. 17). An obliterated self is severed from learning, detached from the circumstances in which learning develops. The interplay of a lost and found self is achieved through an "organic connection between education and personal experience" (Dewey, 1938, p. 25).

Thus, there is a texture and continuity in the actuality of aesthetic encounters that I believe is worth paying closer attention to. The historical sediments surface as necessarily and integrally forming and reforming learning patterns to aesthetically play with ideas, search for connections, and see possibilities for students and teachers. The implications for curriculum, students, and context are interrelated and deserving of further study. Clearly, though, it evidences aesthetic encounters as a pragmatic and philosophical necessity within schooling meriting serious consideration. But teachers must assume the weighty responsibility of addressing this consideration. The primary responsibility is the teacher's to assume, embracing tensions and uncertainties as inherent to teaching and learning, searching for attunement within the development of curriculum itself. Dewey (1938) further claims, "We have no choice but either to operate in accord with the pattern it (experience) provides or else to neglect the place of intelligence in the development and control of a living and moving experience" (p. 88). So, Dewey places teachers at the vortex of this movement, actively facilitating learning connections with students. Dewey claims the educator needs to come to view teaching and learning as a continuous process of reconstruction of experience. *Connectedness* is discussed as the necessary thread that precludes meaningful learning:

> It is part of the educator's responsibility to see equally to two things: First, that the problem grows out of the conditions of the experience being had in the present, and that it is within the range of the capacity of students; and secondly, that it is such that it arouses in the learner an active quest for information and for production of new ideas. (p. 79)

This inquiry reveals this crucial guidance of teachers toward surveying the capacity and needs of students, the formation of ideas, acting upon ideas, fostering connections, seeing potential, making judgments, and arranging conditions. Each aesthetic trace causes me to wonder how teachers learn to create experiences that foster student participation in the world aesthetically. The following considerations surface:

- Given the emphasis in schools on outcomes and results, how do we encourage teachers to focus on acts of mind instead of end products in their work with students?
- Given the orientations toward technical rationality, to fixed sequence, how do we help teachers experience fluid, purpose-

ful learning adventures with students in which the imagination is given room to play?

- Given the tendency to conceive of planning in teaching as the deciding of everything in advance, how do we help teachers and students become attuned to making good judgments derived from within learning experiences?
- How do we help teachers build dialogical multivoiced conversations instead of monolithic curriculum?
- What do we do to recover the pleasure dwelling in subject matter? How do we get teachers and students to engage thoughtfully in meaningful learning as opposed to *covering curriculum*?
- A capacity to attend sensitively, to perceive the complexity of relationships coming together in any teaching/learning experience seems critical. How do we help teachers and students attend to the unity of a learning experience and the play of meanings that arises from such *undergoing* and *doing*?

The traces, patterns, and texture evidenced locate tremendous hope and wondrous possibilities alive within aesthetic teaching/ learning encounters. It is such aliveness I encountered in the grade 4 art classroom that opened this account and continues to compel my attention. Possibilities for teaching, learning, and teacher education emerge. I am convinced they are most worthy of continued pursuit.

Endnote

[1] The data represented in this paper are part of a two-year inquiry conducted at a middle school with a mandate to infuse the arts-making processes across the curriculum as a whole. Twenty-six students and their parents, 3 teachers, and 2 school administrators participated throughout the inquiry. The data consisted of on-going interviews with all participants, student work/artifacts, teacher work/ artifacts, and classroom observations. For a more extensive analysis of the findings arising from this inquiry, refer to Macintyre Latta (2001).

References

Dewey, J. (1934). *Art as experience*. New York: Capricorn.

Dewey, J. (1938). *Experience and education*. New York: Collier.

Field, J. C., & Macintyre Latta, M. (2001). What counts as experience in teacher education? *Teaching and Teacher Education, An International Journal of Research and Studies, 17*, 885–895.

Gadamer, H. G. (1992). *Truth and method*. (J. Weinsheimer & D. Marshall, Trans.) New York: Continuum. (Original work published 1960.)

Greene, M. (1978). *Landscapes of learning*. New York: Teachers College Press.

Hegel, G. W. F. (1964). The philosophy of fine art. In A. Hofstadter & R. Kuhns (Eds.), *Philosophies of art and beauty* (pp. 382–445). Chicago: University of Chicago Press. (Original work published in 1835.)

Kant, I. (1952). *The critique of judgment*. Oxford, England: Clarendon. (Original work published 1790.)

Macintyre Latta, M. (2001). *The possibilities of play in the classroom: On the power of aesthetic experience in teaching, learning, and researching*. New York: Peter Lang.

Marcuse, H. (1978). *The aesthetic dimension*. Boston: Bercuson.

Schiller, F. (1954). *On the aesthetic education of man in a series of letters*. New York: Frederick Unger. (Original work published 1795.)

Snell, R. (1954). Introduction. In F. Schiller (Ed.), *On the aesthetic education of man in a series of letters* (pp. 1–20). New York: Frederick Ungar.

Yinger, R. J. (1987). Learning the language of practice. *Curriculum Inquiry, 17*(3), 293–318.

Chapter 5

An Environment for Developing Souls: The Ideas of Rudolf Steiner

Bruce Uhrmacher

Introduction

The purpose of this chapter is to examine Rudolf Steiner's (1861–1925) holistic approach to the environment—particularly as applied in Waldorf education. In his spiritual ideas and holistic mode of thinking, environments are not merely inert shells. For Steiner, environments possess life. They stimulate thinking. They shape moral possibilities. An understanding of Steiner's view of the environment offers much to inform our thinking about education generally and the educational environment in particular.

To understand Steiner's ideas about the environment, we will employ an appropriately far-reaching Steinerian definition of "environment" which covers the general idea of "surroundings." This definition will allow us to examine not only Steiner's notions as they relate to Waldorf schools but also his relevant architectural and cosmological ideas. Steiner had a great deal to say in these areas which continue to influence Waldorf educators.

Also, in examining Steiner's ideas, we will view the Waldorf classroom using the techniques of educational criticism and connoisseurship (see Eisner, 1991; Uhrmacher, 1991). This presentation juxtaposes descriptions of a Waldorf classroom and interviews with those affiliated with Waldorf schools with explications of Steiner's theories on the Waldorf environment. The descriptions and interviews are intended to illustrate the Steinerian concepts.

Three points are considered in this chapter. First, to understand Rudolf Steiner's ideas about the environment one must know something about Steiner's cosmology because for Steiner cosmic and earthly environments are tightly interwoven. Second, art and architecture provide tools for understanding spirituality. In fact, architecture plays a central role in Steiner's thinking about environments and education. Third, Waldorf educators, who work within Steiner's framework of providing children with a kind of education that embodies what might be termed spiritual functionalism, strive to design a school that is both aesthetic and developmentally appropriate. The analyses here move from macro to micro—from the cosmological to the concrete building of classrooms.

The Cosmic Environment

At 8:00 a.m., about six Waldorf teachers in Sunnyville, California[1] attend "Morning Verse." They meet in the lounge, a small room in the back of one of the buildings filled with an old couch, a large stuffed chair, a coffeemaker, a small refrigerator, and two walls of books. Titles include Russell's *History of Western Philosophy*, Eliade's *Myth and Reality*, Dreikers' *Children the Challenge*, *The Bhagavad-Gita*, Tolstoy's *War and Peace*, *The Dead Sea Scrolls*, as well as an entire bookshelf of Steiner's works. The room's temperature is cool in the early morning as the uninsulated walls do little to keep the cold out. The teachers gather together and form a circle. They hold hands in a moment of silence. One teacher reads from Rudolf Steiner's *Calendar of the Soul* (1988b, p. 36), a book in which Steiner wrote a different verse for each week of the year. Today's verse is:

Can I know what it is "to be"
So that true life can find itself
Again in Soul's creative urge?
I feel that I am granted power
To make my Self, as humble part,
At home within the cosmic Self.

Then, another teacher reads the verse in Steiner's original German. They stand silently together. After a few seconds they switch from the reverent to a more jocular attitude, laughing together as they exit for their classrooms. One teacher tells me that "this ritual prepares our mood of soul to enter the classroom and meet the children." She refers to a passage Steiner wrote,

> Not until we link ourselves in this way to the great facts of the universe do we gain a real understanding of what teaching means. Only out of such an understanding can the right solemnity emerge so that teaching really becomes a kind of service to God, a consecrated service. (Steiner, 1976)

"Man," said Steiner, "is not merely a spectator of the world: he is rather the world's stage upon which great cosmic events continuously play themselves out" (Steiner, 1966, p. 54). For Steiner, the human being is at the center of all things. Steiner maintained that whether we realize it or not, we are intimately linked at all times with the universe at large. Therefore, even in our most mundane moments, we are participating in the cosmic environment. To better understand this perspective, let's examine some basic Steiner premises—ideas Steiner acquired as mystic intuitions.

To begin with, Steiner said, the environment consists of spirit and matter. As a child, Steiner had numerous supersensible experiences (he saw, for example, a vision of a cousin who he later learned had died). Steiner said, "the reality of the spiritual world was to me as certain as that of the physical. I felt the need, however, for a sort of justification of this assumption" (Steiner, 1951, p. 12). He spent the early part of his life seeking such justifications. First, came his work on Goethe (*A Theory of Knowledge Implicit in Goethe's World Conception—Fundamental Outlines with Special Reference to Schiller* [1886]), then his doctoral thesis in 1892 (*Truth and Knowledge*) and finally *Philosophy of Spiritual Activity* (1894). In these texts, Steiner expounded his philosophical ideas. He argued against the Kantian notion that one cannot know things-in-themselves. Kant had postulated two worlds: the phenomenal and the noumenal. The phenomenal is the world of appearances, which the organs of perception, organized by understanding, offer to the mind as reality. Behind this world, said Kant, is the realm of ultimate realities or noumena (things-in-themselves), which the mind can never know. Steiner, however, argued that we could know the noumenal world by entering into it spiritually. "Knowing," said Steiner, "does not consist in a mirroring of something possessing essential being, but the soul's living entrance into this reality of being" (Steiner, 1951, p. 183).

Steiner continued to refine his ideas on the cosmic environment when he encountered Theosophy and later as he developed his own "theosophy" called Anthroposophy. His writing changed from a philosophical discourse to a mystical one, but the ideas were consistent. Steiner claimed the spirit world is real. One could learn from it by observing it closely, like a scientist. The limits on such observation were the limits of our perceptive organs. Plus there existed special organs of spiritual perception, which are atrophied in most individuals but which may be developed. By developing the spiritual organs of perception, people could perceive higher spiritual beings, spiritual evolution, and the manner in which reincarnation works.

As a result of his own spiritual investigations, Steiner maintained that the universe condensed from spirit into matter through successive stages and that it would become spirit again with human assistance. The midpoint in this cosmic evolution occurred with Jesus' crucifixion at Golgotha, which epitomized the possibility of change in the evolution of the soul. The "Christ event," said Steiner, allowed free spiritual activity to be achieved by changing ordinary thinking into pure thinking. "This pure thinking then raises itself to the direct experience of the spiritual world and derives from it the impulses to moral behaviour" (Easton, 1980, p. 90). For Steiner, to accept Christ within is to open up one's powers of perception and moral sensibilities. It would also help humanity return to a world of spiritual beings in a spiritual environment.

Clearly, the cosmic environment is entwined with each soul's earthly life. It is not something detached or distant. In the Waldorf school's morning verse, we see the teachers seeking the cosmic connection. Steiner once said that teachers should consider themselves helpers of the divine-spiritual dimension. Their task, in part, was to help humanity return to a more spiritual world. The cosmic association brought to their consciousness through morning verse reminds them of this fact.

The Role of Art and Architecture

The Sunnyville Waldorf School is tucked away on a farm off the beaten track. I had driven on highway 101 north toward Eureka, and then I made a left turn on Farmington Road, right outside the city of Springfield. I stayed on the new road for about five miles, crossed railroad tracks, made a left turn on Agate Road and drove to the top of the hill. A wood sign points to Sunnyville Waldorf School. I made a right turn onto a gravel drive that took me to a small sandy parking lot. I parked and walked up the gravel path leading to the school.

The school, grades K–10, consists of four buildings that sit on part of Ray Bergen's biodynamic farm. At the far left is a single building that accommodates the kindergarten. Then two long one-story, unadorned buildings sit next to each other. The kindergarten and the two buildings that house grades 1–10 are positioned to form a crescent. Behind the third building is the Eurythmy barn, which also contains the woodworking room. The buildings are certainly pleasant looking and blend into their surroundings. Much work went into raising funds for their construction.

For Steiner, art was not merely for decoration or expressing one's inner emotions. Art was certainly not for art's sake. For Steiner, "Art is a manifestation of higher natural laws that would never be revealed without art" (Steiner, 1999, p. 123). Therefore, one ought to be careful about the kinds of art forms he or she creates—especially in creating architecture. Steiner embraced Goethe's viewpoint that "'Beauty is a manifestation of secret laws of nature, which without art would have remained eternally obscured'" (Nobel, 1996, p. 101). For Steiner, art forms bring the spiritual into the earthly world.

Steiner believed the physical environment should not be taken for granted. Buildings mattered to Steiner. Steiner himself designed and helped construct 17 buildings. Two of the most famous were the Goetheanum I (which burned down in 1922) and the Goetheanum II (the building of which Steiner oversaw from 1923 until his death in 1925), both built in Dornach, Switzerland. Steiner said a lot about architecture and saw himself as the founder of a new style of architecture.

Steiner's ideas about all human-made environments can be summed up in his phrase: "Forms stimulate thoughts" (Steiner, 1999, p. 45). Therefore, anyone wishing to create an environment, whether he or she is an architect or a teacher, must take into account the kinds of thoughts he or she wishes to stimulate. Because Steiner was interested in leading people (adults and children) back to the spiritual and away from an overly materialistic viewpoint, he said that:

> [I]t is not at all unnatural that in a building that belongs to the present and the future we should set out in full consciousness to create forms which will help human beings to conquer their consciousness of merely physical and material actuality, and to feel themselves extended out into the cosmos through the architecture. . . . (Steiner, 1999, p. 123)

Students of architecture have classified Steiner's buildings as an extreme form of expressionism (Pehnt, 1973), organic functionalism (Adams, 1992), or spiritual functionalism (Biesantz & Klingborg, 1979). The last term focuses on Steiner's central concern—that buildings have the power to lead to recognition of the spiritual, but they must also be functional.

What Steiner wanted architects to do was not unlike what he wanted teachers to do—plan for individual contexts, use organic materials, think developmentally (influenced by Goethe, Steiner used the term "metamorphosis" for development) and, of course, think holistically. In essence, Steiner hoped to "attune [the] edifice to living human psychology, to fashion in [the] building an organic 'semblance of consciousness' responsive and sympathetic to what might arise within human beings' own consciousness as they used and experienced the building" (Adams, 1992, p. 191).

As a result of such organic and metamorphic thinking, Steiner foresaw lofty possibilities:

> Peace and harmony will flow into the hearts of men through these forms. Such buildings will be lawgivers. The forms of our building will be able to achieve what external institutions can never achieve. My dear friends, however much study may be given to the elimination of crime and wrongdoing from the world, true healing, the turning of evil into good, will in the future depend upon whether true art is able to send into human souls and human hearts a spiritual medium. (Biesantz & Klingborg, 1979, p. 33)

Steiner provided specific ideas useful for architects who wished to follow his "indications." He discussed technical issues such as doubly curved surfaces (he referred to these as the "simplest Urphanomen of life" [Steiner, 1999, p. 190]), various structural tensions and spatial and load-bearing relationships as well as the kinds of colors one ought to use inside and outside the structure. Steiner believed that there should be a harmonious relationship between buildings and surroundings. It is no accident that the Waldorf school described above with its gravel road, sandy parking lot, and wooden sign blends so nicely into its landscape.

Spiritual Functionalism

Daniel Gregorian is slim, about six feet tall, soft-spoken, and reserved. On most days from 8:00 to 8:30 a.m., Mr. Gregorian stands outside his classroom door waiting for his third-grade students to arrive. Later he tells me, "I stand out there just to receive them. I think it's important." He hugs several children who sidle up to him.

At 8:30 a.m., Marsha, the outreach director and nurse, walks up and down the school yard ringing a bell. Younger students run to their classrooms. Outside Mr. Gregorian's doorway, students take off their shoes and store them underneath long benches. Then they line up outside the door where Mr. Gregorian waits to greet each student formally by shaking his or her hand. Mr. Gregorian's step inside the classroom is not merely a necessary move from outside to inside; for Mr. Gregorian, stepping inside the classroom represents a "crossing of the threshold" that marks the beginning of the school day. After entering, some of the boys conduct last-minute negotiations over baseball cards as they hang up their jackets.

While students take their seats and settle down, Mr. Gregorian strums on a kinderharp. When the room is still, he stands straight, hands at his side, and says with great emphasis, "Good morning class three."

Students, standing behind their desks, respond more slowly, "Good morning, Mr. Gregorian."

"Who would like to write the date today? Bianca?" Bianca goes to the blackboard and prints February 27, 1989. As she writes, Mr. Gregorian says aloud, "Capital f, e, b, r, u, a, r, y. February. Let's spell February together."

Students chorally respond, "Capital f, e, b, r, u, a, r, y." Then they say, "February." Mr. Gregorian's room is large (11 yards, 2 feet, 8 inches long and 7 yards, 2 feet, 8 inches wide, as students measured in their "weights and measurement" unit). The walls are painted with gently swirling yellow colors. The room is bright and airy. The room is also cared for by parents. Mr. Gregorian paints his classroom each year with parent help. He uses the occasion as a way to involve parents in the school. Also, every weekend, students and their families take turns cleaning the classroom.[2]

Mr. Gregorian plays a middle C on his flute. The students hum an ascending scale as Mr. Gregorian signals each rising note with his extended hand. Children hold the last note before descending back down the scale. The students' choral hum has an ancient sound, I think, as I look at the nature table in the front of the room. Pine cones, a candle, a wooden gnome, and a scale rest on the red tablecloth. Slightly elevated, on a blue cloth, is a large Bible. Above the Bible, hanging on the wall, is a picture of an angel. Next to the angel is the blackboard. On the other side of the front wall, behind Mr. Gregorian's desk, is a small round picture of Noah's Ark.

"Morning has come," sing the students, "night is away, rise with the sun and welcome the day." Mr. Gregorian divides students into two groups and has them sing the line in rounds. They do this several times. Afterwards, accompanied by eurythmy movements, Mr. Gregorian and students say, "I feel the power of God, I come from a star afar, I love my earthly home."

Steiner outlined various purposes of Waldorf education depending on the audience he was addressing at a particular time. For example, sometimes he stressed, "The need for imagination, a sense of truth and a feeling of responsibility—these are the three forces which are the very heart of education." Other times, he referred to Waldorf education as an "education towards freedom." Regardless of how Steiner spoke about Waldorf education, I believe his various purposes may be distilled into two major categories: the spiritual/ideal and the social/practical.[3] Together they make up what in the architectural literature is referred to as a "spiritual functionalism." They guide educators in setting up their classroom environments.

The spiritual/ideal emphasizes the point that children are "spiritual gifts from heaven." Steiner put it this way:

> [E]very single child becomes for us a sacred riddle, for every single child embodies this great question—not, how is he to be educated so that he approaches some "idol" which has been thought out.—But, how shall we foster what the gods have sent down to us into the earthly world? (Steiner, 1967, p. 20)

The spiritual/ideal reminds educators that "Waldorf School Education is not a pedagogical system but an Art—the Art of awakening what is actually there within the human being. Fundamentally, the Waldorf School does not want to educate, but to awaken" (p. 23). Awakening students to become nobler, higher beings is Steiner's goal. Ogletree (n.d.) views Steiner's educational system in the idealistic tradition—a cooperative art in which the teacher works with nature and assists it through the "development of watchful attention and timely prodding."

To create free, imaginative, noble human beings is one major goal of Waldorf education. To create social and practical human beings is another. Steiner was concerned that people in his day did not know, for example, how some "modern" technology worked: "Imagine even how many people see a steam engine rushing by without having any clue as to the workings of physics and mechanics that propel it. Consider what position such ignorance puts us in as regards our relationship with our environment" (Steiner, 1976, p. 165). He warned teachers not to approach idealism with sentimentality. Rather, he stated: "Every single thing a child learns during the course of his schooling should in the end be presented so broadly that threads may everywhere be found linking it with practical human life" (Steiner, 1976, p. 168). General classroom curricula should have practical ramifications, Steiner thought, and in addition, some activities to which all children would be exposed, such as knitting or woodwork, are practical through and through.

What is the role of the teacher in achieving Steiner's aims? From the outset, Steiner was very clear that everything depended upon the teacher in the classroom. In one of his many lectures on Waldorf education, Steiner said, "There are no prescribed rules for teaching in the Waldorf School....The teacher is autonomous. Within this one unifying spirit [Anthroposophy] he can do entirely what he thinks right" (Steiner, 1988, p. 46). Steiner preferred to provide "indications" of what to do rather than prescribing rules. Teachers were charged with fostering the divine-spiritual. "What may be the result if we approach education with this attitude of mind?" (Steiner, 1967, p. 20).

Regarding the preceding description of the classroom, we see that Mr. Gregorian's waiting for students each morning, his students taking off their shoes before entering the room, the playing of the kinderharp to settle the students, the cleaning of the room, the singing of songs and the learning of dates are all examples of a practical/social pedagogy. Some of these activities, however, also present spiritual/ideal dimensions. Walking into the classroom, for example, may be seen as a practical activity of moving from one space to another, but it can also be seen as the "crossing of a threshold." Likewise, singing can be seen in its loftier sense of evoking in the children their inherent spirituality. Certainly the Old Testament curriculum and the short prayer ("I feel the power of God...") provide students with opportunities to explore their sense of spirituality and their ideals.

The Aesthetic Environment

Once a week from 1:15 to 2:00 p.m., Mr. Gregorian teaches form drawing. He starts by handing out large paper mats so that students can cover their desks, and then he distributes large white sheets of paper—Strathmore 400—a thick, high-quality paper with a smooth feel. Mr. Gregorian tapes one sheet on the blackboard for himself as he tells students to fold their paper into two, creating a top and bottom half. The form Mr. Gregorian draws on his own paper looks like the following:

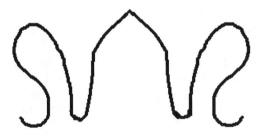

Next, Mr. Gregorian asks several students to come to the front of the class and walk the form "with their feet" while facing the chalkboard. The class watches. Then Mr. Gregorian has all the students "draw" the form in the air. They do this several times, and then with a gold block crayon, they draw the form on their paper. Mr. Gregorian walks around the room, observing the students' form drawings. When students are almost done, Mr. Gregorian asks what they think the form looks like. Students answer, "a periscope," "a tower with waves around it," and "one of those big ole things that's on freighter ships." Mr. Gregorian may comment on students' answers, but he does not say that any is right or wrong. Next, Mr. Gregorian has students complete the form by drawing its mirror image on the bottom half of their papers. While students work on their mirror images, Mr. Gregorian continues to study their pictures. When they are more than half done, he tells them to finish their form drawing by first going over the gold with "a warm color" and then coloring the picture in "with colors that go together."

A great deal could be said about Steiner's recommendations to teachers for creating an aesthetic environment (see Uhrmacher, 1993). He not only provided an overarching conceptual framework but also gave specific advice down to the kinds of pictures that could be hung on classroom walls at each grade level (see Steiner, 1998b). Because several of Steiner's indications for an artistic environment were utilized in Mr. Gregorian's classroom, we can continue our analysis by examining these.

First, we saw a number of carefully placed artifacts (i.e., the Bible, the picture of Noah, and the picture of the angel), which reflected the curriculum being presented. This shows how the aesthetic environment harmonizes with what the students study. Said Steiner:

> How it is to be deplored…that the schoolrooms for our children are a veritably barbaric environment for their young hearts and minds. Imagine every schoolroom…shaped by an artist in such a way that each single form is in harmony with what his eye should fall upon when the child is learning his tables. (Stockmeyer, 1965, p. 238)

A congruence between the class environment and the curriculum is an important foundation for Steiner. However, his comment that every schoolroom ought to be shaped by an artist also indicates more about his concern for the aesthetic environment. Steiner sought artistry—an environment imbuing the practical with the spiritual.

Gregorian's classroom was painted in swirling strokes of yellow. Color is also fundamental to Steiner's thinking. He first used the method of lazure painting in 1907 at the Munich Conference of the

doing. They are not quite settled...always there is this questioning, this pushing against the parameters of the world whether it be physical or psychological. And so in this class it's the same kind of thing. There's all this arguing, this whole thing yesterday with the baseball cards. How do you work it out? And there needs to be a space to work it out to experience the pain, because this separation from this all-one consciousness now brings pain. But anytime there's pain there is a possibility of consciousness—the child is trying to come to full adult consciousness and it is a painful experience.

I also asked Mr. Gregorian what defined a Waldorf school. He replied, "The teachers are free in the classroom; that's one of our main features. Second is the way we look at the human being and how he or she develops. We educate the child in wholeness. We look at the child from birth to adulthood."

By the age of twenty-two, Steiner had edited Goethe's scientific works for the popular book series, *Deutsche Nationalliteratur (German National Literature)* and as a result had become quite familiar with Goethe's idea of "metamorphosis." According to Goethe, there is a creative purpose in the universe that may be intuited and seen in life around us. Distinct species, he argued, are really an illusion produced out of the ever-changing flux by the shortness of human life. Goethe had spent a lot of time studying plants, and he came to believe that underlying all plant forms was an archetypal plant. What interested Goethe was the way plants contracted and expanded in the process of living. All organisms, he believed, grow and are transformed rhythmically.

Steiner applied Goethe's observations in countless ways. Perhaps the most important was his theory of child development. Steiner postulated three ways of thinking about the school environment based on his three stages of child development. Much has been written about Steiner's ideas on child development, so I will not go into depth about them here, but I would like to emphasize a few aspects of how Waldorf teachers mold the classroom environment for each developmental stage.[4]

According to Steiner, "From birth to about the sixth or seventh year, the human being naturally gives himself up to everything immediately surrounding him in the human environment, and thus, through the imitative instinct, gives form to his own nascent powers" (Steiner, 1985a, p. 3). During this period, children learn through empathy and action. Learning absorbs all the child's energies. A Waldorf preschool may look somewhat austere with a minimum of objects, though scarves abound. The walls are red; the small amount of furniture in the room is made of wood. If there are toys, they are usually incomplete. Steiner approved of unfinished toys, such as rag dolls without facial features, so that children could "finish" the objects using their own imaginations.[5]

The second developmental stage, which starts around the age of seven when children lose their baby teeth, may be labeled the time of feeling. This period, which lasts until the age of fourteen, requires teaching through vivid pictures, images, and rhythm since these awaken the forces of feeling. Steiner argued that "everything that one brings to a child at this age must be given in the form of fairy tales, legends and stories in which everything is endowed with feeling" (Steiner, 1988, p. 49). The environment is filled with pictures (Noah, the angel) and items (a wooden gnome, a candle, a scale, and the Bible) to reflect this phase of feeling and imagination.

Finally, abstract thinking denotes the third stage, from the onset of puberty to the age of twenty-one. Whereas before this stage, teachers try to teach pictorially and rhythmically, now they can employ abstractions more freely. In her dissertation, Joan Armon describes a Waldorf classroom for adolescents. While studying biology, the classroom has little more than a framed photograph of a Greek bas-relief figure. There are no posters, skeletons, or specimens of body parts. The curriculum employs anatomy drawings by Leonardo da Vinci, chalkboard drawings, and an occasional photograph from a book on anatomy. According to Armon, the teacher believes the mainstream biology curriculum materials contribute to a "deadening rather than awakening [of the] students' sense of wonder and awe at the beauty of the human body" (Armon, 1997, p. 113). Armon describes the classroom further:

> The physical classroom environment is sparse, in the Waldorf tradition....Waldorf educators do not believe it is psychologically or

spiritually healthy to fill a room with a myriad of materials....Waldorf educators believe that an overabundance of...materials creates conditions that contribute to chaos. Mr. Hoechter is particularly concerned about avoiding chaotic conditions for his adolescent students who are already immersed in the chaotic process that results from their immersion in the lonely desert of adolescence. (pp. 112–113)

Whatever one may think about Mr. Hoechter and other Waldorf educators' ideas, one can see that a great deal of thought has gone into shaping the classroom environment.

One last point to be made concerning all the grade levels is the lack of advanced technological implements in the classroom. In her study of Waldorf classrooms, Armon also observed that one teacher "deliberately avoids technological devices such as video or audio recordings, television, computers, or calculators, believing with other Waldorf educators that such tools and their messages lead children toward materialism, consumerism, competition, and addictions in a variety of forms" (p. 178).

Conclusion

I had an opportunity to interview Waldorf parents. One in particular had much to say that was insightful and pertinent about Waldorf education and its use of "natural" or organic materials in schools. She said:

I was always talking about Waldorf [education]...and I remember this one man got up and said that he wanted to know why in a Waldorf kindergarten there were all these pine cones and pieces of wood and shells and rocks and things like that. Why weren't there regular kindergarten kinds of equipment? And I just thought that was such an amazing question....[I]n this day and age you would get up and ask why do you have all these completely natural objects in your classroom as if it was some kind of abnormality, and why didn't we have the Formica, and the plastic and the Legos, you know, and things like this that were completely artificial. That really spoke to the kind of condition of our society where these natural objects are now considered abnormal.

Waldorf education started as an alternative to the traditional German educational system in 1919. Alternatives often come into existence out of dissatisfaction with the status quo. Steiner was concerned that materialistic forms of thinking and acting were overshadowing spiritual ones. The cosmic was becoming divorced from the mundane, he thought; a realist style of education was overtaking an ideal one; educators were becoming more concerned with thinking scientifically rather than artistically, and they were teaching with linear piecemeal development in mind rather than holistic transformation. Moreover, technology was overtaking nature, with the examination of universal processes obscuring individual contexts.

Steiner was not wrong. Germany then and America now have not addressed Steiner's concerns. Does he therefore present a solution? On the one hand, Steiner's ideas truck in the spiritual (e.g., reincarnation, karma, angels) in a way the public at large is not likely to embrace anytime soon. Consequently, Steiner's notions are prone to remain at the margins. On the other hand, Steiner does offer a powerful critique of mainstream culture. Materialism, whether manifested through science, consumerism, or technology is a pervasive problem. More specific to education, the preoccupation with prediction and control currently manifested through standards-based education is a concern. The idea that students are to absorb what is all about them (and be measured as to how short of that goal they are) rather than to cultivate what is inherently within them (and be evaluated for what they may offer society) would have appalled Steiner. Also, the idea that advanced technology, with its full graphics and its next-to-being-there potential could replace adults telling stories to children from one soul to another would have been anathema to Steiner. Steiner's ideas as embodied in Waldorf education provide an example to mainstream educators that things can be different. For these reasons, among others, educators can profit from examining his ideas.

Whatever we may think about Steiner's spiritual viewpoint and the philosophical foundations of his theories on child development and his notions about art and architecture, his prescriptions do present a valuable alternative to mainstream culture and educational practices.

What are the specific lessons to be learned from Steiner and Waldorf schools? Staying close to our examination of the environment, I believe there are four in particular. First, a spiritual or cosmic perspective suggests that all environments may be richer than they seem. One does not need to be an Anthroposophist to embrace the viewpoint that a feeling of mystery and awe is a valuable consequence of a recognition of the spiritual. From his process philosophy viewpoint, Donald Oliver also suggests that the spiritual or cosmic should not be cut off from the way we learn about or understand the world around us. Referring to this phenomenon as "ontological knowing," Oliver maintains that "the central quality of ontological knowing is one's feeling for tentative connection—the way in which a novel occasion is to relate, harmoniously or destructively—to the larger world" (Oliver, 1989, p. 14). Like Steiner, Oliver believes that a technical knowing, which privileges prediction and control, has dominated our thinking. We have neglected placing our knowledge in broader contexts grounded in some notion of our place in the universe, and the consequences of that fragmenting of knowledge have been great. Oliver believes that a lack of connection to the larger cosmos is a major part of students' feelings of anomie, isolation, and carelessness. The same lack of connection, by the way, also affects teachers. Whether one embraces Steiner or Oliver's ideas, one would do well to recognize that there is more than one way of understanding.

Second, Steiner's central architectural idea that the kinds of forms one creates stimulate the kinds of thoughts one is likely to have is as powerful as it is simple. Although I find Steiner's (and even more so, his protégé Erik Assmussen's) organic structures to be beautiful and even inspirational, I doubt that such buildings will spring up across this country. However, we may take Steiner's ideas to a simpler level and ask, what kinds of environments are students exposed to? Considering this question in terms of Noddings's philosophy of "care" (Noddings, 1984) as Armon did in her dissertation (1997), we may ask, do the environments model caring or do they reveal carelessness, neglect, and indifference? If the former, do students feel—to use Noddings' term—cared for in their environments? Although Steiner did not use the language of caring, I believe he would agree that if forms stimulate thoughts of care, that would certainly be good for education and for society. Waldorf educators clearly exhibit care by trying to create beautiful forms (e.g., buildings, classroom walls, etc.) and purposefully placing them (as was seen in Mr. Gregorian's placement of objects).

Third, Steiner's developmental perspective on preparing an aesthetic environment is one that has been discussed theoretically over the years (Eisner, 1976; Gardner, 1994), but it has not truly penetrated public school classroom life. Although I am not convinced that Steiner's aesthetic is the one we all need to embrace, I do believe that paying attention to aesthetics is definitely better than not doing so. Dewey, in fact, puts it this way: "If their eye is constantly greeted by harmonious objects, having elegance of form and color, a standard of taste naturally grows up" (Dewey, 1916, p. 18). We may, of course, debate issues of taste (whose sense of taste should we embrace?), but such debate would be good. Currently, I do not believe much thought is going into any sense of taste. Moreover, when we discuss issues of *developmentalizing* aesthetics or taste, there is, at the public school level, even less discussion.

One reason of course that there may be little discussion about aesthetic environments is because the issue is not seen in the way Waldorf educators see it—as cognitively charged. Whereas Steiner believed that art was an avenue to knowing the world's spiritual mysteries—hence color was so important, because as he stated, the cosmos reveals itself through color—most teachers today see color and art as mere decoration.

Our fourth consideration then is that art is a way of knowing the world. Steiner placed art at the center of Waldorf education's curriculum, pedagogy, and crafting of the school or classroom environment. His ideas may be summarized this way:

> When we direct our attention to the elements of form, color, or other fields of perception and make a comparative observation of two colors or forms,

we can awaken to a direct inner experience of their relative qualities....What is speaking to us through color and form? These practical activities lead us toward an answer to Steiner's question: When will the gods speak to us? Such an orientation to color and form develops an organ of perception in us whereby soul and spirit substance become as real for us as physical substance is already. (Michael Howard in Steiner, 1998a, p. 35)

The argument that art is a form of spiritual cognition is not one that mainstream educators are likely to embrace precisely because of its spiritual aspect. But the idea that art is a powerful cognitive activity has been ardently and comprehensively discussed by Eisner (1991, 1998) without the spiritual overtones. Briefly, Eisner argues that people express themselves through "forms of representation," each of which reveals and conceals. For example, we can express certain thoughts through the visual arts in ways that would be difficult in poetry. Likewise, other thoughts are better in poetry than in propositional discourse. Although Waldorf educators articulate the role of art in very different ways from Eisner, the educational implications are similar. For this reason, too, mainstream educators may look to Waldorf educators for inspiration and novel ideas (e.g., form drawing, wet-on-wet watercolor drawing, and much more—see Uhrmacher [1991]).

Some predicted that when Steiner died, his ideas would die with him. They were clearly wrong. Waldorf education survives and prospers—perhaps because what Steiner worried about in his day is still of concern today. Steiner himself was aware that his ideas were unusual and even perceived by some as mad. But his reply to critics in 1919 still holds true today:

It is all too easy for the world to laugh at our saying that the human being consists of a physical body, etheric body, astral body, and ego. As long as one judges these matters only with the yardstick of customary science, one cannot help laughing....But considering the serious tangle in which our civilization finds itself, one would expect at least some readiness to seek for what cannot be found elsewhere. (Steiner, 1988, p. 110)

Endnotes

[1] I have used pseudonyms for the school and teachers' names.

[2] By having parents and children take turns cleaning the classroom, Mr. Gregorian distributes feelings of responsibility and ownership. The most important outcome, I think, is that students learn to care for their classroom and, therefore, do not become disconnected from their environment. They must clean the mess they make. Each Monday, Mr. Gregorian makes a point of noticing how nice the room looks and thanks the appropriate children.

[3] The spiritual and the ideal are two sides of the same coin, but they have slightly different connotations, and they hint at slightly different Waldorf aims. The spiritual reminds educators of the cosmic world; the ideal reminds them of cultivating the inner child. The same goes for practical and social. Practical endeavors yield social consequences. When students make something, they use it. Also, in the making, there is a social atmosphere. I prefer to insert a backslash between the words in order to keep all four aspects in mind.

[4] Almost any text that discusses Waldorf education examines Steiner's ideas on child development. Among others, see the following for an overview (Ginsberg, 1982; Harwood, 1958; Uhrmacher, 1991, 1995).

[5] "As the muscles of the hand grow firm and strong in performing the work for which they are fitted, so the brain and other organs of the physical body of man are guided into the right lines of development if they receive the right impression from their environment. An example will best illustrate this point. You can make a doll for a child by folding up an old napkin....Or else you can buy the child what they call a 'pretty' doll, with real hair and painted cheeks....If the child has before him the folded napkin, he has to fill in from his own imagination all that is needed to make it real and human. This work of the imagination moulds and builds the forms of the brain. The brain unfolds as the muscles of the hand unfold when they do the work for which they are fitted. Give the child the so-called 'pretty' doll, and the brain has nothing more to do" (Steiner, 1965, p. 26).

References

Adams, D. (1992). Rudolf Steiner's first Goetheanum as an illustration of organic functionalism. *Journal of the Society of Architectural Historians, 51*(2), 182–204.

Armon, J. (1997). Teachers as moral educators: A study of caring. Unpublished doctoral dissertation. University of Denver.

Biesantz, H., & Klingborg, A. (1979). *The Goetheanum: Rudolf Steiner's architectural impulse*. Trans: Jean Schmid. London: Rudolf Steiner.

Dewey, J. (1916). *Democracy and education*. New York: Free Press.

Easton, S. C. (1980). *Rudolf Steiner: Herald of a new epoch.* Spring Valley, NY: Anthroposophic.

Eisner, E. W. (Ed.). (1976). *The arts, human development, and education.* Berkeley: McCutchan.

Eisner, E. W. (1991). *The enlightened eye.* New York: Macmillan.

Eisner, E. W. (1998). *The kind of schools we need.* Portsmouth, NH: Heinemann.

Gardner, H. (1994). *The arts and human development.* New York: Basic.

Ginsberg, I. (1982, Winter). Jean Piaget and Rudolf Steiner: Stages of child development and implications for pedagogy. *Teachers College Record, 84,* 327–337.

Harwood, A. C. (1958). *The recovery of man in childhood: A study in the educational work of Rudolf Steiner.* New York: Anthroposophic.

Niederhäuser, H. R., & Frohlich, M. (1970). *Form drawing.* Translated by M. Frohlich, Mimeo.

Nobel, A. (1996). *Educating through art: The Steiner school approach.* Trans. E. Waldenstrom. Edinburgh: Floris.

Noddings, N. (1984). *Caring: A feminine approach to ethics & moral education.* Berkeley: University of California Press.

Ogletree, E. J. (no date). *Creativity and Waldorf education: A study.* Mimeo.

Oliver, D. (1989). *Education, modernity and fractured meaning.* Albany, NY: State University of New York Press.

Pehnt, W. (1973). *Expressionist architecture.* London: Thames and Hudson.

Steiner, R. (1951). *The course of my life.* Trans.: O. D. Wannamaker. [Published in installments from December 9, 1923–April 5, 1925.] New York: Anthroposophic.

——— (1965). *The education of the child in the light of Anthroposophy.* Trans: G. Adams, & M. Adams [first printed in 1927]. London: Rudolf Steiner.

——— (1966). *Study of man.* Trans: D. Harwood, & H. Fox. Revised by A. C. Harwood. [In Stuttgart, August 21–September 5, 1919.] London: Rudolf Steiner.

——— (1967). *Human values in education.* Trans: C. Davy. [In Holland, July 17–24, 1924.] London: Rudolf Steiner.

——— (1976). *Practical advice to teachers* (2nd ed.). Trans: J. Collis. [In Stuttgart, August 21–September 5, 1919.] London: Rudolf Steiner.

——— (1985a). *An introduction to Waldorf education.* Trans: E. Bowen-Wedgewood. Revised by F. Amrine. [1919] Spring Valley, NY: Anthroposophic.

——— (1985b). *An introduction to Waldorf education* (2nd ed). Trans: Hans Pusch and Ruth Pusch. Spring Valley, NY: Anthroposophic.

——— (1988). *The kingdom of childhood* (2nd ed.). [In Holland, August 12–20, 1924] London: Rudolf Steiner.

——— (1998a). *Art as spiritual activity.* Edited and introduced by M. Howard. [Lectures given between 1888 and 1923.] Hudson, NY: Anthroposophic.

——— (1998b). *Faculty meetings with Rudolf Steiner* (Volume 2), 1922–1924. Hudson, NY: Anthroposophic.

———— (1999). *Architecture as a synthesis of the arts.* Trans: J. Collis, D. Osmond, R. Raab, & J. Schmid-Bailey. [Eight lectures given between 1911 and 1914; extracts from two lectures given in 1923 and 1924.] London: Rudolf Steiner.

Stockmeyer, E. A. K. (1965). *Rudolf Steiner's curriculum for Waldorf schools* (2nd ed.). Trans: R. Everett-Zade. Michael Hall, Forest Row, East Sussex, UK: Steiner Schools Fellowship.

Uhrmacher, P. B. (1991). Waldorf schools marching quietly unheard. Unpublished doctoral dissertation, Stanford University.

———— (1993). Coming to know the world through Waldorf education. *The Journal of Curriculum and Supervision, 9*(1), 87–104.

———— (1995). Uncommon schooling: A historical look at Rudolf Steiner, anthroposophy, and Waldorf education. *Curriculum Inquiry, 25*(4), 381–406.

Chapter 6

School as Parkland: The Re-invention of a "Story of School"

Cheryl J. Craig

Building on the generative nature of Clandinin and Connelly's (1996) "professional knowledge landscape" of schools metaphor, Diamond (2000) proposed the idea of schools and educational inquiry being re-formed—and contextual inquiries being re-conceptualized—as parkland. In advancing his perspective, Diamond drew on the re-landscaping of a barren area of New York City in 1858 to create what is currently known as Central Park. The restoration was done to promote social reconciliation and add to the developing sense of community. He explained:

> Crafted to offer dense woodland, open formal spaces, artificial lakes and terraces, 30 elegant bridges and arches, bridle paths and rambles, the park was created on an unpromising site of quarries, shacks, and swampland. Ten million cartloads of stone and earth and a half a million trees and shrubs transformed the landscape into a lush series of composed views. The park with its captured sense of nature is arguably the 19th-century America's great work of art. (Diamond, 2000)

In this chapter, I borrow Diamond's idea of schools transformed as parkland and blend it with Clandinin and Connelly's (1996) professional knowledge landscape conceptualization. Within that theoretical frame, I narrate the story of how Martha Maude Cochrane Elementary School, now Martha Maude Cochrane Academy, a grade 4–5 campus located in a historically African American community in

a mid-southern state, was altered—re-landscaped, so to speak—
to address historical inequities and injustices. This work brings
"the pedagogy of place," the explicit theme of this book and
"the politics of space," an underlying theme of this chapter, to
the forefront.

To begin, I elaborate my theoretical framework, then use different
story perspectives to survey Clandinin and Connelly's professional
knowledge landscape over time. I relate Cochrane Academy to
parkland landscape and discuss the political situation surrounding
Cochrane Elementary School that led to its transformation. I end with
cautionary notes concerning how parks and schools, the people who
inhabit them, and the communities they serve must be cared for and
nurtured. Without a conscious sense of "watching over" (Aoki, 1989),
parks and schools can easily become landscapes of despair,
characterized by unresolved tensions and human development that
falls short of possibility.

Theoretical Framework

Situating the Study in the Literature

Clandinin and Connelly's (1996) metaphor of schools as
professional knowledge landscapes sheds important light on the

contexts of teaching. It provides a narrative way of thinking about school milieu. In the authors' words,

> a landscape metaphor allows us to talk about space, place, and time. Furthermore, it has a sense of expansiveness and the possibility of being filled with diverse people, things, and events in different relationships.... Because we see the professional knowledge landscape as composed of relationships among people, places, and things, we see it as both an intellectual and moral landscape. (p. 5)

School landscapes are storied landscapes made up of in-classroom and out-of-classroom places as well as in-school and out-of-school places. This chapter explores how politically and socially charged out-of-school places historically shaped in-school and in-classroom places for students and educators at Cochrane Elementary.

A number of stories shape the contours of Cochrane's school landscape. Stories of community—community stories (Craig, 2000)—are integral narratives because they reach back in time and portray historical and social legacies. They also account for differences between the narratives given to communities and narratives told by community members. Similarly, stories of school are stories given to schools while school stories are narratives told about schools (Clandinin & Connelly, 1996). In this work, these two different narratives are conjoined and then interfaced with stories of reform—narratives of reform expected to be lived and told—and reform stories—narratives of reform authentically told (Craig, 2001). These story variations are brought together to illustrate how the story of school at Cochrane Elementary School was dramatically changed to become the story of Cochrane Academy.

Associated with the professional knowledge landscape idea is Diamond's (2000) metaphor of school landscapes revitalized as parkland. As implied earlier, the word *landscape* can also be used as a verb to connote "the re-forming or artistic rearranging of a view" (p. 3). Diamond strongly advocates for new stories of schools "to be lived by" in situations where unpromising circumstances prevail. He additionally proposes that school landscapes be considered fields of inquiry where researchers, school-based educators, and the public linger and thoughtfully derive experiential meaning in context.

Story Constellations: The Research Method

The methodological roots of "story constellations" (Craig, in press), the matrix of narratives I have briefly sketched, connect directly with my "telling stories" (Craig, 1997) and "parallel stories" approaches (Craig, 1999). In the story constellations narrative approach, the research of Carr (1986) and Polkinghorne (1988) provides additional support for the construction of institutional narratives; that is, the creation of "stories of school."

This inquiry offers a partial view of Cochrane Academy's nuanced landscape. It is based on the field texts collected during a particular period of time and my interpretations of them. Considerable attention is paid to a shifting story of community, a developing story of school, as well as a federally mandated story of reform. Meaning is excavated through uncovering individual and shared stories lived and told over time, especially before and after the landmark *Brown v. Board of Education* decision.

Introducing the Study

My contact with what is currently known as Cochrane Academy began in early 1998. The principal and faculty requested that I assist them in understanding and recording their experiences of a locally interpreted national reform movement. Two years later, I, with the support of a research assistant, was invited to write a case study of Cochrane Academy to capture the changes that had taken place. The school continues to be my research site in the formal evaluation of the locally based initiative.

Introducing the Researcher

A former teacher, curriculum consultant, and doctoral and postdoctoral fellow, I had previously conducted program and school evaluations and personal and professional landscape research studies in Canada. My contact with organized reform efforts, however, began in the United States. Also, when I moved from Western Canada to a mid-southern state, I came to know desegregation as something other than a historical fact when I experienced how the policy deeply shaped human lives.

The Story of Hardy Community — Hardy Community Stories

The Hardy Community, where Cochrane Academy is located, was developed during World War I when African American citizens purchased one-acre plots of land, built homes, and assumed agrarian lifestyles. Livestock such as chicken and horses were raised, and produce was grown for personal consumption. Highly popular, the neighborhood increased in size to the point where a 1950s newspaper called it "the largest all-Negro community in the United States."

The Hardy Community currently covers an expanse of 7,600 acres, crosses three school districts, and reflects striking contrasts in terms of old and new, rural and urban, and poverty and wealth. In the vicinity of Cochrane Academy, spacious homes sit alongside subsidized apartments and seemingly endless cottages, the majority of them showing advanced signs of aging. Some properties look abandoned while others appear to be inhabited by temporary dwellers. In short, the neighborhood around Cochrane is, as a current educator describes it, "about as far removed from a cookie cutter community as one could possibly imagine."

Two thoroughfares pass through the Hardy neighborhood near Cochrane Academy. The one located immediately in front of the school was completed as recently as 1998. All other roads near Cochrane are more like rambling lanes and bear names reflecting the history and folklore of the local people. Roads such as Salvation Corner, Pecan Street, and Banjo Lane abound.

Small churches and businesses are sprinkled abundantly throughout the Hardy neighborhood. They continue to exist because some citizens walk to such institutions and businesses as they go about their daily routines. Thrift is the order of the day where stores are concerned, and spiritual revival is a common theme of the churches. Hence, signs like "Bargain Basement Prices" appear next to "A New Day Coming...."

To individuals born and raised in the community, the neighborhood around Cochrane is a place where African American citizens "put down roots" and "grew wings." An important community leader, for example, spoke of the neighborhood in the following manner: "I was reared here and am very proud. No community is any greater. There are outstanding people, personalities, resources, and leaders here. I am blessed to be a part of it."

Another local leader, also raised in the community, concurred. She also emphasized the "dignity and sense of pride in community" and "the tight connection between family and community." She particularly referred to a specific street that was closed for parades, homecomings, and other festivities. For her, the Hardy neighborhood was fondly recalled as a community "with a lot going on for children."

But the neighborhood surrounding Cochrane Elementary School changed dramatically in the decades that followed. It regrettably declined to the point where it was openly talked about as "plagued with poverty, unemployment and crime." The street once distinguished for its parades and celebrations became known for drug dealing.

A retired African American educator agreed with this portrayal of the community transition. To him, a common public perception of the neighborhood around Cochrane was that it was "a rough, drug-infested, crime-riddled neighborhood." At the same time, though, the individual recognized the historical roots linking Cochrane Elementary School and its community. He explained:

> Prior to forced desegregation, the community had a lot to do with education. It had a rich history, not in terms of dollars, but in terms of the value the community placed on education. In the neighborhood, schools were highly prized. Everyone knew about the academic, social, and athletic contributions of schools. (Cochrane Academy).

The school faculty delicately stated a similar view in Cochrane's *Year 2 Reform Movement Proposal*: "Education has always been important in this African American community, but African American people in

America historically have been denied the right to empower themselves through education" (Cochrane Academy, p. 1).

This combined sketch of stories of community—community stories set the stage for the Cochrane Academy story of school—Cochrane Academy school stories that follow. Narrative threads that link Cochrane to its community will soon become vividly apparent.

Cochrane's Story of School—Cochrane School Stories

The history of Cochrane Elementary's story of school precedes the construction of the building. A prominent 66-year-old city and community leader noted that early in the segregation years, the Hardy Community had only one school that was crowded to the extent that students attended in, first, two shifts, then, three shifts. Due to school overcrowding, one black father of three children "crossed over" to a white neighborhood of his own accord. The voluntary crossover resulted in the recognition of the educational needs of the African American community. As a result, more schools were built in the neighborhood, Cochrane Elementary School being one such construction. These developments addressed the over-crowding situation while allowing racially segregated schools to continue to exist.

Named after a prominent African American educator, Cochrane Elementary School was originally designed to educate poor black children in a segregated setting, in which community, academics, and athletics were of vital importance. Later, when it became apparent that schools in the urban area were going to desegregate, the vast majority of people in the vicinity of Cochrane embraced Martin Luther King's "I Have a Dream" vision. They desired equal education and access to facilities. They longed for well-appointed schools and new instructional material for teachers and students. They did not want "hand-me-down sports equipment" and "discarded books filled with other people's names."

At this point in time, however, the community members did not know lending support to school desegregation would mean that the campuses in their neighborhood would be drastically changed, even eliminated. In what later became a "forced scenario," African American students were redistributed throughout a large school district that was mainly white, but which soon would be dominated by minorities. For instance, in one year, 1,850 Hardy students were transported to schools outside the neighborhood. This enormous flight from the community resulted in Cochrane's feeder junior high school being turned into an alternative behavior campus, Cochrane Elementary School serving rotating grades of students, and the closure of the feeder high school. Many of the high school's trophies, photographs, and certificates were destroyed (community members salvaged some), and the symbol on the building—rumored to be an early work of a student who became a professional artist—was taken down, and later reported to be stolen.

These developments, among others, gave rise to serious, almost irreparable, mistrust between the formal institution of schooling and the African American community that the local schools had once served. It also divided the Hardy Community into a number of factions represented by rivaling Chambers of Commerce and civic groups that have yet to reconcile.

In the aftermath of the initial wave of desegregation, many African American people felt "taken advantage of." Additionally, parents and community leaders who were once united had now split into factions. Contact with black youngsters also was not maintained to the same degree. Black youth were scattered throughout the school district, and some parents did not have the necessary transportation to travel to schools in order to attend to problems as they previously had done when they were able to walk to community schools.

Seventeen years passed. During this time of rapid socioeconomic change, the educational possibilities for neighborhood children did not expand as anticipated. When some African American leaders gathered to formally consider the academic progress of the students in their new settings, it was readily apparent that the schools and children had been stripped of "community and family support." Furthermore, the attitude that "certain kids could learn and certain kids could not learn" formed a pervasive "psychological barrier." Students additionally found few African American teachers with whom to identify in their new school settings. There were not only changing laws but also changing modes of discipline with which to come to terms. As one prominent African American educator from the segregation period put it:

> We were pretty strict—both the school and the community . . . .[In the crossover], a generation of children learned freedom away from the watchful eyes of teachers and community members. The youngsters did not understand it well. In handling freedom, the students neglected to do what they should have done academically.

In this individual's opinion, the transition adversely affected student achievement and enormously influenced the lives and stories of the African American students, who then became the next generation of parents. Concerns for the educational growth of black students at Cochrane Elementary (now Cochrane Academy) and other neighborhood schools continue to reverberate.

In addition to the lower-than-expected academic performance of African American students, other information pertaining to the Hardy Community was made public. As with other urban neighborhoods, relationships were shown to exist between and among intergenerational illiteracy and poverty, inadequate housing, and poor community infrastructure. In 1990, for example, 32% of the citizens in the vicinity of Cochrane Elementary School were found to be living below the poverty level. Included in this number were 1,650 single-parent families, a figure that suggests a high incidence of child poverty. Furthermore, 40% of the residents aged twenty-five and over in the neighborhood around Cochrane had not graduated from high school.

Alarming statistics such as these prompted community leaders and the school district to return to the federal justice system in 1994 to explore better ways to serve the educational needs of black youth. A number of plans were entertained. A district official who worked diligently to regenerate the schools explained how events unfolded in the following conversation:

> First of all, the district was under court order since 1977 for desegregation purposes. That court order required busing....There was no choice. In 1994, some [Hardy] community members...approached the district about re-looking at that plan to see if there was something we could do to have

neighborhood schools so that elementary children particularly would not
have to be bussed across the district....So we began that process with a visit
to the Justice Department....The Department would not allow us to do that
because we would return basically to a one-race school....And so we looked
at various plans, held various focus group meetings in the community, and
decided on the magnet school plan. [Cochrane Academy] became one of the
first of two magnet schools.

This was the birthing process that gave rise to a new story of
school for the former Cochrane Elementary School. The magnet
school concept struck a compromise between the culturally relevant,
intimate campus (Ladson-Billings, 1992) that community leaders
desired for African American children and the legal options. This led
to the school being renewed and re-named Cochrane Academy for
Mathematics, Science, and Fine Arts. This development left other
district schools with regular programs and all of the competitive
sports teams in the district, a turn of events that represented a
significant departure from the founding story (Craig, 2000) put in
place at Cochrane decades earlier.

Having traced the concurrent development of Cochrane's story of
school and school stories told over time, I will introduce Cochrane's
story of reform and reform story separately. Attention to students'
interests, the celebration of cultural and ethnic diversity as well as the
fostering of student achievement within an environment of choice—
the hallmarks of a magnet story of reform—will be described, then
illuminated.

The Magnet "Story of Reform"

The different iterations of educational struggle that took place in
the Hardy Community over time gave rise to a grassroots, second-
wave attempt to re-story Cochrane's story of school through a legally
mandated story of reform. The bottom up/top down effort set its
sights on "making the community a safer place to live, aggressively
returning education to the community, and focusing relentless
attention on children and the special conditions that might scaffold
their learning" (Cochrane Academy, p. 1). Because community

members living around the academy wanted to restore neighborhood schools, and the school district was already working under a 1977 desegregation order, the Justice Department was necessarily consulted. A very complex process began. In 1995, the Justice Department stipulated eleven objectives that the school district needed to meet in a five-year period (1995–2000) in order to successfully comply with the desegregation order. These objectives have been summarized here from evaluation and legal documents.

Objective

1 To establish a procedure to address the ethnic composition so that black pupils in each school, to the extent practical, are in proportion to the district average. The district will use strategies that include, but are not limited to, magnet schools, year-round schools, majority to minority transfers, and boundary changes.

2 To establish a procedure for professional staff employment campus by campus so that black staff at each building is in proportion to the district wide average plus or minus 10 percentage points at the secondary level.

3 To utilize focus groups for the purpose of soliciting parent and community input into magnet themes.

4 To establish procedures for magnet programs so that admissions are equitable and contribute to desegregated enrollment in sending and receiving schools.

5 To establish a public information strategy to keep all segments of the community informed, especially as to the district's desegregation objectives, methods, and results.

6 To establish strategies for ongoing community involvement in effectively stabilizing desegregated schools.

7 To establish strategies for staff development for magnet program implementation and desegregation, and to continue to provide staff development for instructional strategies for a diverse population.

8 To provide a plan for continued construction and capital improvement that is consistent with the district's desegregation objectives.

9 To establish a contemporary facility as a high school and community resource facility that is unique in the district and is utilized year round on an extended-day basis.

10 To establish an ongoing evaluation process that will include monitoring and reporting on the implementation of the desegregation plan.

11 To develop a five-year timeline for the full implementation of this plan.

To finance the expansive story of reform mandated for Cochrane's story of school and other stories of school in the particular district, a major magnet school proposal was written and submitted to the United States Department of Education. In the fall of 1995, the school district was awarded a $7 million grant from the federal Magnet Assistance Program. The award provided the funds for the development of the original magnet schools (of which Cochrane Academy was one) and start-up funds for five additional magnet campuses.

From the very beginning, the magnet schools were meant to meet the needs of all students as opposed to those of a specialized population, although a portion of the students living in the Hardy Community would be guaranteed admittance to Cochrane and other neighborhood schools. To ensure a balanced racial population at Cochrane Academy and other schools, an electronic lottery was instituted that determined who would attend. The theory of action (Argyris & Schon, 1978; Hatch, 1998; Schon & McDonald, 1998) underlying the magnet school approach was to provide enhanced educational experiences for African American youth in their home community setting within a desegregated school population. This would be accomplished through attracting non-black students from elsewhere in the school district to the unique programs, top-notch facilities, and state-of-the-art equipment that distinguished Cochrane Academy from other district schools. This narrative turn formed a sharp contrast to the way the 1977 desegregation order was lived by students educated in the school district.

The Magnet Themes of Cochrane Academy

Community members in the vicinity of Cochrane Academy participated in focus groups in which they determined the magnet themes for the new school programs that would be located in the facilities to be updated. For Cochrane Academy, the math, science, and fine arts combination was favored. The fact that one of America's most well-known African American artists resided in the urban core may have influenced the choice of the third element. What follows are abbreviated descriptions of the specific curricula in Cochrane's three magnet strands as outlined in documents approved by the Justice Department.

Science and Mathematics

National Standards for Mathematics and Science and the Benchmarks for Scientific Literacy form the cornerstones on which the Cochrane science and mathematics programs are built. Students have the opportunity to explore areas of interest and gain insights into career opportunities existing for those who excel at science and mathematics.

Students can use enhanced technologies to gather data through the Internet. As a result of the access and the tools available, students are able to develop a deeper understanding of mathematical and scientific concepts and are able to recognize them as tools for problem solving and components of a specialized language for communication. In this way, real-world challenges and issues are interpreted, and feasible and desirable solutions are sought.

Other methods of study include acquiring mathematical and scientific data, selecting experimental designs, drawing inferences and making generalizations, forming hypotheses, using logical reasoning, making conclusions, evaluating the impact of mathematics and science and technology on society, and employing group investigation, dialogue, and debate. Some of the special topics of study include mathematical relations, function and concepts, geometry, measurement, problem solving, and probability/statistics. Space/astronomy studies allow students to view the night sky at school with STARLAB, a portable planetarium.

Fine Arts

The Fine Arts magnet focus centers on the performing and visual arts, advanced dance and theatre programs, creative writing and literature. The curriculum is designed to teach children of different social, economic, ethnic, and racial backgrounds an appreciation of many cultures through the study of various art works, music, dance, and drama. Students receive individual and group instruction and opportunities to express their individuality through the arts. The objectives include participation in dance, music, theatre, and visual mediums; development of an appreciation of creative writing and literature; investigation of various careers in the arts; participation in arts and writing contests; and publication of art and writing pieces in order to qualify for scholarship opportunities.

Reform Story

The student-painted wooden lounge chairs, bright benches, and primary-colored poles supporting the external walkways between classrooms at Cochrane Academy signal that an arts-centered place of learning is being entered.

An enormous John Biggersinspired mural on an external wall confirms the passing hypothesis. Anchored with seasonal sketches of the pecan trees that line the internal courtyard, the mural projects the magnet themes of the campus. The pecan trees, so revered by the local African American community, serve as a reminder of how Cochrane's social narrative history reaches into the past, is lived in the present, and projects into the future (Dewey, 1938).

Upon entering Cochrane Academy, one is not only captivated by the sights of learning but also confronted by the sounds of learning. Walking down the corridors, one hears students practicing piano, violin, and tap dancing and singing joyfully in a chorus. Echoes of dramatic productions in the black box theatre/classroom can also be heard.

As one peers into classroom windows, one sees students practicing ballet and developing perspective in art class under the thoughtful direction of their teachers.

One also views students using manipulatives in mathematics and high-quality microscopes in new high-technology science labs.

Walking on, other expressions of learning become visible. A Japanese "Garden of Silence" and an insect sanctuary, for example, are found in the internal courtyard spaces.

Also evident is a Hispanic Plaza of Knowledge, whose design reflects the Alamo and a Spanish mission. It will soon display Diego Riverainspired panels designed and painted by Cochrane youth. The plaza symbolizes the culture of Hispanic-speaking citizens and immigrants who have recently taken up residence in the Hardy community. Student created and maintained, these gardens and spaces extend learning beyond the conventional four walls of class-rooms and the generic box called "school."

Inside Cochrane Academy classrooms, hands-on, multi-disciplinary learning is evident. Students can be seen learning mathematical terms like "diagonal," "square," "line," and "circle" by studying works of art. They also create dance movements to popular tunes like "Rocky Top" that students in cooperative learning groups later perform. Overseeing this activity is a mathematics teacher and a choreographer who was born and raised in the Hardy community and who has worked with many nationally recognized black artists. Her presence at Cochrane is made possible by a grant from the local office of a national reform movement, a grant focused on repairing relationships between the institution of schooling and members of the Hardy community. Later, the students meet with their mathematics teacher and the "learning through the arts" teacher to artistically depict the shapes they have studied.

In another classroom, students analyze Stuart Davis' 1938 picture, "Gloucester Harbor" and borrow Davis's style to form their own works of art. Below is one student's artistic rendition, which is followed by the student's written response to Davis's and his own artistic representation.

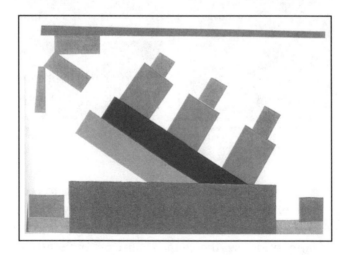

(Stuart Davis's picture, Gloucester Harbor, *was made in 1938 with oil on canvas....It is a very bright, bold and colorful picture. He*

uses different kinds of shapes in his picture. He uses mostly rectangles. Every time you look at it, you see something different. I see two boats with ladders in them sometimes. Other times what stands out to me is a mountain. It is a very bright yellow.

The picture that I made is a red, black, orange, and yellow boat sinking in the ocean. It is kind of like the Titanic. *I used brown and green for the land, and I used yellow rectangles for the sun.*

Elsewhere on the campus, Cochrane students may be actively participating in experiments like "the marble launch," which brings together skills in mathematics, technology, and science. Students are required to roll marbles at given angles and to record the distance the marbles travel. They then use computers to create spreadsheets and line graphs from which they will make a series of predictions.

In another classroom, other students are learning to recognize the difference between point of view and perspective as commonly defined in literature and art. After reading the story, *Hey, Little Ant* by Phillip and Hannah Hoose, their teacher invites the students to write their own versions of a stanza in the story, a stanza that will represent the point of view of both the boy and the ant. Here is one student's artistic representation and response:

Kid: Well, you seem very funny.
And I don't want to make you putty.
I made my decision to set you free
But please remind the ants not to bite me.

Not only is instruction experiential at Cochrane Academy, so, too, is evaluation. The science rubric featured next, together with the image, illustrates students immersed in an authentic assessment task that demonstrates what they have come to know about the properties of structures, how they are constructed, and how to work cooperatively in a group.

Structures Rubric

Participated in the planning and construction of the tower (40 pts)   _____

Cooperated with team members in the construction process (10 pts)   _____

Ability of tower to stand without aid (5 pts)   _____

Detailed description of the building process written in complete
sentences (20 pts)   _____

Detailed and accurate diagram of tower drawn and labeled (20 pts)   _____

Conclusion and summary written of the important concepts
learned (5 pts)   _____

Bonus points: Height of Tower (every 10 cm = 1 point)   _____

   Total Points (Grade)   _____

In the previous pages, photographs and narrative passages capture "composed views" of Cochrane's arts-based landscape and convey the essence of the school's magnet story of reform. The walking tour makes it readily apparent that the school context has been infused with arts-based learning and a mathematics, science, and fine arts program that is possibly the late twentieth century America's greatest achievement in the field of education. However, what never should be forgotten is the fact that the school did not evolve in a typical fashion. Rather, it came into being through legal intervention and vigilant monitoring related to the politics of space which, in turn, gave rise to the pedagogy of place.

Parting Reflections

The particular matrix of stories assembled in this chapter challenge a story that is tacitly present in society: the unspoken meta-narrative that poor urban minority students are incapable of learning. The intersecting narratives soundly debunk this myth by clearly showing how the re-landscaping of a school—coupled with an encompassing focus on experiential, arts-infused learning—restories the possibilities available to youth. These narratives amply show that human learning is not thwarted in a dynamic environment that sparks students' interests and nurtures their development.

At the same time, however, the danger of a Hollywood plot line exists in this "school as parkland" inquiry. For this reason, discussions of Cochrane Academy's "success" must always be firmly grounded in the social, narrative history of the African American community, the story of a people's ongoing struggle for high-quality education and equal access, and the narratives of the unanticipated consequences that added to the complexities of the educational situation in the aftermath of *Brown v. Board of Education*. Furthermore, the poverty in the Hardy community cannot be dismissed. Neither should the fact that a significant portion of Cochrane's student population remains at risk be overlooked. Stark realities such as these remind one that Cochrane's story, embedded in the formidable challenges present in the community context, has merely begun. The extent to which the mathematics, science, and fine arts magnet theme assists in bringing about a sense of social justice that historically has been missing remains to be seen.

This discussion provides an important segue to a second major point: the fact that Cochrane Academy is only in its fifth year of existence and so has only a fledgling institutional narrative. In those five years, huge sums of money have been funneled into the school district by the federal government, and great attention was understandably paid to the school. This occurred because of the court order but also due to the novel opportunity to revitalize a school context with little financial constraint. Questions regarding Cochrane's future automatically arise. For example, what will happen to Cochrane as funding and attention are directed to the reland-scaping of other district schools that also deserving of attention? And what changes will occur in magnet school stories of reform as they become commonplace in the district? Over time, will they, too, become storied as "run of the mill," "status quo"?

Mention of the term, status quo, leads to a final point that needs to be raised: Cochrane challenges status quo learning for students, but the school and its students are nevertheless subjected to paper-and-pencil standardized evaluation measures that have historically not served African American youngsters well (Madaus & Clarke, 1998). Will Cochrane's rich academic program become stunted over the long haul by the press for conventional results and "the limitations of evaluation technology"? (Eisner, 2001). In a strange narrative twist, might Cochrane end up conforming to the prevailing conditions of the larger landscape that necessitated its re-landscaping in the first place?

Using the professional knowledge landscape and parkland metaphors, I have captured how Cochrane Academy changed directions through the re-invention of its story of school. I have also shown how I, with the help of my field-based research assistants, have become immersed in the complexities of one school context and deciphered meaning from it. In the process, my research direction changed as photographic images became favored over conventional text in conveying the creation of Central Park and Cochrane's magnet story of reform. Diamond's (2000) call for the artistic re-formulation of contextual inquiries deeply influenced how the research text was presented.

My research inquiry at Cochrane Academy began with a fascination with "the unique programs, the top-notch faculties, and state of the art equipment" (Cochrane Academy Year 2 Reform Proposal) that set the school apart from any other I have experienced, a similar impetus to the one that compels parents of non-black students to enroll their children in a school located in the Hardy community. Shortly afterward, however, the pedagogy of place and the politics of space themes became abundantly apparent. The narratives shared here provide promising evidence that Cochrane is a transformed school landscape. However, the way that Cochrane Academy shapes lives and the stories told by students who attend it and inspires other struggling campuses and school districts serving poor urban minority students to re-story their pedagogical plot lines in the pursuit of social justice will ultimately speak to the school's influence.

Endnote

The author acknowledges the centrality of the experiences of the educators and community members who participated in this research study. She deeply appreciates the opportunity to conduct the collaborative inquiry at Cochrane Academy. Special thanks are extended to research assistants, Cazilda Steele and Sreekanth Nadella, and to the local office of a national reform movement that funded the work.

References

Aoki, T. (1989). Beyond the half-life of curriculum and pedagogy. *One World, 27*(2), 3–10.

Argyris, C., & Schon, D. (1978). *Organizational learning: A theory of action perspective.* Reading, MA: Addison-Wesley.

Carr, D. (1986). *Time, narrative, and history.* Bloomington: University of Indiana Press.

Clandinin, D. J., & Connelly, F. M. (1996). Teachers' professional knowledge landscapes: Teacher stories—stories of teachers—school stories—stories of school. *Educational Researcher, 25*(3), 24–30.

Cochrane Academy. (1998). *Cochrane Academy Year 2 Reform Movement Proposal.*

Craig, C. J. (1997). Telling stories: A way to access beginning teacher knowledge. *Teaching Education, 9*(1), 61–68.

——— (1999). Parallel stories: A way of contextualizing teacher knowledge. *Teaching and Teacher Education, 15*(4), 397–412.

———— (2000). Stories of schools/Teacher stories: A two-part invention on the walls theme. *Curriculum Inquiry, 30*(1), 11–44.

———— (2001). The relationships between and among teachers' narrative knowledge, communities of knowing, and top-down school reform: A case of "The Monkey's Paw." *Curriculum Inquiry, 31*(3).

———— (in press). Story constellations: A way to characterize school contexts and contextualize teacher knowledge. *Curriculum and Teaching Dialogue.*

Dewey, J. (1938). *Experience and education.* New York: Collier.

Diamond, C. T. P. (2000). Turning landscape into parkland: Difficulties in changing direction. *Curriculum Inquiry, 30*(1), 1–10.

Eisner, E. (2001). *What does it mean to say that a school is doing well?* April 4th Keynote Address delivered in the Epiphany Lecture Series, University of Houston.

Hatch, T. (1998). The differences in theory that matter in the practice of school improvement. *American Educational Research Journal, 35*(1), 3–31.

Ladson-Billings, G. (1992). Culturally relevant teaching: The key to making multicultural education work. In Carl A. Grant (Ed.), *Research and multicultural education: From the margins to the mainstream.* London: Falmer.

Madaus, G., & Clarke, M. (1998). *The adverse impact of high stakes testing on minority students: Evidence from 100 years of test data.* Paper presented at The Civil Rights Implications of High Stakes K–12 Testing Conference sponsored by The Civil Rights Project at Harvard University, Teachers College, and Columbia Law School.

Polkinghorne, D. E. (1988). *Narrative knowing and the human sciences.* New York: SUNY Press.

Schon, D., & McDonald, J. (1998). *Doing what you mean to do in school reform.* Providence, RI: Annenberg Institute.

Steiner, R. (1988). *Calendar of the soul.* Spring Valley, NY: Anthroposophic.

Part III

Place as Political and Historical

Photograph by Anna Latta

Chapter 7

Away with All Teachers: The Cultural Politics of Home Schooling

Michael W. Apple

If one of the marks of the growing acceptance of ideological changes is their positive presentation in the popular media, then home schooling has clearly found a place in our consciousness. It has been discussed in the national press, on television and radio, and in widely circulated magazines. Its usual presentation is that of a savior, a truly compelling alternative to a public school system that is presented as a failure. While the presentation of public schools as simply failures is deeply problematic,[1] it is the largely unqualified support of home schooling that concerns me here. I am considerably less than sanguine about it.

Data on home schooling are not always accurate and are often difficult to compile. However, a sense of the extent of home schooling can be found in the fact that the National Home Education Research Institute has estimated that as of the 1997–1998 school year, 1.5 million children were being home schooled in the United States. The Institute also has suggested that there has been a growth of 15 percent annually in these numbers since 1990. Although these data are produced by an organization that is one of the strongest supporters of home schooling, even given the possible inflation of these figures, it is clear that this is a considerable number of students.[2]

In a relatively short chapter, I cannot deal at length with all of the many issues that could be raised about the home schooling movement. I want to ask a number of critical questions about the dangers associated with it. Although it is quite probable that certain children and families will gain from home schooling, my concerns are larger. They are connected to the more extensive restructuring of this society that I believe is quite dangerous and to the manner in which our very sense of public responsibility is withering in ways that will lead to even further social inequalities. In order to illuminate these dangers, I shall have to do a number of things: situate home schooling within the larger movement that provides much of its impetus; suggest its connections with other protectionist impulses; connect it to the history of and concerns about the growth of activist government; and, finally, point to how it may actually hurt many other students who are not home schooled.

At the very outset of this article, let me state as clearly as I can that any parents who care so much about the educational experiences of their children that they actively seek to be deeply involved are to be applauded, not chastised or simply dismissed. Let me also say that it is important not to stereotype those individuals who reject public schooling[3] as unthinking promoters of ideological forms that are so deeply threatening that they are—automatically—to be seen as beyond the pale of legitimate concerns. Indeed, as I have demonstrated in *Cultural Politics and Education* (Apple, 1996), there are complicated reasons behind the growth of anti-school sentiments. There are elements of "good" sense as well as "bad" sense in such beliefs. All too many school systems *are* overly bureaucratic, are apt not to listen carefully to parents' or community concerns, or may act in overly defensive ways when questions are asked about what and whose knowledge is considered "official." In some ways, these kinds of criticisms are similar across the political spectrum, with both left and right often making similar claims about the politics of recognition (see Fraser, 1997). Indeed, these very kinds of criticisms have led many progressive and activist educators to build more community-based and responsive models of curriculum and teaching in public schools (Apple & Beane, 1995, 1999).

This said, however, it is still important to realize that the intentions of such critics as home schoolers may be meritorious, but the effects of their actions may be less so.

Although many home schoolers who have not made their decision based on religious convictions, a large proportion have (see Detwiler, 1999; Ray 1999). In this chapter, I shall focus largely on this group, in part, because it constitutes some of the most committed parents and, in part, because ideologically it raises a number of important issues.

Many home schoolers are guided by what they believe are biblical understandings of the family, gender relationships, legitimate knowledge, the importance of "tradition," the role of government, and the economy (Detwiler, 1999; Kintz, 1997).[4] They constitute part of what I have called the "conservative restoration" in which a tense alliance has been built among various segments of "the public" in favor of particular policies in education and the larger social world. Let me place this in its larger context.

Education and Conservative Modernization

Long-lasting educational transformations often come not from the work of educators and researchers but from larger social movements which tend to push our major political, economic, and cultural institutions in specific directions. Thus, it would be impossible to fully understand educational reforms over the past decades without situating them within, say, the long struggles by multiple communities of color and by women for both cultural recognition and economic redistribution (e.g., Fraser, 1997). Even such taken-for-granted things as state textbook adoption policies—among the most powerful mechanisms in the processes of defining "official knowledge"—are the results of widespread populist and anti-northern movements and especially of the class and race struggles over culture and power that organized and re-organized the polity in the United States a century ago (Apple, 2000).

It should, then, come as no surprise that education is again witnessing the continued emergence and growing influence of powerful social movements. Some of these may lead to increased democratization and greater equality, while others are based on a fundamental shift in the very meanings of democracy and equality and are more than a little retrogressive socially and culturally. Unfortunately, it is the latter that have emerged as the most powerful.

The rightward turn has been the result of years of well-funded and creative ideological efforts by the right to form a broad-based coalition. This new alliance, what is technically called a "new hegemonic bloc," has been so successful in part because it has been able to make major inroads in the battle over common sense.[5] That is, it has creatively stitched together different social tendencies and commitments and has organized them under its own general leadership in issues dealing with welfare, culture, the economy, and, as many of you know from personal experience, education. Its aim in educational and social policy might best be described as "conservative modernization" (Dale, 1989). In the process, democracy has been reduced to consumption. Citizenship has been reduced to possessive individualism. And a politics based on resentment and a fear of the "Other" has been pressed forward.

There are a number of major elements within this new alliance (see Apple, 1996, for a more detailed discussion). The first, neo-liberals, represent dominant economic and political elites who are intent on "modernizing" the economy and the institutions connected to it. They are certain that markets and consumer choice will solve all of "our" social problems, because private is necessarily good and public is necessarily bad—hence, their strong support of vouchers and privatized choice plans. Although there is clear empirical evidence about the very real inequalities that are created by such educational policies (Lauder & Hughes, 1999; Whitty, Power, & Halpin, 1998), this group is usually in leadership of the alliance. If we think of this new bloc as an ideological umbrella, neo-liberals are holding the umbrella's handle.

The second group, neo-conservatives, are economic and cultural conservatives who want a return to "high standards," discipline, "real" knowledge, and what is in essence a form of Social Darwinist competition. They are fueled by a nostalgic and quite romanticized vision of the past. It is often based on a fundamental misrecognition of the fact that what they might call the classics and "real" knowledge gained that status as the result of intense past conflicts and often had been seen as just as dangerous and just as morally destabilizing as any of the new elements of the curriculum and culture they now castigate (Levine, 1996).

The third element is made up of largely white working-class and middle-class groups that mistrust the state and are concerned with security, the family, gender and age relations within the home, sexuality, and traditional and fundamentalist religious values and knowledge. They form an increasingly active segment of authoritarian populists, who are powerful in education and in other areas of politics and social and cultural policy. They provide much of the support from below for neo-liberal and neo-conservative positions, because they see themselves as disenfranchised by the "secular humanism" that supposedly now pervades public schooling. They are also often among those larger numbers of people whose very economic livelihoods are most at stake in the economic restructuring and capital flight that we are now experiencing.

Many home schoolers combine beliefs from all three of these tendencies, but it is the last one which seems to drive a large portion of the movement (Detwiler, 1999; Kintz, 1997).

Satan's Threat

For many on the right, one of the key enemies is public education. Secular education is turning our children into "aliens," and, by teaching them to question our ideas, is turning them against us. What are often accurate concerns about public schooling that I noted earlier—its overly bureaucratic nature; its lack of curriculum coherence; its disconnection from the lives, hopes, and cultures of many of its communities; and more—are here often connected to more deep-seated and intimate worries. These worries echo Elaine Pagels argument that Christianity has historically defined its most fearful satanic threats as coming not from distant enemies but from very intimate ones (Pagels, 1995). "The most dangerous characteristic of the satanic enemy is that though he will look just like us, he will nevertheless have changed completely" (quoted in Kintz, 1997, p. 73).

Some of the roots of this point of view can be found much earlier in the conservative activist Beverly LaHaye's call for the founding of an organization to counter the rising tide of feminism. In support of Concerned Women of America, she spoke of her concern for family, nation, and religion.

> I sincerely believe that God is calling the Christian women of America to draw together in a spirit of unity and purpose to protect the rights of the family. I believe that it is time for us to set aside our doctrinal differences to work for a spiritually renewed America. Who but a woman is as deeply concerned about her children and her home? Who but a woman has the time, the intuition, and the drive to restore our nation?...They may call themselves feminists or humanists. The label makes little difference, because many of them are seeking the destruction of morality and human freedom. (quoted in Kintz, 1997, p. 80)

It is clear from the above quote what is seen as the satanic threat and what is at stake here. These fears about the nation, home, family, children's "innocence," religious values, and traditional views of gender relations are sutured together into a more general fear of the destruction of a moral compass and personal freedom. "Our" world is disintegrating around us. Its causes are not the economically destructive policies of the global economy (Greider, 1997), not the decisions of an economic elite, and not the ways in which, say, our kind of economy turns *all* things—including cherished traditions (and even our children)[6]—into commodities for sale. Rather, the causes are transferred onto those institutions and people which are themselves being constantly buffeted by the same forces—public sector institutions, schooling, poor people of color, other women who have struggled for centuries to build a society that is more responsive to the hopes and dreams of many people who have been denied participation in the public sphere, and so on.[7]

As I noted at the beginning of this chapter, however, it is important not to stereotype individuals involved in this movement. For example, a number of men and women who are activists in rightist movements believe that some elements of feminism did improve the conditions of women overall. By focusing on equal pay for equal work and opening up job opportunities that had been traditionally denied to women who had to work for pay, women activists had benefited many people. However, for authoritarian populists, feminism and secular institutions in general still tend to break with God's law. They are much too individualistic and misinterpret the divine relationship between families and God. In so doing, many aspects of civil rights legislation, of the public schools' curricula, and so many other parts of secular society are simply wrong. Thus, for example, if one views the Constitution of the United States literally as divinely inspired, then it is not public institutions but the traditional family—as God's chosen unit—that is the core social unit that must be protected by the Constitution (Kintz, 1997, p. 97). In a time of seeming cultural disintegration, when traditions are under threat and when the idealized family faces ever more externally produced dangers, protecting our families and our children is a key element in returning to God's grace.[8]

Even without these religious elements, a defensive posture is clear in much of the movement. In many ways, the movement toward home schooling mirrors the growth of privatized consciousness in other areas of society. It is an extension of the "suburbanization" of everyday life that is so evident all around us. In essence, it is the equivalent of gated communities and of the privatization of neighborhoods, recreation, parks, and so many other things. It provides a "security zone" both physically and ideologically. Linda Kintz describes it this way.

> As citizens worried about crime, taxes, poor municipal services, and poor schools abandon cities, the increasing popularity of gated communities... fortress communities...reflects people's desire to retreat...They want to spend more of their tax dollars on themselves instead of others. Further, they take comfort in the social homogeneity of such communities, knowing that their neighbors act and think much as they do. (Kintz, 1997, p. 107)

This "cocooning" is not just about seeking an escape from the problems of the "city" (a metaphor for danger and heterogeneity). It is a rejection of the entire *idea* of the city. Cultural and intellectual diversity, complexity, ambiguity, uncertainty, and proximity to "the Other," all these are to be shunned (Kintz, 1997, p. 107). In place of the "city" is the engineered pastoral, the neat and well-planned universe where things (and people) are in their "rightful place" and reality is safe and predictable.

Yet in so many ways such a movement mirrors something else. It is a microcosm of the increasing segmentation of American society in general. As we move to a society segregated by residence, race, economic opportunity, and income, "purity" is increasingly apt to be found in the fact that upper classes send their children to elite private schools; where neighborliness is determined by property values; where evangelical Christians, ultra-orthodox Jews, and others only interact with each other and their children are schooled in private religious schools or schooled at home (Kintz, 1997, p. 108). A world free of conflict, uncertainty, the voice and culture of the Other—in a word I used before, cocooning—is the ideal.[9]

Home schooling, thus, has many similarities with the Internet. It enables the creation of "virtual communities" which are perfect for those with specialized interests. It gives individuals a new ability to "personalize" information, to choose what they want to know or what they find personally interesting. However, as many commentators are beginning to recognize, unless we are extremely cautious, "customizing our lives" could radically undermine the strength of local communities, many of which are already woefully weak. As Andrew Shapiro puts it,

> Shared experience is an indisputably essential ingredient [in the formation of local communities]; without it there can be no chance for mutual understanding, empathy and social cohesion. And this is precisely what personalization threatens to delete. A lack of common information would deprive individuals of a starting point for democratic dialogue. (Shapiro, 1999, p. 12)

Even with the evident shortcomings of many public schools, at the very least they provide "a kind of social glue, a common cultural reference point in our polyglot, increasingly multicultural society" (Shapiro, 1999, p. 12). Yet, whether called personalizing or cocooning, it is exactly this common reference point that is rejected by many within the home schooling movement's pursuit of "freedom" and "choice."

This particular construction of the meaning of freedom is of considerable moment, because there is a curious contradiction within such conservatism's obsession with freedom. In many ways this emphasis on freedom is, paradoxically, based on a *fear* of freedom (Kintz, 1997, p. 168). It is valued, but also loathed as a site of danger, of "a world out of control." Many home schoolers reject public schooling out of concern for equal time for their beliefs. They want "equality." Yet it is a specific vision of equality, because coupled with their fear of things out of control is a powerful anxiety that the nation's usual understanding of equality will produce uniformity (Kintz, 1997, p. 186). But this feared uniformity is not seen the same as the religious and cultural homogeneity sponsored by the conservative project. It is a very different type of uniformity—one in which the fear that "we are all the same" actually speaks to a loss of religious particularity. Thus, again there is another paradox at the heart of this movement: we want everyone to be like "us" (this is a "Christian nation"; governments must bow before "a higher authority") (Smith, 1998); but we want the right to be different—a difference based on being God's elect group. Uniformity weakens our specialness. This tension between knowing one is a member of God's elect people and thus by definition different and also so certain that one is correct that the world needs to be changed to fit one's image is one of the central paradoxes behind authoritarian populist impulses. For some home schoolers, the paradox is solved by withdrawal of one's children from the public sphere in order to maintain their difference. For still others, this allows them to prepare themselves and their children with an armor of Christian beliefs that will enable them to go forth into the world later on to bring God's word to those who are not among the elect. Once again, let us declare our particularity, our difference, in order to better prepare ourselves to bring the unanointed world to our set of uniform beliefs.

Attacking the State

At the base of this fear both of the loss of specialness and of becoming uniform in the "wrong way" is a sense that the state is intervening in our daily lives in quite powerful ways, ways that are causing even more losses. It isn't possible to understand the growth of home schooling unless we connect it to the history of the attack on the public sphere in general and on the government (the state) in particular. In order to better comprehend the anti-statist impulses that lie behind a good deal of the home schooling movement, I need to place these impulses in a longer historical and social context. Some history and theory are necessary here.

One of the keys to this is the development of what Clarke and Newman (1997) have called the "managerial state." This active state combined bureaucratic administration and professionalism. The organization of the state centered around the application of specific rules of coordination. Routinization and predictability are among the hallmarks of such a state. This was to be coupled with a second desirable trait, that of social, political, and personal neutrality rather than nepotism and favoritism. This bureaucratic routinization and predictability would be balanced by an emphasis on professional discretion. Here, bureaucratically regulated professionals such as teachers and administrators would still have an element of irreducible autonomy based on their training and qualifications. Their skills and judgment were to be trusted if they acted fairly and impartially. Yet fairness and impartiality were not enough; the professional also personalized the managerial state. Professionals such as teachers made the state "approachable" by not only signifying neutrality but by acting in non-anonymous ways to foster the "public good" and to "help" individuals and families (Clarke & Newman, 1997, pp. 5–7).

Of course, such bureaucratic and professional norms existed not only to benefit "clients." They acted to protect the state, by providing it with legitimacy. (The state is impartial, fair, and acts in the interests of everyone.) They also served to insulate professional judgments from critical scrutiny. (As holders of expert knowledge, we—teachers, social workers, state employees—are the ones who are to be trusted because we know best.)

Thus, from the end of World War II until approximately the mid-1970s, there was a "settlement," a compromise, in which an activist welfare state was seen as legitimate. It was sustained by a triple legitimacy. There was (largely) bi-partisan support for the state to provide and manage a larger part of social life, a fact that often put it above a good deal of party politics. Bureaucratic administration promised to act impartially for the benefit of everyone. And professionals employed by the state, such as teachers and other educators, were there to apply expert knowledge to serve the public (Clarke & Newman, 1997, p. 8). This compromise was widely accepted and provided public schools and other public institutions with a strong measure of support since by and large the vast majority of people continued to believe that schools and other state agencies did, in fact, act professionally and impartially in the public good.

This compromise came under severe attack, as the fiscal crisis deepened and as competition over scarce economic, political, and cultural resources grew more heated in the 1970s and beyond. The political forces of conservative movements used this crisis, often in quite cynical and manipulative—and well-funded—ways. The state was criticized for denying consumers the opportunity to exercise choice. The welfare state was seen as gouging the citizen (as a taxpayer) to pay for public handouts for those who ignored personal responsibility for their actions. These "scroungers" from the underclass were seen as sexually promiscuous, immoral, and lazy as opposed to the "rest of us" who were hard working, industrious, and moral. They supposedly are a drain on all of us economically and state-sponsored support of them leads to the collapse of the family and traditional morality (Apple, 2000). These arguments may not have been totally accurate (e.g., Fine & Weis, 1998), but they were effective.

This suturing together of neo-liberal and neo-conservative attacks led to a particular set of critiques against the state. For many people, the state was no longer the legitimate and neutral upholder of the public good. Instead the welfare state was an active agent of national decline as well as an economic drain on the country's (and the family's) resources. In the words of Clarke and Newman:

> Bureaucrats were identified as actively hostile to the public—hiding behind the impersonality of regulations and "red tape" to deny choice, building bureaucratic empires at the expense of providing service, and insulating themselves from the "real world" pressures of competition by their monopolistic position. Professionals were arraigned as motivated by self-interest, exercising power over would-be consumers, denying choice through the dubious claim that "professionals know best." Worse still...liberalism...was viewed as undermining personal responsibility and family authority and as prone to trendy excesses such as egalitarianism,

anti-discrimination policies, moral relativism or child-centeredness. (Clarke & Newman, 1997, p. 15)

These moral, political, and economic concerns were easily transferred to public schooling, since for many people the school was and is the public institution closest to them in their daily life. Hence, public school and the teaching and curricula found within it became central targets of attack. Curricula and teachers were not impartial but elitist. School systems were imposing the Other's morality on "us." And "real Americans" who were patriotic, religious, and moral—as opposed to everyone else—were suffering and were the new oppressed (Delfattore, 1992). Although this position fits into a long history of the paranoid style of American cultural politics and it was often based on quite inaccurate stereotypes, it does point to a profound sense of alienation that many people feel.

Much of this anti-statism, of course, was fueled by the constant attention given in the media and in public pronouncements to "incompetent" teachers who are overpaid and have short working days and long vacations.[10] We should not minimize the effects of the conservative attacks on schools for their supposed inefficiency, wasting of financial resources, and lack of connection to the economy. After years of well-orchestrated attacks, it would be extremely odd if one did not find that the effects on popular consciousness were real. The fact that a number of these criticisms may be *partly* accurate should not be dismissed. There undoubtedly is a small group of teachers who treat teaching as simply a job that gives them many holidays and free time in the summer. Administrative costs and bureaucratic requirements in schools have risen. Parents and local communities do have a justifiable right to worry about whether their daughters and sons will have decent jobs when they leave school, especially in a time when our supposedly booming economy has left millions of people behind, and many of the jobs being created are anything but fulfilling and secure (Apple, 1996). (The fact that the school has very little to do with this is important.)

Yet, it is not only worries about teachers that fuel this movement. As I point out in my book, *Educating the "Right" Way* (Apple, 2001), public schools themselves are seen as extremely dangerous places. These schools were institutions that threatened one's very soul.

Temptations and Godlessness were everywhere within them. God's truths were expunged from the curriculum, and God's voice could no longer be heard. Prayers were now illegal, and all of the activities that bound my life to scriptural realities were seen as deviant.

Even with the negative powerful emotions that such senses of loss and disconnection create, an additional element has entered into the emotional economy being created here with a crushing force. For an increasingly large number of parents, public schools are now seen as threatening in an even more powerful way. They are seen as filled with physical dangers to the very life of one's children. The spate of shootings in schools in the United States has had a major impact on the feelings of insecurity that parents have. Stories of violence-ridden schools (worrisome but viewed as largely an "urban problem" involving the poor and children of color) had already been creating an anti-public school sentiment among many conservative parents. The horrors of seeing students shoot other students, now not in those supposedly troubled urban schools but in the suburban areas that had grown after people fled the city, exacerbated the situation. If even the schools of affluent suburbia were sites of danger, then the *only* remaining safe haven was the fortress home.[11]

Fears, no matter how powerful they are or whether they are justified or not, are not enough, however. That a person will act on her or his fears is made more or less probable by the availability of resources to support taking action. It is almost taken for granted, but important nonetheless, that the growth of home schooling has been stimulated by the wider accessibility to tools that make it easier for parents to engage in it. Among the most important is the Internet (see Bromley & Apple, 1998). There are scores of websites available that give advice, provide technical and emotional support, tell the stories of successful home schoolers, and are more than willing to sell material at a profit. The fact that, like the conservative evangelical movement in general (Smith, 1998), a larger portion of home schoolers than before seems to have the economic resources to afford computers means that economic capital can be mobilized in anti-school strategies in more flexible and dynamic ways than in earlier periods of the home schooling movement.

Since home schooling is often done using the web, it is useful to see what some of the sites say. The Teaching Home, based in Portland, Oregon, is one of the central resources for conservative Christians who wish to home school.[12] On its website the question "Why do families home school?" is asked, and a number of answers are given.

> Many Christian parents are committed to educating their children at home because of their conviction that this is God's will for their family. They are concerned for the spiritual training and character development as well as the social and academic welfare of their children.

Among the advantages of home schooling listed are:

- Parents can present all academic subjects from a biblical perspective and include spiritual training.
- "The fear of the LORD is the beginning of wisdom, and the knowledge of the Holy One is understanding" (Prov. 9:10 NAS).
- Home schooling makes quality time available to train and influence children in all areas in an integrated way.
- Each child receives individual attention and has his unique needs met.
- Parents can control destructive influences such as various temptations, false teachings (including secular humanism and occult influences of the New Age movement), negative peer pressure, and unsafe environments.
- Children gain respect for their parents as teachers.
- The family experiences unity, closeness, and mutual enjoyment of one another as they spend more time working together.
- Children develop confidence and independent thinking away from the peer pressure to conform and in the security of their own home.
- Children have time to explore new interests and to think.
- Communication between different age groups is enhanced.
- Tutorial-style education helps each child achieve his full educational potential.

- Flexible scheduling can accommodate parents' work and vacation times and allow time for many activities.

This list is broader than might be allowed in some of the stereotypes of what home schooling advocates—particularly religiously conservative ones—are like. There is a focus on wanting their children to explore, to achieve their full academic potential, to have "his" needs met. Yet, in this diverse list of advantages, certain themes come to the fore. At the top is biblical authority, with knowledge and understanding connected with "fear of the LORD." "Real" knowledge is grounded in what the Holy One has ordained. The role of the parent is largely one of "training," of influencing one's children in all areas so that they are safe from the outside influences of a secular society. God/home/family is pure; the rest of the world—secular humanism, peers, popular culture—are forms of pollution, temptations, dangers. That the male pronoun is used throughout is indicative of God's wish for the man of the house to be God's chosen leader (Kintz, 1997).

Yet, one cannot deny the elements of concern that parents such as these express. They are *deeply* worried about the lives and futures of their children, children they are fully willing to sacrifice an immense amount for. They do want a caring environment for their children, one in which all family members respect and care for each other. There are powerful positive moments in these statements. In a time when many groups of varying religious and political sentiments express the concern that children are ignored in this society, that they are simply seen as present and future consumers by people who only care whether a profit is made off of them, that our major institutions are less responsive than they should be, and that elements of popular culture are negative as well as positive—all of these sentiments are central to the concerns of home schoolers as well.

Given what I have just said, we do need to recognize that there are elements of good sense in the critique of the state made by both the left and the right, such as the home schoolers I have discussed above. The government has assumed all too often that the only true holders of expertise in education, social welfare, etc., are those in positions of formal authority. This has led to over-bureaucratization.

It has also led to the state being partly "colonized" by a particular fraction of the new middle class that seeks to ensure its own mobility and its own positions by employing the state for its own purposes (Bourdieu, 1996). Some schools have become sites of danger given the levels of alienation and meaninglessness—and the dominance of violence as an "imaginary solution" in the "popular" media. However, there is a world of difference between, say, acknowledging that there are some historical tendencies within the state to become overly bureaucratic and not listen carefully enough to the expressed needs of the people it is supposed to serve and a blanket rejection of public control and public institutions such as schools. This has not only led to cocooning, but it threatens the gains made by large groups of disadvantaged people for whom the possible destruction of public schooling is nothing short of a disaster. The final section of my analysis turns to a discussion of this situation.

Public and Private

We need to think *relationally* when we ask who will be the major beneficiaries of the attack on the state and the movement toward home schooling. What if gains made by one group of people come at the expense of other, even more culturally and economically oppressed, groups? As we shall see, this is not an inconsequential worry.

A distinction that is helpful here is that between a politics of redistribution and a politics of recognition. In the first (redistribution), the concern is for socioeconomic injustice. Here, the political-economic system of a society creates conditions that lead to exploitation (having the fruits of your labor appropriated for the benefit of others), and/or economic marginalization (having one's paid work confined to poorly paid and undesirable jobs or having no real access to the routes to serious and better-paying jobs), and/or deprivation (being constantly denied the material that would lead to an adequate standard of living). All of these socioeconomic injustices lead to arguments about whether this is a just or fair society and whether identifiable groups of people actually have equality of resources (Fraser, 1997, p. 13).

The second dynamic (recognition) is often related to redistribution in the real world, but it has its own specific history and differential power relations as well. It is related to the politics of culture and symbols. In this case, injustice is rooted in a society's social patterns of representation and interpretation. Examples of this include cultural domination (being constantly subjected to patterns of interpretation or cultural representation that are alien to one's own or even hostile to it), nonrecognition (basically being rendered invisible in the dominant cultural forms in the society), and disrespect (having oneself routinely stereotyped or maligned in public representations in the media, schools, government policies, or everyday conduct) (Fraser, 1997, p. 14). These kinds of issues surrounding the politics of recognition are central to the identities and sense of injustice of many home schoolers. Indeed, they provide the organizing framework for their critique of public schooling and their demand that they be allowed to teach their children outside of such state control.

Although both forms of injustice are important, it is absolutely crucial that we recognize that an adequate response to one must not lead to the exacerbation of the other. That is, responding to the claims of injustice in recognition by one group (say, religious conservatives) must not make the conditions that lead to exploitation, economic marginalization, and deprivation more likely to occur for other groups. Unfortunately, this may be the case for some of the latent effects of home schooling.

Because of this, it is vitally important not to separate the possible effects of home schooling from what we are beginning to know about the possible consequences of neo-liberal policies in general in education. As Whitty and colleagues (1998) have shown in their review of the international research on voucher and choice plans, one of the latent effects of such policies has been the reproduction of traditional hierarchies of class and race. That is, the programs clearly have differential benefits in which those who already possess economic and cultural capital reap significantly more benefits than those who do not. This is patterned in very much the same ways as the stratification of economic, political, and cultural power produces inequalities in nearly every socioeconomic sphere (Whitty et al., 1998). One of the hidden consequences that is emerging from the expanding conservative critique of public institutions, including schools, is a growing anti-tax movement in which those who have chosen to place their children in privatized, marketized, and home schools do not want to pay taxes to support the schooling of "the Other" (Apple, 1996).

The wider results of this are becoming clear—a declining tax base for schooling, social services, health care, housing, and anything "public" for those populations (usually in the most economically depressed urban and rural areas) who suffer the most from the economic dislocations and inequalities that so deeply characterize this nation. Thus, a politics of recognition—I want to guarantee "choice" for my children based on my identity and special needs—has begun to have extremely negative effects on the politics of redistribution. It is absolutely crucial that we recognize this. If it is the case that the emergence of educational markets has consistently benefited the most advantaged parents and students and has consistently disadvantaged both poor parents and students and parents and students of color (Lauder & Hughes, 1999; Whitty et al., 1998), then we need to critically examine the latent effects of the growth of home schooling in the same light. Will it be the case that social justice loses in this equation just as it did and does in many of the other highly publicized programs of "choice"?

We now have emerging evidence to this effect, evidence that points to the fact that social justice often does lose with the expansion of home schooling in some states. A case in point is the way in which the ongoing debate over the use of public money for religious purposes in education is often subverted through manipulation of loopholes that are only available to particular groups. Religiously motivated home schoolers are currently engaged in exploiting public funding in ways that are not only hidden but raise serious questions about the drain on economic resources during a time of severe budget crises in all too many school districts.

Let me say more about this, because it provides an important instance of my argument that gains in recognition for some groups (say, home schools) can have decidedly negative effects in other spheres, such as the politics of redistribution. In California, for example, charter schools have been used as a mechanism to gain public money for home schoolers. Charter school legislation in California has been employed in very "interesting" ways to accomplish this. In one recent study, for example, 50 percent of charter schools were serving home schoolers. "Independent study" charter schools (a creative pseudonym for computer-linked home schooling) have been used by both school districts and parents to gain money that otherwise might not have been available. Although this does demonstrate the ability of school districts to strategically use charter school legislation to get money that might have been lost when parents withdraw their children to home school them, it also signifies something else. In this and other cases, the money given to parents for enrolling in such independent study charter schools was used by the parents to purchase religious material produced and sold by Bob Jones University, one of the most conservative religious schools in the entire nation (Wells, 1999).

Thus, public money not legally available for overtly sectarian material is used to purchase religious curricula under the auspices of charter school legislation. Yet unlike all curricula used in public schools which *must* be publicly accountable in terms of content and costs, the material purchased for home schooling has no public accountability whatsoever. This does give greater choice to home schoolers and does enable them to act on a politics of recognition, but it takes money away from other students who cannot afford computers in the home and denies them a say in what the community's children will learn about themselves and their cultures, histories, values, and so on. Given the fact that a number of textbooks used in fundamentalist religious schools expressly state such "facts" as Islam is a false religion and embody similar claims that many citizens would find deeply offensive,[13] one can seriously question the appropriateness of public money being used to teach such content without any public accountability.

Thus, two things are going on here. Money is being drained from already hard-pressed school districts to support home schooling. Just as importantly, curricular materials that support the identities of religiously motivated groups are being paid for by the public *without* any accountability, even though these materials may act in such a way as to deny the claims for recognition of one of the fastest-growing religions in the nation, Islam. This raises more general and quite serious issues about how the claims for recognition by religious conservatives can be financially supported when they may at times actually support discriminatory teaching.

I don't wish to be totally negative here. After all, this is a complicated issue in which there may be justifiable worries among home schoolers that their culture and values are not being listened to. But it must be openly discussed, not lost in the simple statement that we should support a politics of recognition of religiously motivated home schoolers because their culture seems to them to be not sufficiently recognized in public institutions. At the very least, the possible dangers to the public good need to be recognized.

Conclusion

I have used this chapter to raise a number of critical questions about the economic, social, and ideological tendencies that often stand behind significant parts of the home schooling movement. In the process, I have situated it within larger social movements that I and many others believe can have quite negative effects on our sense of community, on the health of the public sphere, and on our commitment to building a society that is less economically and racially stratified. I have suggested that issues need to be raised about the effects of its commitment to "cocooning," its attack on the state, and its growing use of public funding with no public accountability. Yet, I have also argued that there are clear elements of good sense in its criticisms of the bureaucratic nature of all too many of our institutions, in its worries about the managerial state, and in its devotion to being active in the education of its children.

The task is to disentangle the elements of good sense evident in these concerns from the selfish and anti-public agenda that has been pushing concerned parents and community members into the arms of the conservative restoration. The task of public schools is to listen much more carefully to the complaints of parents such as these and to rebuild our institutions in much more responsive ways. As I have argued in much greater detail elsewhere, all too often public schools push concerned parents who are not originally part of conservative cultural and political movements into the arms of such alliances by their defensiveness, lack of responsiveness, and silencing of democratic discussion and criticism (Apple, 1996). Of course, sometimes these criticisms are unjustified or are politically motivated by undemocratic agendas (Apple, 1999). However, this must not serve as an excuse for a failure to open the doors of our schools to the intense public debate that makes public education a living and vital part of our democracy.

We have models for doing exactly that, as the democratic schools movement demonstrates (Apple & Beane, 1995, 1999). While I do not want to be overly romantic here, there *are* models of curricula and teaching that are related to community sentiment, that are committed to social justice and fairness, and that are based in schools where both teachers and students want to be. If schools do not use these models, all too many parents may be pushed in the direction of anti-school sentiment. This would be a tragedy both for the public school system and for our already withered sense of community, which is increasingly under threat. Even though state-supported schools have often served as arenas through which powerful social divisions are partly reproduced, at least in the United States, such schools have also served as powerful sites for the mobilization of collective action and for the preservation of the very possibility of democratic struggle (Hogan, 1985; Reese, 1986). As one of the few remaining institutions that *are* still public, struggles over it are crucial. This is obviously a tightrope we need to negotiate. How do we uphold the vision of a truly public institution at the same time that we rigorously criticize its functioning? In the United States, this is one of the tasks that the critical educators involved in *Democratic Schools* and the National Coalition of Education Activists have set for themselves (Apple & Beane, 1995, 1999).[14] They have recognized that schools have contradictory impulses and pressures upon them, especially in a time of conservative modernization. It is not romantic to actively work on and through those contradictions so that the collective memory of earlier and partly successful struggles is not lost. Nor is it romantic to engage in what I have elsewhere called "non-reformist reforms," reforms to expand the space of counter-hegemonic action in public institutions (Apple, 1995). Yet, to do this, it is necessary to defend the public nature of such public spaces.

Raymond Williams (1989) may have expressed it best when— positioning himself as an optimist without any illusions—he reminded us of the importance of the *mutual* determination of the meanings and values that should guide our social life. In expressing his commitment toward "the long revolution," his words are worth remembering. "We must speak for hope, as long as it doesn't mean suppressing the nature of the danger" (Williams, 1989, p. 322). There are identifiable dangers to identifiable groups of people in public schooling as we know it. But the privatizing alternatives may be much worse.

Endnotes

[1]It is important that we remember that public schools were and are a victory. They constituted a gain for the majority of people who were denied access to advancement and to valued cultural capital in a stratified society. This is not to claim that the public school did not and does not have differential effects. Indeed, I have devoted many books to uncovering the connections between formal education and the recreation of inequalities (see, for example, Apple, 1990, 1995). Rather, it is to say that public schooling is a site of conflict but one that also has been a site of major victories by popular groups (Reese, 1986). Indeed, conservatives would not be so angry at schools if public schools has not had a number of progressive tendencies cemented in them.

[2]For further information on the National Home Education Research Institute and on its data on home schooling, see the following website: http://www.nheri.org.

[3]In the United States, the term "public" schooling refers only to those schools that are organized, funded, and controlled by the state. All other schools are considered "private" or "religious."

[4]In part, the attractiveness of home schooling among religiously motivated parents is also due to a structural difference between schools in the United States and those in many other nations. Historically, although at times mythical, the separation between state-supported schooling and an official state religion has been a distinctive feature of education here. Thus, the absence of religious instruction in schools has been a source of tension among many groups and has generated even more anti-school sentiment (see Nord, 1995). I have discussed some of the history of

the growth of conservative evangelical movements and their relationships with anti-school sentiment in Apple (in press).

[5]I have demonstrated elsewhere the success of this movement both historically and empirically. See Apple (2000) and Apple (1996). For a history of the tensions surrounding the forces of conservative modernization, specifically in the United States, see Foner (1998).

[6]I am thinking here of Channel One, the commercial television show that is in an increasingly large percentage of our middle and secondary schools. In this "reform," students are sold as a captive audience to corporations intent on marketing their products to our children in schools. See Apple (2000) and Molnar (1996).

[7]Of course, the very distinction between "public" and "private" spheres has strong connections to the history of patriarchal assumptions (see Fraser, 1989).

[8]This is a *particular* construction of the family. As Coontz (1992) has shown in her history of the family in the United States, it has had a very varied form, with the nuclear family that is so important to conservative formulations merely being one of many.

[9]Of course, it is important to realize that there may be good reasons for some groups to engage in cocooning. Take the example of indigenous or colonized groups. Given the destruction of cultures (and bodies) of oppressed peoples, it is clear that for many of them a form of cocooning is one of the only ways in which cultures and languages can be preserved. Because dominant groups already have cultural and economic power, the relative lack of such power among oppressed peoples creates the need for protection. Thus, in cases such as this, cocooning may have a more positive valance.

[10]Anti-teacher discourse has a long history, especially in the United States. It was often employed to legitimate centralized and standardized curricula and centralizing decision-making about textbooks within the state. See, for example, my discussion of the growth of state textbook adoption policies in Apple (2000).

[11]There have been a number of highly publicized shootings in schools in the past few years in the United States. The most well known occurred in Columbine High School in a relatively affluent community in Colorado where two alienated students killed a teacher and twelve other students and also planted pipe bombs throughout the building. This followed other shootings in suburban schools. In a recent instance, in a suburban but much less affluent community in Michigan, a six-year-old boy killed a six-year-old girl classmate after an altercation on the playground. Violence is now seen as a very real possibility in schools throughout the United States.

[12]This and other similar material can be found at the following website for The Teaching Home: <http://www.teachinghome.com/qa/why/htm>.

[13]See Moshe Re'em (1998) for an interesting analysis of some of this content.

[14]One of the best places to turn for an understanding of the more progressive movements surrounding education and social justice in public schools in the United States is the fast-growing newspaper *Rethinking Schools*. It represents one of the

most articulate outlets for critical discussions of educational policy and practice in the country and brings together multiple activist voices: teachers, community activists, parents, academics, students, and others. It can be contacted at *Rethinking Schools*, 1001 E. Keefe Avenue, Milwaukee, Wisconsin 53212, USA or via email at RSBusiness@aol.com.

References

Apple, M. W. (1990). *Ideology and curriculum*. New York: Routledge.

—————— (1995). *Education and power* (2nd ed). New York: Routledge.

—————— (1996). *Cultural politics and education*. New York: Teachers College Press.

—————— (1999). *Power, meaning, and identity*. New York: Peter Lang.

—————— (2000). *Official knowledge* (2nd ed). New York: Routledge.

—————— (2001). Educating the "right" way: Marketing, standards, God, and inequality. NY: Routledge/Falcon.

—————— (in press). Bringing the world to God. *Discourse*.

—————— & Beane, J. A. (Eds.). (1995). *Democratic schools*. Washington, DC: Association for Supervision and Curriculum Development.

—————— & Beane, J. A. (Eds.). (1999). *Democratic schools: Lessons from the chalk face*. Buckingham: Open University Press.

Bourdieu, P. (1996). *The state nobility*. Stanford: Stanford University Press.

Bromley, H., & Apple, M. W. (Eds.). (1998). *Education/technology/power*. Albany: State University of New York Press.

Clarke, J., & Newman, J. (1997). *The managerial state*. Thousand Oaks: Sage.

Coontz, S. (1992). *The way we never were: American families and the nostalgia trap*. New York: Basic Books.

Dale, R. (1989). The Thatcherite project in education, *Critical Social Policy, 9*(3), 4–19.

Delfattore, J. (1992). *What Johnny shouldn't read*. New Haven: Yale University Press.

Detwiler, F. (1999). *Standing on the premises of God: The Christian right's fight to redefine America's public schools*. New York: New York University Press.

Fine, M., & Weis, L. (1998). *The unknown city: The lives of poor and working-class young adults*. Boston: Beacon.

Foner, E. (1998). *The story of American freedom*. New York: Norton.

Fraser, N. (1989). *Unruly practices*. Minneapolis: University of Minnesota Press.

—————— (1997). *Justice interruptus*. New York: Routledge.

Greider, W. (1997). *One world, ready or not*. New York: Simon and Schuster.

Hogan, D. J. (1985). *Class and reform: School and society in Chicago, 1880-1930*. Philadelphia: University of Pennsylvania Press.

Kintz, L. (1997). *Between Jesus and the market*. Durham: Duke University Press.

Lauder, H., & Hughes, D. (1999). *Trading in futures: Why markets in education don't work*. Philadelphia: Open University Press.

Levine, L. (1996). *The opening of the American mind*. Boston: Beacon Press.

Molnar, A. (1996). *Giving kids the business.* Boulder: Westview.

Nord, W. (1995). *Religion and American education.* Chapel Hill: University of North Carolina Press.

Pagels, E. H. (1995). *The origin of Stan.* New York Random House.

Ray, B. (1999). *Home schooling on the threshold: A survey of research at the dawn of the new millennium.* Salem, OR: National Home Education Research Institute.

Re'em, M. (1998). Young minds in motion: Teaching and learning about difference in formal and non-formal settings. Unpublished Ph.D. dissertation, University of Wisconsin, Madison.

Reese, W. (1986). *Power and the promise of school reform.* New York: Routledge.

Shapiro, A. (1999, June). The net that binds. *The Nation, 268,* 11–15.

Smith, C. (1998). *American evangelicalism.* Chicago: University of Chicago Press.

Wells, A. S. (1999). *Beyond the rhetoric of charter school reform.* Los Angeles: Graduate School of Education and Information Studies, UCLA.

Whitty, G., Power, S., & Halpin, D. (1998). *Devolution and choice in education.* Philadelphia: Open University Press.

Williams, R. (1989). *Resources of hope.* New York: Verso.

Chapter 8

Identity, Literature, Schools, and Race: Southern Writers and Literature as a Metaphor for Place

David M. Callejo Pérez

One morning during the writing of *Southern Hospitality* (Callejo Perez, 2001), I decided to blow the day off, so I walked to the Chevron Food Mart on the corner of the busiest street in Oxford, Mississippi, home of Ole Miss and William Faulkner.[1] I became involved in a conversation about Ole Miss football, the rebel flag, and July in Mississippi with Clyde Goolsby and my friend John Morgan King while buying a *USA Today* in hopes that the newspaper would help to take my mind away from the everyday life of writing and editing. As I debated to the evils of the flag and the stupidity of racism, I came across an interesting article titled, "Is School Desegregation Fading?" (Henry, 1999). After reading Tamara Henry's piece, I discovered that districts were still attempting to integrate schools 20 years after *Mecklenberg* without much success. Instead of integrating schools, critics, especially parents, wanted schools to increase the amount of money and new programs for minority students. The article reminded me of Raymond Wolters' 1984 book on the effects of the *Brown* decision 30 years later, in which he saw white flight as a negative perception of blacks that linked them with drugs and violence that would surely follow them to school. For example, Cincinnati's school system is 70 percent black and 30 percent white, which does not reflect the base of its student population (Henry, 1999). Another more interesting issue was that of community education. To encourage whites to attend inner-city schools, districts have created magnet schools that ultimately restricted neighborhood kids from attending their own community schools. Black parents interviewed in the article wanted to take back their community schools. The cry was for more money and better teachers and not for integration.

This story allowed me to make a connection to my own research on schooling and literature and their role in the formation of identity. I had been staying in Oxford, Mississippi, a mecca for writers including Barry Hannah, John Grisham, Willie Morris, and Larry Brown. It had been the home of William Faulkner and at the time was hosting the *74th Yoknapatawpha Conference* on "Faulkner and Postmodernism." I walked toward the university and decided to sit in on a presentation on Faulkner's characters as neither good nor bad, right nor wrong, but of their time. In between the catchy postmodern terms, *differance* and *existenz*, I managed to dismiss the presenter as misunderstanding Southern literature and its position identity. "Southern identity is very specific," I thought to myself and, as Allen Tate described it, very pertinent to the existence of the individual.

In *The Writer in the South* (1972), Louis Rubin introduces his thesis through the recounting of one night of dining and drinking, during which he introduced a friend to Donald Davidson and John Donald Wade, who spoke like "good ol' boys." As Rubin retired, his companion expressed his astonishment at the crass behavior of these literary icons, these men of letters. Rubin responded that what they "were doing was demonstrating to each other, but most of all to themselves, that they were still Southern boys. They were, to put a more formal construction upon it, asserting their community identity" (Rubin, 1972, p. 85). Benedict Anderson (1991) states that "awareness of being imbedded in secular, serial, time, with all its implication of continuity, yet of 'forgetting' the experience of continuity...engenders the need for a narrative of 'identity.'" Identity for Anderson was not innate but culturally and historically created by narratives that cooperated with each other (literature with history), while, at the same time, being conscious of each other.

Southern identity, C. Vann Woodward writes, is consciousness of the past in the present (1993, p. 33). This is resonated by Eudora Welty when she tells Woodward that

> I am myself touched off by place. The place where I am and the place I know, and other places that familiarity with and love for my own make strange and lovely and enlightening to look into, are what set me to writing my stories. (pp. 23–24)

The Southern phenomenon of identity is not limited by race. Woodward observed that blacks involved in the Second Reconstruction had a "tendency to look back upon the First Reconstruction as if it were in some ways a sort of Golden Age. In this nostalgic view that period takes the shape of the race's finest hour...with no bowing to compromises of 'deliberate speed'" (p. 107).

Southern identity is tied to place, and past, more so than any other region, especially in its literary canon (Kreyling, 1998). The richness of local color through description, and of characters formed from the region's past and place, separate it from the rest of regional literature. In years before, Southern literature and its regionalism, was out of step with the beliefs of the American nation. Today, however, Southern literature is more in step with the beliefs of the American nation and its obsession of individual identity and group belonging, based on ethnicity and lineage. Today, Philip Roth's (1998) description of the Mid-Atlantic region, and his attention to the same problems of place and past that concerned Southerners after the Southern literary renaissance of 1930 are not unusual. In Southern literature, there is an attempt at defining an identity that Southerners are not sure existed even though they lived it. It is here that young boys relive the Civil War, young blacks the psychological burdens of slavery and segregation, and young women are debutantes. It is here that an entire region has tied itself to the land in the face of its own growing industrialism, refusing to face the realities of their world head on.

After overanalyzing the moment, I thought about the importance of literature, schooling, and identity as I heard the speaker dwell in the fictional world of Faulkner, and as I saw Faulkner's nephew listen intently to the conversation. His face, and others' too, lit up with a dark red shade of anger at the presenter's statement that *The Sound and the Fury* house "only existed in the mind of Faulkner, and in his reader's interpretation," when for him, and every resident of Oxford, that house had always been the big white house at 1206 Jefferson. Identity runs deep in every individual, especially when, as Woodward (1993) describes, that individual is carrying the burden of an entire region.

The richness of place and past from which Southern authors invent identity as they are confronted with their realities is what I wish to discuss in this chapter, especially in the works of Faulkner, Robert Penn Warren, Richard Wright, Ralph Ellison, and Alice Walker. However, I also realize that Southern literature was no longer a product of past and place, it was only real in terms that the reader made it real. I hope to use the ontological journey of Southern literature as a metaphor for schooling and curriculum, from the particular notions around one's local experiences to the imagined transregional experiences of media culture. The transculturalization of American society in the past 30 years has been phenomenal. The old regionalism of place that limited personal identity has been replaced by one that transcends borders, that can be constructed and changed by the individual without regard to the Other. It is a new distinct problem of individual identity that always existed in the South, which has for now become one of the main concerns of an entire nation. The problem of identity under such conditions is not unique to America. In Latin America, the works of Gabriel García Márquez, Pablo Neruda, Jose Martí, Isabel Allende, and Octavio Paz demonstrate some of the same issues of place and past that Southerners struggled with and that the American nation is currently struggling with today. An example of the current tensions in individual identity is the idea that a Hispanic individual, whether Puerto Rican or Dominican, in New York City could build a bond with a Hispanic in Miami, whether Cuban or Nicaraguan, and then sever that tie immediately when the two cities meet in a sporting event or when politics are involved or their two cultures collide.

Tamara Henry's (1999) article in *USA Today* also forced me to reconsider my beliefs on the role of schools and identity formation.

As Southerners, writers, such as Faulkner were trying to define their place in terms of their past. Their writing reflected this Southern regionalism so pervasive in Southern life, from politics to economics to culture, based on the burdens of the Lost Cause and slavery (Silver, 1964). Their work served to define the region. As culture changed, so did the role of schooling. The regional interpretation ceased to be localized, and cultural identity became national and individual. Today, the literature of the South can be a metaphor for the changing nature of education and its role in the formation of identity. Southern literature represented an attempt by a group of persons to come to grips with their past and place. The regional construction resulting from their work has been changed into a meaning that is invented and unique to each reader, which, in turn, has been constructed by their imagined communities. The power of the imagined community to which the individual surrenders hinges on the importance and need for racial identification as the basis for individual freedom in today's media-influenced society and its obliteration of regional boundaries, leaving individuals with only their past as a means of identification. However, the structure upon which that past is built is the value of racial identification.

Southern literature was always concerned with place and past, especially regional and racial identities. American society, busy with acculturation and assimilation, did not openly deal with those problems in its social institutions. At the time of the Civil Rights Movement, individual racial identity was prompted to the forefront, making the Southern literary example more poignant. America began to encounter the same problems the South had faced and had to invent new forms of expression from which to define the new social roles it had created. Louis Castenell and William Pinar (1993) state that it is an "understatement to observe that issues of race are paramount in contemporary curriculum debates in the public sphere" (p. 2). They then suggest that curriculum is "racial text" because debates about what we teach youngsters are "debates over who we perceive ourselves to be, and how we will represent that identity, including what remains as 'left over,' as 'difference'" (p. 2). Curriculum as race, text, and identity implies understanding the "American national identity, and vice versa" as racial text (p. 2). Race and identity are terms that are constantly changing, one grows out of the individual's past, as, say, for example, "black" from slavery, whereas identity comes from how the individual deals with her past and what role society assigns that past.

As the repression of individual identity softened by social changes, so, too, did the school respond to these changes, allowing marginal groups to do things that would separate them from the dominant social elite. Thus, African Americans in a quest for their African identity no longer saw themselves as extremities of Europeans, ultimately leading to a new definition of self as African. In Southern literature, the black individual was always subject to an autobiographical experience that would make an attempt at separation from a dominant political and social structure that oppressed individual freedom and identity. Therein lies the appeal of the Southern literary character's struggle for independence in current society. Second, the individual's search for her identity in terms of the larger base of knowledge and tradition comes to fruition in characters' attempts to discover themselves as Southern or black or feminine or worthy in the face of the hammer-like closed society of the South. The release through literature for these authors finds a receptacle in marginalized groups outside the South, particularly women and persons of color. Third, education has traditionally marginalized the importance of these groups while providing a place for them to exist. In the literature they find there is no place for them, that others, too, have tried and become ostracized for their attempts to become free by the social order.

Schooling is merely an institutional representation of the social milieu that encompasses it. The nature of the change in schools as a response to the social milieu is that the repression of African Americans in our society has not been properly addressed. As the curriculum has become national, it has excluded aspects of individual identity, forcing marginalization through the public policy of integration. Although the media tells us that we have similar needs and wants, Castenell and Pinar state that "all Americans are racialized beings; knowledge of who we have been, who we are, and who we will become is a story or text we will construct" (Castenell & Pinar, 1993, p. 8).

The focus of schooling has changed from regional to national as the culture has also shifted from regional to national. The new black identity was the result of the re-interpretation of Southern literature based on the construction of individual meaning after the individual achieved liberation from the collective group as manifested in the changing definition of the individual characters and the stories of Southern literature, the changing nature of regional culture, and the birth of a national media-oriented culture.

Southern literature will never cease to be Southern, as the schools will never cease to be local. However, new questions arise. How have the rise of individual freedom and the power of individual identity been formed by the national media? How has the new national media construct of an individual with its social norms and values affected institutions as traditional as Southern literature, stuck in its burden of the past and place, or the school, stuck in the eternal dialogue between the need of the student and the need of the region? "Success" was very regional before the media blitz of the past 30 years. Today, national ideas of success are found on television shows like *Friends*, Lexus commercials, and MTV's *Cribs*. In California as well as in Louisiana, an imported car, a house with digital cable, and vacations to Disney are now transregionally created truths that imply success. What then can we see in the literature of the South and in the changing role of the school?

The struggle of the writer for self-purification and, hence, for a way to deal with the burden of the past (slavery and the Lost Cause) and the place (the Depression and racial segregation) through the creation of works that seem more autobiographical than fictional at first was difficult for those readers who could not relate to characters because of regional borders they could not overcome. However, these readers could construct a stereotype of that character who, for them, only lived in the South. The Southerners who read these works found that they signified someone from their past or in their town. Transregionalization of culture through the construction of an imagined community with the individual at the center has changed the focus of the social order from place to character. That change is also true for the school. It is no longer the domain of the Southern white school to teach Faulkner or the domain of the Southern black school to teach Wright, these authors belong, first, to every individual who can relate to them, and, second, to the entire nation. The characters are only real in terms of the individual's interpretation. The individual's interpretation has been facilitated by the technological advances of the media, which allows them to transcend region and focus on race, ethnicity, gender, sexual preference, and class.

The focus for the individual is that, in defining themselves and their world, these figures of Southern literature have, in turn, defined the roles of individuals and their region in terms of race, demonstrating the power of their words beyond their time, and the role education has had in defining them as regional and their readers as transregional.

Southern Construction

School desegregation was the most visible result of the Civil Rights movement in the South. After 1954, the federal government began to integrate schools. Mississippi became the national battleground of the Civil Rights movement, as thousands of Northerners poured into the South to take the mantle of the movement to the people. The actual battle occurred much earlier. What happened before desegregation and Civil Rights? In that period (1920–1948), Southern literature foretold a new identity that would arise as a result of change. It provided a preview of what occurred as Negroes became blacks, striking out to build a new identity forged by the pressures of being outsiders living in the norm and yet not being able to participate. The school served as the ultimate battleground for desegregation as literature foretold. School desegregation was slow, as few blacks participated in the movement. Most chose to stay within their own schools (Curry, 1995). The issue of race and desegregation, a Southern problem, transcended Southern borders and became a national concern centered on racial identification as a group and individual identification as part of that group. The first state of being was concerned with region or place, the second with past.

School integration was an individual act, dependent on each child's family. White academies arose all over the South, as whites left the schools rather than integrate with blacks (Morris, 1971). The federal government would not enforce the law, causing desegregation to actually occur only in places that were already moving toward desegregation (Woodward, 1974). At the time, in the United States racial problems were "regarded as largely a Southern peculiarity" (p. 164). C. Vann Woodward (1974) believes that 1960 was the year of the great awakening of Southern Negroes, as they formed Afro-centric organizations, such as the Student Nonviolent Coordinating Committee (SNCC), to help Southern blacks take full advantage of the *Brown* decision. Because integration was an individual choice, blacks had to deal with the psychological and social burden of being the outsider in the school. However, those who survived were now able to move into the mainstream and did not return to the local community as they would have in the past (Callejo Pérez, 2001). The loneliness of integration shaped a new individual, who constantly dealt with the resistance to change from himself and from white and black society. This new individual felt pressure to succeed and "get out" from himself and from black society as well as from Northern white society, which had pushed for desegregation in the South.

The integration of blacks into the Southern school system led to a new black identity, a defense mechanism against the white society that was based on a definition of Southern blacks that ultimately caused blacks to separate from the "Negro" collective identity. The new identity stretched across the traditional boundaries of the South, to inner-city blacks in the North, and to other oppressed groups who could relate to the oppression suffered by the black collective. The literature and music of the Southern black, which along with religion had provided the only release for the collective, now transcended Southerners and formed an imagined bond of all those individuals who could relate to the individual singer or character in the novel.

For Southern blacks, integration led to the realization of being an individual in society and the conflict with being part of the Negro South. The black individual was born as a response to the white definition of Southern society, begotten in the days of slavery, based on a fictional code of chivalry and honor developed as a response to the conditions which the plantation system presented. The system corralled the individual through political, economic, and social restrictions that came from above and doubly enforced the system's cruelty and codes for blacks. The new "man became this false reconceptualization of a hegemonic definition" based on the tenets of the Civil Rights Laws that emphasized the individual over the collective rights of the "Negro" citizenry which represented the Old South. Civil Rights held as its central tenet the advancement of the individual over the group. Thus, it transcended the South and gave hope to all those individuals who felt oppressed and voiceless. At the same time, it was not only normal to be different, but being different was more important than conforming to the group. Individualism was not based on action; it was based on belonging to an imagined community of individuals struggling to speak against social oppression.

The prevailing argument and social milieu of Southern society played out through the work of individual Southern authors as they voiced Southern uniqueness, frustration, and hopes. The writers provided a script for whites and blacks from all classes and political orientations to follow in their dialogue during the social upheaval that began after World War II. Whites such as Faulkner and Warren and blacks such as Wright, Ellison, and Walker made it clear that the construct of black and white in the South came from a redemptive reconstruction (both black and white) and also from economic frustration and a desire for change in the region. However, the reality of that construction transcended the region because of social changes in American society, inspired by the social justice movements of the 1960s, carried through by the rise of the powerful new medium of television, and synthesized regional culture into national culture. The changing nature of the characters in Southern literature demonstrate that like society's changing norms and values, Southern authors changed the role of the black character from Faulkner's Isaac McCaslin or Benjy-like "Negroes" to Wright's existentialist black man, and, finally, Walker's feminist radical.

Southern literature, especially that of William Faulkner, serves as a metaphorical representation of the reality of the Southern condition. The congruency of interaction, of what is espoused and acted between the defined role of the individual and society, is the main concern of Faulkner's stories. The literary interpretation of the social reality is central to Faulkner's writing. The result of the commemoration of the Lost Cause and the economic and social realities of the New South led to the expression of the South as a land of incongruence between what was echoed for the outsider and what was lived by the participant. A mask on the local community hid the realities of society, similar to the metaphor Franz Fanon (1967) uses in *Black Skin, White Masks* to describe being black in a postcolonial state. The five Southern authors invented a social construct of racial relations in the South as well as the role of the blacks that paralleled the shift in social culture, dominated by media in creating in schooling and curriculum, a need for identity formation by individuals and groups that transcended boundaries or region, based on oppression, both physical (political) and psychological (prejudice and racism). The literary analysis will show how the construction of the racial identity changed over time as did the cultural interpretation of that role and how as society changed from communal social maintenance to transregional individual identity, schools were left behind.

Manifestations of Southern Identity Construction

Henry Allan Bullock (1970) stated that the verbal protest developed in the early twentieth century was shaped through literary effort as American blacks

> were to find a new conception of themselves and a deeper spiritual orientation. The new group aspired to reestablish the Negro's racial heritage....The Negro must remake his past in order to make his future. And so they wrote of African Kings, black warriors, black leaders of slave rebellions, Negro jockeys, and the problems of being Negro. (p. 199)

The first shift occurred through literary interpretation, based on the historical rejection of a past. This reinterpretation is similar to that of white Southerners' self-interpretation after the Civil War as they began to see themselves as English gentry and Arthurian heroes. Robert Penn Warren captured the ideology in *The Legacy of the Civil War* with the term "Great Alibi." "By the Great Alibi the Southerner explains, condones, and transmutes everything. By a single reference to the "'War'...laziness becomes the aesthetic sense...and resentful misery becomes divine revelation...he turns defeat into victory, defects into virtue" (Warren, 1961).

The South was an honor culture, with chivalric undertones derived from the romantic literature, especially Tennyson's King Arthur (Brown, 1986). One of the most popular works was Sir Walter Scott's *Ivanhoe*. Rollin Osterweis (1971) stated that "there existed a natural affinity in all this [Southern romanticism] for the theme of medieval chivalry, emphasized by Scott's brand of romanticism" (p. 17). *I'll Take My Stand* (Twelve Southerners, 1930) outlines Southern tradition as tied down to an agrarian practice which emphasized honor, chivalry, bravery, slavery, and womanhood. The point of womanhood is part of "the most profound change in the Southern self-image...involved the romantic role hitherto prescribed for Southern women" (Thomas, 1971, p. 225).

A second factor is the economic determinism, illustrated by the large number of sharecroppers of both races who struggled for a voice against the landowners, the federal government, and the Northern industrial complex's control structures where, first, through the ideology behind the Progressive nature of the New South; second, through the Depression and the New Deal; and, third, through the federal control of the post-World War II economy, their dependence was solidified (Bartley, 1995). For Faulkner and Warren, their black characters faced the hopelessness of a structure impossible to overcome, while their white characters were either victims or beneficiaries of the system. However, whereas whites used the structure, blacks could only fail in their attempts to become free. The unfair nature of the structure was a determinant of the role blacks were forever to play in the South. Wright, Ellison, and Walker all had something in common. Like, Faulkner and Warren they saw the structure as debilitating. Unlike Faulkner and Warren, they believed that it could be overcome. Also, they saw the black social structure as a product of Jim Crow, and, therefore, just as debilitating as the white structure. Their hope was to "get out" and achieve a voice. The individualistic nature of their characters' struggle to get away from the controlling structures that oppressed them is for many individuals reminiscent of their current struggle in society to be recognized, to be part of the new national culture of media.

The maturing of this generation came with their tribute to their lost through monuments and literature. It was their attempt to partake in the epiphany that was the Lost Cause. They had grown old with the myths but had not lived the experience. They were the early existentialists, suffering in angst through a life which they had been forced into with choice, not realizing or having the courage to realize that freedom was just a thought away. The individuality won by humans against traditional society led to the isolation and alienation of the individual that only the bonds of that traditional society alleviated (Fromm, 1941). Once the traditional society was broken, only artificially created myths could replace the comfort of community. This was the case of the Lost Cause myth, the driving force behind the New Southerner, black and white, created as a defense mechanism for a defeated people, where honor was the center, and the battle dead were immortalized through communal commemoration in mind, body, and spirit. The Southern way of life "involved a combination of states' rights, agrarianism, racial slavery, aristocracy, and habits of mind including individualism, personalism toward God and man, provincialism and romanticism" (Thomas, 1971, p. 21). Recalling this notion of Southernness, many whites feared that "broader educational opportunity for blacks...could profoundly unsettle the patterns of southern life" (McMillen, 1989, p. 90). The social order, black and white, wanted black education to remain largely manual labor-oriented and unique for the "Negro" race (p. 91).

It is from this fabricated society that the Southerner redefined his existence in order to match his imagined world. Thus, came a change in the Southern states' constitutions, Jim Crow Laws, lynching, and other methods of separation, including economic control that did not allow blacks the ability to sustain themselves or leave for the North to look for employment. The South was out of step with the rest of America, as Southerners' existence depended on their obsession with their past and place and how they were losing control of their own future. The second issue was that blacks as well as whites had to deal with race every day and with the social roles of based on racial identification. Civil Rights, forced on the South in order to bring justice to the oppressed individuals, made the crutch of past and place fall apart. Blacks received the tools for individual advancement; they realized that their individual social freedom had come with a price: the end of their collective memory as oppressed people under the structure of segregation. Thus, began self-recreation based on an African past and on the idea of being black first and Southern second. Black Power was reminiscent of the turn-of-the-century movements led by men like Marcus Garvey. Other groups also joined blacks in their struggle to rediscover their past. However, media and schools did not create a place for these people in their structures. And like the Southern blacks, these groups now needed a voice to express their struggle, and as Southern literature had, the American nation now had to deal with race and individual identity. The example of Swede Levov in *American Pastoral* (Roth, 1998) is one such case as he deals with the collapse of his world and identity when his place and family change and he remains static. Thus, in Southern literature the reader can find himself at different stages of the struggle for voice, from the voiceless Benjy in Faulkner to the women in Walker's *Everyday Use*.

William Faulkner: Savage South and Noble Savages

William Faulkner is the most notable twentieth-century writer of the tradition of darkness, sin, guilt, and internal self-conflict. Faulkner grew up surrounded by tales of glory from the Mississippi frontier and the Civil War (Williamson, 1993). Faulkner's period of grandeur began in 1929 with the publication of *The Sound and the Fury* although the novel did not receive as much attention as Thomas Wolfe's *Look Homeward, Angel*. Faulkner's stream of consciousness style was difficult and did not fit into the panorama of early twentieth-century American writers such as Hemingway or Lewis or Fitzgerald. *The Sound and the Fury* is an intense tragedy of Greek proportions, expounding the perils of pride and the failures of love. The story is that of the decline of the once-powerful Compson family whose love for each other is non-existent. There is no father or mother to love; the siblings do not love each other nor anyone else. However, there are several love stories in this novel, that of Benjy for the constant attention of his sister, Caddy, and the paternalistic possessiveness of older brother Quentin for Caddy; finally, Caddy's desperate search for love through sexual promiscuity. Their father takes refuge in alcohol and the neurotic mother in self-pity. The key character is Quentin, an insecure Harvard student obsessed with family honor, afraid of his sexuality, searching for the childhood innocence he shared with Caddy; he finally commits suicide at Harvard. He represents the Southern elite male, and his world, the Lost Cause and the past, the attempt to recapture that time that never existed in the face of Northern industrialism and capital. He feels somehow insecure in comparison with the black male, whom he imagines to be sexually superior and, thus, happier.

Caddy represents the female in the South. The changing world and her position "upon a pedestal," as Janiewski (1985) describes, force the Southern woman to seek alternatives to two types of love— one, very paternalistic and controlling, which places her as the central piece of Southern culture; and the second, which views her as a coveted possession. The third character, Benjy, a castrated boy, retarded, a grotesque creation that should never have existed, is Faulkner's representation of the black after Reconstruction. The perceived white idea of the black male coveting the white woman is exemplified by Benjy, who has no voice and no sense of being human in his relation with Caddy.

A second Faulkner novel, *Light in August*, is a world of grotesqueness. There is Hightower, the cast-out Presbyterian minister who lives in the heroic past, obsessed by the foolish Civil War charge of his grandfather; Joanna Burden, possessed of a mission to shape, reform, and redeem blacks; Joe Christmas, the wanderer and sufferer whose lifelong search for his racial identity ends with his murder of Joanna Burden, and, nine days later, his own death; and a collection of other racial and religious fanatics. As a foil to these characters, Lena Grove, the pregnant wanderer, responds viscerally and concretely to life and is taken in by the community. Faulkner's women fall into two categories. Lena is the pure abstraction, the Earth mother while Joanna is the concrete reformer. This grotesqueness that drives Faulkner is now a reality of the interracial mixing that is currently making headlines as the "face" of America is changing with popular singers like Mariah Carey, anchorwomen like Soledad O'Brien, actors like Cameron Diaz or Jimmy Smits, and the violence against people who intermarry or interracial children in society and, especially, in school.

Absalom! Absalom! (1936) is a unique novel, in that Thomas Sutpen and his sons are such a mystery, especially the murder by the younger, Henry the puritan, of the older, mixed-blood hedonist Charles Bon. The intriguing character is once again Quentin Compson, who in Sutpen's story finds himself and his Southern past, which haunts him as much as it draws him. He is blessed and cursed with Sutpen's past and its larger meaning—what happened to the South during the nineteenth century. He returns in his mind to what Woodward calls the Southern burden of its past, values, and myths on his family and himself. The Southerner must live with his past as well as his present, which he influences as he is influenced by his past. However, he is only one of the characters created by Faulkner obsessed and tormented by their Southern past. In *Go Down, Moses* (1983), especially in "The Bear" chapter, Isaac McCaslin is keenly aware of the racial sins of his fathers and tries to make amends for them. In *Intruder in the Dust* (1975), Faulkner introduces us to a story of racial violence and one of its victims, Lucas Beauchamp, of *Go Down, Moses*, who refuses to sacrifice his pride to conform to southern racial conventions.

Robert Penn Warren: Power and Innocence and Growing up Southern

Robert Penn Warren was the South's most versatile writer. After attending school in Clarksville, Tennessee, he entered Vanderbilt at age sixteen, in 1921. In the early 1920s Vanderbilt was alive with literary activity, including his freshman English professor, John Crowe Ransom, his sophomore instructor Donald Davidson, and

Allen Tate, who launched the poetry magazine, *The Fugitive* with Warren, who was considered a prodigy by the other poets. He received a masters from Berkeley and went to Yale for a doctorate, where he wrote a biography of martyr John Brown, which was published in 1929. It was the study of the power of an abstract idea on a historical figure, who sacrificed himself and all else for an ideological goal. He then left on a Rhodes scholarship to Oxford University. He was one of the 12 writers of *I'll Take My Stand*, subtitled the *South and the Agrarian Tradition* (1930), a defense of the rural way of life against the Northern industrial environment; it was also a critique of progress in many forms. Warren's essay was a defense of racial segregation as a result of his reluctant approach to change in the South, a mistake that he would later repent. He never plunged into the Agrarian Movement. Warren, more than any other white writer, represents the growth of the South as a region, as it begins to deal with its past and its racial identity. He is the moderate Southern white. In 1935, he founded the *Southern Review*, known for its fiction and literary criticism. He believed, along with Cleanth Brooks, that literary work should be historical and biographical. His work, especially *Understanding Poetry* (Warren, 1938) is where he, along with John Crowe Ransom developed the influential literary criticism style known as New Criticism.

After *Night Rider* (1992), Warren wrote *At Heaven's Gate* (1943/ 1995), the story of the destructive nature of power. The protagonist, Bogan Murdock, is a businessman who ultimately destroys those all around him, including his own daughter. Warren's next work, *All the King's Men* (1990), is the story of Deep South demagogue Willie Stark, who, although Warren denied it, was believed to be based on Huey Long. He was interested in power, acquisition, and, especially, the capacity to destroy. Stark's counterpoint in the novel was Jack Burden, a cynical former history student and newspaper reporter. Burden is on a quest for truth, weighing the meaning of human life and history and the deterministic view (individuals not responsible for their actions) versus the humanistic (where the choices made must be lived with). After Burden examines the Civil War diary of a relative, Cass Mastern, and his present family and friends, he chooses humanism, to constantly make choices and live with their consequences.

His 1942 collection of poems, *Eleven Poems of the Same Theme*, deals with the loss of innocence. Much of Warren's poetry, especially "Brother to Dragons" (1953/1990) is historical, as he traces the move west to Kentucky of one of Thomas Jefferson's nephews. He is able to deal with terms such as slavery and race relations from the point of view of the protagonist and himself. Thus, he links the Old South and its burden to the more recent problems of racial tension and desegregation. In "Blackberry Winter," a story of murder and revolution in Kentucky tobacco country, he describes little Jebb as

> a mean and fiery Negro. Jebb killed another Negro in a fight and got sent to the penitentiary, where he is yet, the last I heard tell. He probably grew up to be mean and feisty from just being picked on so much by the children of the other tenants, who were jealous of Jebb and Dellie for being thrifty and clever and being whitefolks' niggers.

Warren gives the reader an insight into the classes and social relationships among the blacks and toward the whites. Jebb lived with the choices made first by the whites who created Southern society and the institution of slavery, which was replaced by sharecropping and segregation. And then his parents' chose to be good blacks in order to leave and survive. Finally, the other children saw in him what whites had done to them and, in their hatred for the system in which they lived, took out their frustrations on him. It seems that his only choice was the violent murder that landed him in prison.

Richard Wright: Searching for Identity in America

Richard Wright is a study in contrast to Warren and Faulkner. He was malnourished for most of his early life and never received a formal education. Yet, he believed that in books he would find his freedom. His father abandoned the family when Wright was five. Later he was placed in an orphanage. He spent most of his youth traveling between Arkansas, Jackson, Memphis, and Chicago. In

Arkansas, his uncle, a saloonkeeper, was murdered by a white mob. In *Black Boy* (1945/1998), an autobiographical sketch, he exaggerates his position as an outsider in his homeland. When he discovered H.L. Mencken (1934), Wright was shocked that anyone was able to attack the South and used him as a moral and spiritual guide. Wright began to believe that words could be weapons to express his bitterness and frustration toward the Jim Crow South. He joined the Communist Party because of its stance on Civil Rights and support for blacks. He wrote *Long Black Song*, the story of a proud black salesman who goes on a murder rampage after learning about a white man's seduction of his wife and his wife's complicity to that seduction. He ultimately is killed by a white mob. For very different reasons, Wright joins Faulkner in painting a picture of a savage and benighted South.

His first great work, *Uncle Tom's Children* (Wright, 1937/1998), exposed the life and racial conflicts of Southern living. In *Native Son* (1943), Bigger Thomas, a young black man from Mississippi, like Wright, encounters the racial prejudice, tension, and hypocrisy of Chicago. Thomas, a character inspired by the farce of a trial and conviction of nine black males accused of rape in Scottsboro, Georgia, works for a wealthy Hyde Park family and accidentally kills a white girl in what looks like a murder. He is then tried and executed. The story is a commentary not only on Scottsboro but on the inequalities and injustices of the American justice system. Wright was accused by black critics of reinforcing the white stereotype of blacks as savage and violent. The defense lawyer, Boris Max, is a communist whom Wright portrays as a Party mouthpiece, with little individual liberty and expression apart from the Communist Party.

Wright had begun *Black Boy* (1945) in 1943, after a visit to the segregated South. Wright portrayed black life as unrelievedly bleak, sterile, and nearly hopeless. He not only described the white oppression but the black community without the social supports that Zora Neale Hurston had described as sustaining African American life in the South—a strong family, rich folk culture, a creative religious impulse, and a sense of place and community, of which Wright had none. He is the heroic loner who escaped the horror of the South and found freedom because he never learned to, as Wright (1937/1995) defiantly writes, "live Jim Crow." This was due to his detachment from any sense of community, black or white, in the early years of his life. He also dealt with his move to Chicago in a later volume which did not appear until 1977 as *American Hunger*. In 1953, he published *The Outsider*, an existential story of a black American who is also a Communist and is able to transcend racial and political concerns. In the United States, black Southerners like Ralph Ellison and Northerners like James Baldwin were beginning to be more widely read as a result of Wright's success.

In *The Ethics of Living Jim Crow* (1937), an autobiographical sketch, which had laid the foundations for *Black Boy*, Wright stated that he "never fully realized the appalling disadvantages of a cinder environment till the day the gang to which [he] belonged found itself engaged in a war with the white boys who lived beyond the tracks." After a crucial rock- and bottle-throwing barrage, he realized that they were losing because unlike the white boys who were able to hide "behind trees, hedges and sloping embankments of their lawns," they had to run back to their homes. Apart from the aesthetic difference, his mother, who worked for a white family, punished him because he had fought with the white boys. As she beat him, he described her as "impart[ing] to me the gems of Jim Crow wisdom." He later described the scene from the white part of town as representing white society, and after his beating, he began to fear anything that resembled those white houses and monuments.

Ralph Ellison: Struggle for Identity in America

Ralph Ellison was influenced more by Freud, Eliot, Hemingway, Malraux, and Twain than by Wright, with whom he disagreed as to the purpose of literature. In *Invisible Man* (1952), Ellison, like Wright, drew on his own life, especially at Tuskegee, to tell the story of a naive young man searching for identity, only to find himself the victim of history, circumstance, and malice. Haunted by the advice of a grandfather who pretended to be acquiescent to whites, the narrator wins a scholarship to a Tuskegee-like school by surviving the indignities imposed on him by the good white citizens of his hometown (he is forced to fight before receiving his scholarship and a briefcase). He then becomes involved in the struggles between an unscrupulous black president and a white trustee who believes it his destiny to shape the lives of young black people. He is expelled from the college after he drives the trustee to Trueblood's shack, where he told a harrowing tale of incest. He then moves to New York, where he becomes a speaker for an organization that resembles the Communist Party. The association leads to a clash between the organization (the Brotherhood) and Black nationalists in Harlem that results in a riot. He vows not to return to college, then becomes a militant by living underground and stealing power from the electric company.

The "Trueblood" chapter is the most famous. It takes place in the South and deals with the shaping of black lives through white as well as black racist practices. It parodies the tradition of accommodation and uplifting education of Booker T. Washington, makes clear the economic base of interracial relations, and posits the acquiescence to author accommodation as a life-denying attribute. The chapter also captures the power and spirit of black folk culture and oral traditions, both storytelling and music. This work is a response to the state of African American leadership and its failure to unite the nation. The influence of Twain is seen, as this work represents the ultimate battle between the powerful and the powerless, as Twain's *Huckleberry Finn* did. The novel represents the coming together of the rich Southern tradition of writing as well as the episodic nature of black writing in the South. It is the union of the two worlds of Southern history between the fight for a black voice and the love of place, the influences of both Faulkner and Wright.

Alice Walker: Transcending the South

Alice Walker was born in 1944 to sharecroppers in Georgia and today is the best-known voice of the Southern woman. She is to the black woman what Eudora Welty was to the white upper-class Southern woman. She combines activism with literature to make the world aware of the plight of women and children. She attended Spellman on a scholarship before transferring to Sarah Lawrence, where, with the help of Muriel Rukeyser, she was able to publish her first book of poetry. She cited her influences as the traditional Southern writers such as Faulkner, Flannery O'Conner, Zora Neale Hurston, and Jean Toomer. Walker also became pregnant one summer while studying in Africa and contemplated suicide. Her experience ultimately inspired the publication of *Once* (Walker, 1968). She worked in Mississippi on voter registration and married Jewish lawyer Melvyn Leventhal, a civil rights activist, in Jackson (they were the first legally married interracial couple in the state). The marriage led to the cold reception of her writing by black intellectuals until the couple separated. In her first novel, *The Third Life of Grange Copeland* (1970), Walker discusses how the sharecropping system affects black men and their social role, which, in turn, leads to the destruction of the women in their lives. The novel posits that black men cannot advance themselves or the black race until they take responsibilities for all the women in their lives and advance them as well.

In her next great work, *The Color Purple*, Walker (1992) explores the enslavement of women in marriage, the exploitation of their creativity, controlling patriarchal love, the influence of education, the power of folk traditions, and the uplifting of persons who have nothing to live for. The story revolves around an abused black woman, who through the help of another woman, finds her inner strength. The work was criticized by the black community for its critical views on incest by the father and abuse by the husband. The two women in *The Color Purple* as well as the young educated woman who becomes interested in family quilts in the short story "Everyday Use" (1994), depict the Southern woman's battle between the militant ideology of both the feminist and civil rights movements and the traditional role of the woman in both the South and black society. The second concern for Walker arises in *Possessing the Secret of Joy* (1993), and *Warrior Marks* (1996), where she deals with female circumcision, its psychological and physical effects. Society circumcises women psychologically by taking away their creativity and independence, and by physically forcing them to become baby machines. This practice has led to the larger worldwide issue of female circumcision as physical abuse.

In a conversation with author Willie Morris, Walker wonders if "integration is really worth the effort." She believes in "the children working it out together, but worries if all the pressures on them right now might finally prove to be destructive" (Morris, 1971, p. 145). She describes the looks she and her husband got as they took their daughter to Sears. She later confronts her husband's optimism by telling Morris that "I'm not at all optimistic that we'll have one society. And what worries me is that if we're not going to have one society, school integration may not be worth it" (Morris, 1971, pp. 145–146). Morris described her as a "Southerner—and in fact reminds me a little of myself—but I doubt if she gets out of the house very much in Jackson" (p. 146).

Literature and Curriculum: Living Out the Metaphor

Blacks in the South can best be described through Faulkner's Benjy, in *The Sound and the Fury* (1992), alone in his world, yet a human being, defined by the Other. The deprived Southerner created Benjy, a combination of surreal inbreeding and an imagined romantic past who became a retarded, castrated being with no identity except the one given him. Benjy loved three things: his pasture, his sister Candace, and firelight. Upon this falseness, he became a new Benjy, a sight too grotesque even for a Botero painting. He was committed to an asylum, returned home, "where sure enough in less than two years he not only burned himself but completely destroyed the house too." Benjy became what did not previously exist; what was imagined now became real. The collective created the individual without thought or realizations of the consequences.

Faulkner spoke of Benjy as:

> Without thought or comprehension; shapeless, neuter, like something eyeless and voiceless which might have lived, existed merely because of its ability to suffer, in the beginning of life; half fluid, groping: a pallid and helpless mass of the mindless agony under [the] sun, in time yet not of it save that he could nightly carry with him that fierce, courageous being who was to him but a touch and a sound that may be heard on any golf links and a smell like trees, into the slow bright shapes of sleep. (Blotner, 1974, p. 571)

Like Benjy, the Mississippi "Negro" was isolated from the social world by his inability to acquire the ultimate act of social behavior and freedom: speech. For Arendt (1998), action, through speech, was a way out of oppression. Speech, or language, the ability to express oneself, requires action, and the ability to control one's place (Habermas, 1973). Speech, also referred to as voice, is the only authentic existence for humans and, thus, the way to liberation (Foucault, 1970, 1977). An attempt at lingual liberation is also evident in Southern black literature.

In *Black Boy* (1945/1998), Richard Wright wrote of his love of place and of the hate of the people in the same breath. James Baldwin (1955), a Harlem author, articulated for white America what it meant to be an American and a black American at the same time. However, Baldwin spoke for the urban black; he could not articulate Wright's voice in describing Roxie, Mississippi, or the disappointment of leaving the South to discover the unfriendliness of Chicago. In *The Outsider* (1953/1993), Wright discovers that the collective Negro support in the South allowed him to overcome the hate for the color of his skin, whereas Chicago offered no such communal refuge. For Wright, like other Southerners, specifically Warren and the twelve Southerners (1930) in *I'll Take My Stand*, the classic Neo-Jeffersonian attempt to reconcile their existence as Southern agrarians in a modern world offered no contradiction between their love of place and its grotesque absurdity. They manifested this in their critical "dark" comedic prose with the kind of love only a mother could show toward a Southern child like Benjy. The black individual was and always will be a Southern black, tortured by membership in the oppressed caste as well as by membership to the larger American community.

In individualism, the black individual finds power, the power of speech. Black discourse is based on an invented creation traced to a source that had long disappeared, Africanness. The South's definition did not represent reality. Southerners defined their world not from observation—they based their definition on experiences and theorized about the source. Central to this theorized definition of a lived experience was the Southern black (Genovese, 1974; Jordan, 1969).

As major social changes have occurred, they have radically affected education, as witnessed by the power of the media in causing the regional boundaries to disappear. The power of the media lies in its ability to synthesize the experiences of all persons, regardless of region or autobiography. Thus, the oppressed black woman in Alice Walker's *The Color Purple* (1992) is no longer a product of place and past but a martyr for all women and their struggle for equality. Faulkner's Benjy represents all victims of social repression. The shift in the reader's interpretation is significant because of the change in the social milieu, resulting from the social revolution that swept through schools in America—first, desegregation and bussing; second, the movements by oppressed groups (Hispanics, Asians, Women, Gays, and Lesbians); and, third, grassroots movements such as PARC, multiculturalism, and bilingualism.

The acceptance of these persons first into the curriculum and later into popular culture occurred as regional boundaries were traversed by cultural events, especially Jimmy Carter's election in 1976 and shows like *Dallas* in the 1980s. The literature of the South was rediscovered as Faulkner, Warren, Ellison, Wright, and Walker as well as others once again received national attention. However, the second time around, their works invented culture of place and time was now seen as character driven. In the social revolution of the 1960s, ethnicity and individual identity replaced community and regionalism as the two most important drives for Americans.[2] As literary interpretation shifted from place-based to character-based, a new imagined community was formed as cultural and regional boundaries fell, and reading the work was just as good as being there. Identity was not only place but individual. The reader could now build an imagined bond between themselves and the characters. Benedict Anderson provides a model for this type of connection only possible in the new world order of the postcolonial era that began in the 1950s and ran concurrently with the Cold War. After the Cold War's end, it was heightened by the rise of new ethnic minorities asserting their voices. Anderson states that "members of even the smallest nation will never know most of their fellow-members, meet them, or even hear of them, yet in their minds of each lives the image of their communion" (Anderson, 1991, p. 6).

The roles of the writers never changed; their job, as they saw it, was to write about what they knew. In the Southern case, the past and place weighed very much on their work. This was a reality that America did not have to deal with until after the emphasis on the individual, especially their race, after the cultural and social revolution of the 1960s.

The five authors discussed here were very regional and driven by place as evidenced by the characters who seem dependent on past and place for their identity. The same could be said of education. The idea of the community school was the central unit of learning for the student, with ultimate control coming with the people of the community. The social revolution of the 1960s brought certain changes that were augmented by technological advances. Technology augmented the power of the media, which caused the interpretation of literature to change from regional to cultural centrality. Media replaced local culture as contemporary culture. Thus, the idea that those characters in Faulkner or in any other writer's work were not good or bad or the place was not real is correct. Although the *Sound and the Fury* (Faulkner, 1992) house had always been there, the role it played is up to the reader. In 1936, the Compson house was the center of the story. In 1999, the Compson house is merely the place where the characters play out their lives.

In order to discuss identity and its place in literature, I find myself turning to Neil Postman's (1996) question of whether schools create a *public*. He states that the "answer to this question has nothing to do with computers, testing, with teacher accountability, with class size, and with the other details of managing schools" (Postman, p. 18). The right answer, continues Postman, rests on "the existence of shared narratives and the capacity of such narratives to provide an inspired reason for schooling" (p. 18). The problem in today's schooling lies in the false assumption that we have made: multiculturalism does not allow for shared meanings; therefore, shared narratives cannot provide an inspired reason for schooling. Yes, we all interpret Alice Walker's characters but only insofar as they relate to ourselves and not to the larger collective mindset. The role of the imagined community enters into the equation of interpretation. Although all women can relate to the character's oppressed state, it is only relevant to their state of being, not to any other woman's. The importance of individuality makes it easy for all of us to see ourselves in the character, but we cannot see anyone else in that character. Cultural identity does not allow us to see others; it is not about you, it is about me.

The South always had dealt with race and construction of social roles for its people, a problem the United States has never dealt with until the power of individual identity transcended regionalism, ultimately transmitted by media. As society changed, so did the role of schools and curriculum, a fact lost on American society. Schooling has not dealt with the changing nature of American society like the Southern authors did with the construction of social roles for Blacks. Thus, the critics of the schools have a point in the fact that schools have not changed with society. The construction of individual identity is now based on race, a problem the school and curriculum are not dealing with today.

Endnotes

[1] I hope to not only tell a story of the richness in literature in giving words to our thoughts and actions but of the complexity of race relations, not only in the South, but for all individuals.

[2] As I write this, Louis Menand (2001) comes to mind. He states that individualism was always a part of our identity after the Civil War and that we tried to control it through reform movements. In other words, individualism, not community have been our nature as Americans.

References

Anderson, B. (1991). *Imagined communities*. London: Verso.

Arendt, H. (1998). *The human condition*. Chicago: University of Chicago Press.

Baldwin, J. (1955). *Notes of a native son*. Boston, MA: Beacon Press.

Bartley, N. (1995). *The new south, 1945–1980*. Baton Rouge, LA: Louisiana State University Press.

Blotner, J. (1974). *Faulkner: A biography* (Vol. 1). New York: Random House.

Brown, B. W. (1986). *Honor and violence in the Old South*. New York: Oxford University Press.

Bullock, H. A. (1970). *A history of Negro education in the south*. New York: Praeger.

Callejo Pérez, D. (2001). *Southern hospitality: Identity, schools, and the civil rights movement in Mississippi, 1964-1972*. New York: Peter Lang.

Castenell, L., Jr., & Pinar, W. (Eds.). (1993). *Understanding curriculum as racial text: Representations of identity and difference in education*. Albany, NY: SUNY Press.

Curry, C. (1995). *Silver rights*. Chapel Hill, NC: Algonquin.

Ellison, R. (1952). *Invisible man*. New York: Vintage.

Fanon, F. (1967). *Black skin, White masks*. New York: Grove.

Faulkner, W. (1964). *Absalom! Absalom!* New York: Vintage.

———— (1975). *Intruder in the dust*. New York: Vintage.

———— (1983). *Go down, Moses and other stories*. Birmingham, AL: The Southern Classics Library.

———— (1992). *The sound and the fury*. New York: Vintage.

Foucault, M. (1970). *The order of things*. New York: Pantheon.

———— (1977). *Discipline and punish: The birth of the prison*. (A. Sheridan, Trans.). New York: Pantheon.

Fromm, E. (1941). *Escape from freedom*. New York: Holt.

Genovese, E. (1974). *Roll, Jordan, roll: The world the slaves made*. New York: Pantheon Books.

Habermas, J. (1973). *Theory and practice* (J. Viertel, Trans.). Boston, MA: Beacon.

Henry, T. (1999, July 22). "Is school desegregation fading?" *USA Today*, A1.

Janiewski, D. (1985). *Sisterhood denied: Race, gender, & class in a New South community*. Philadelphia: Temple University Press.

Jordan, W. (1969). *White over Black: American attitudes toward the Negro, 1550–1812*. New York: Norton.

Kreyling, M. (1998). *Inventing southern literature*. Jackson, MS: University of Mississippi Press.

McMillen, N. (1989). *Dark journey*. Chicago: University of Illinois Press.

Menand, L. (2001). *The Metaphysical Club*. New York: Farrar, Straus and Giroux.

Mencken, H. L. (1934). *The Sahara of the Bozart*. New York: Norton.

Morris, W. (1971). *Yazoo: Integration in a deep-southern town*. New York: Harpers Magazine Press.

Osterweis, R. (1971). *Romanticism and nationalism in the Old South*. Baton Rouge, LA: Louisiana State University Press.

Postman, N. (1996). *The end of education: Redefining the value of school*. New York: Vintage.

Roth, P. (1998). *American pastoral*. New York: Vintage.

Rubin, L (1972). *The writer in the South*. Athens, GA: University of Georgia Press.

Silver, J. (1964). *Mississippi: The closed society*. New York: Harcourt, Brace & World.

Thomas, E. (1971). *The Confederacy as a revolutionary experience*. Englewood Cliffs, NJ: Prentice-Hall.

Twelve Southerners. (1930). *I'll take my stand: The South and the Agrarian tradition*. NY: Harper & Row.

Walker, A. (1968). *Once*. New York: Harcourt Brace.

———— (1970). *The third life of Grange Copeland*. New York: Harcourt Brace.

———— (1992). *The color purple*. New York: Harcourt Brace.

———— (1993). *Possessing the secret of joy*. New York: Harcourt Brace.

———— (1994). *Everyday use*. New Brunswick, NJ: Rutgers University Press.

———— (1996). *Warrior marks: Female genital mutilation and the sexual blinding of women*. New York: Harvest.

Warren, R. P. (1938). *Understanding poetry*. New York: Norton.

———— (1942). *Eleven poems of the same theme*. New York: Norton.

———— (1943/1995). *At heaven's gate*. New York: Norton.

———— (1990). *All the king's men*. New York: Harvest Books.

———— (1992). *Night rider*. New York: J.S. Sanders.

———— (1990). "Brother to dragons," in *The Collected Poems of Robert Penn Warren*. Baton Rouge, LA: Louisiana State University.

———— (1961). *The legacy of the civil war*. New York: Random House.

Williamson, J. (1993). *William Faulkner and southern history*. New York: Oxford University Press.

Wolters, R. (1984). *The burden of Brown: Thirty years of school desegregation*. Knoxville, TN: University of Tennessee Press.

Woodward, C. V. (1974). *The strange career of Jim Crow*. New York: Oxford University Press.

———— (1993). *The burden of southern history*. Baton Rouge, LA: University of Louisiana Press.

Wright, R. (1937/1995). *The ethics of living Jim Crow*. New York: Perennial.

———— (1937/1998). *Uncle Tom's children*. New York: Perennial.

———— (1943/1997). *Native son*. New York: Perennial.

———— (1945/1998). *Black boy*. New York: Perennial.

———— (1953/1993). *The outsider*. New York: Harper.

———— (1977/1998). *American hunger*. New York: Perennial.

Chapter 9

Getting from Farmhouse to Schoolhouse: School Consolidation, Pupil Transportation, and the Limits of Educational Reform in Mississippi

Corey Lesseig

Mississippians registered, licensed, and operated over a quarter million automobiles in 1929. Near-universal agreement exists among scholars and laypeople alike that the introduction of the automobile profoundly affected life in the state, region, and nation. Quantifying the specific societal changes that automobile adoption effected remains a tricky business.

In Mississippi from the end of World War I until the beginning of World War II, school enrollments mushroomed, literacy improved, life expectancy increased, and infant mortality decreased. During this same period, thousands of Mississippians purchased automobiles. Were these merely concurrent phenomena, or did some sort of relationship exist between these social changes and the adoption of the automobile?

Automobile registration numbers can be collected, tabulated, and analyzed in comparison to other social indicators. From such data, the sociologist and demographer can create a rough outline, but to breathe life into the portrait, to flesh out the real substance and relationship between automobility and social change, requires incorporating personal accounts from memoirs and interviews as well as contemporary observations garnered from newspapers and correspondence. In sum, it requires the artistry of the historian.

"Let us ever remember that that blessed trinity of good roads, good schools, and good churches are one and inseparable," proclaimed the Carthage, Tennessee *Courier*. Indeed, while the fervor of national progressivism may have fizzled in the wake of the Versailles Treaty, various progressive reforms continued in the South in the postwar period. During the 1920s, reform-minded Southerners led campaigns for improvements to the region's roads, schools, and public health and social welfare programs and facilities. The automobile played an integral role in the institutionalization, professionalization, and implementation of each of these crusades (Brownwell, 1975; Keith, 1995; Tindall, 1967).

At the turn of the century, Mississippi's educational system ranked among the nation's worst. Teacher's salaries provide some insight into the health of the state's educational system. For the 1901–02 school year, white teachers in Mississippi's rural schools could expect a salary of just under $34 a month. The school term averaged 110 days, thus, these same teachers received an annual compensation of $186. Black teachers received approximately $20 monthly and worked fewer than 100 days annually. "Full-time" black Mississippi teachers often made less than $100 a year from their professional calling (*Biennial Report of the State Superintendent of Public Education, 1901–02 and 1902–03,* 1904).

State Superintendent of Public Education and future governor, Henry L. Whitfield, put it best in his 1903 annual summary of the condition of Mississippi's woeful educational system.

> As a rule our terms are too short, the compensation received by our teachers for a year's work is too small for them to make the preparations to be skilled in their work, and our school-houses in the main are uncomfortable and poorly equipped. (*Biennial Report of the State Superintendent of Public Education, 1901–02 and 1902–03,* 1904)

Subsequent reports from the superintendent reveal little progress in rectifying the ills outlined by Whitfield. Beginning in 1909, however, school reformers increasingly clamored for school consolidation as the answer to Mississippi's educational woes. J.N. Powers, Whitfield's successor as the head of the state's educational bureaucracy, enthusiastically supported the "consolidation of weak one-teacher schools into strong, efficient graded ones."

In the 15 years following Powers 1909 rallying cry, Mississippians created 927 white consolidated schools with a total enrollment of 150,000 pupils. Fully two-thirds of white rural schools consolidated from 1909 to 1924. Black school consolidation moved more slowly than white. Nevertheless, 20 percent of the state's black children attended one of Mississippi's 250 black consolidated schools by 1924 (*Biennial Report and Recommendations of the State Superintendent of Public Education, 1909–10 and 1910–11*, 1911).

Consolidation supporters often faced stiff opposition to their programs. Willard F. Bond oversaw the peak years of consolidation in Mississippi while serving as state superintendent of public education from 1916 until 1936. During his tenure, Bond and other educational reformers often met with concerned Mississippians to discuss the merits of school consolidation in a less-than-cordial atmosphere. In his autobiography, Bond recounts several humorous and many heated encounters between local residents and state officials at countywide educational reform meetings. One such incident occurred during a meeting of Lafayette County residents over the recently passed compulsory attendance law.

> One trustee got up and expressed himself as being very much opposed to such a law, stating that although he had been a life-long resident of Lafayette County, he would move out of the county before he would put up with such a law. He was informed that this law was not only for Lafayette County but for the State as a whole. He then said he would move out of the State. When told that Mississippi was the last state to have such a law, shaking his fist and speaking with considerable emotion, he said that he would go to hell before he would put up with it. (Bond, 1958, pp. 95–96)

Consolidation opponents responded violently in defense of their local schools. Defenders of one-room community schools feared the symbolic as well as material change that consolidated institutions augured for their society. Consolidation required that schools built, maintained, staffed, and attended by local citizens be closed. In their stead, new "better schools" would be built often miles away in another town, village, or city. Reform legislation passed concurrently with the consolidation movement lengthened the school term, raised teacher salaries, increased minimum certification requirements, and provided for the transport of children living beyond walking distance (two miles) (Bond, 1958; Danbom, 1979).

Thus, in addition to giving up a treasured cornerstone of their society, Mississippians faced new taxes to lengthen the school term, build educational edifices, and fund pupil transportation. The combination proved too much for many to bear. Several outraged citizens burned schools; others shot, stabbed, or beat school officials (Bond, 1958).[1]

Localism in education died hard in Mississippi, yet Bond and his supporters made huge strides in consolidating the state's rural schools. By 1925, two out of three rural white pupils attended consolidated schools. As early as 1909, consolidation supporters recognized the paramount importance of pupil transportation in their educational program. In his initial call for consolidation in 1909, J.N. Powers concluded that

> The success of the consolidated school depends in very large measure upon transportation. If the transportation is safe, comfortable, rapid, and in the charge of men of high character, no troubles result from it. (*Biennial Report and Recommendations of the State Superintendent of Public Education, 1909–1910 and 1910–1911*, p. 6).

Mississippi law required that transportation be provided free of charge to any child living farther than two miles from school. Thus, the exponential growth of consolidated schools from 2 in 1910 to 862 in 1925 required an equally explosive growth in the number of children transported to school. The inaugural report on consolidation submitted by Powers featured a photograph of a typical "school wagon on [the] way home." Pulled by a sturdy-looking team of horses, the "transportation wagon" afforded its youthful passengers a mode of transport as well as protection from "the danger of those offences to decency and good morals, so common on the road going to and from school." Slowly over the next decade automobiles and trucks customized for pupil transportation began to replace horse-drawn wagons (*Biennial Report and Recommendations of the State*

Superintendent of Public Education, 1909–10 and 1910–11, 1911; Biennial Report of State Superintendent of Education, 1923–25; Danbom, 1979; Link, 1986; O'Shea, 1924).[2]

The 1924 law empowered local school boards to award transportation contracts to the lowest "responsible bid." The extent of rules and regulations went no further than requiring buses to come to a complete stop at all rail crossings. The only other provisions dictated that all students living beyond a two-mile radius of the school building were to be picked up by bus or wagon no farther than a mile and a half from their residence. The laxity of state safety regulations and requirements coupled with the embryonic state of Mississippi's roadways produced in the early years of school bus travel an almost frontier air of excitement and automobile adventure (O'Shea, 1924).

Travis Moore Gray experienced those years as both driver and student. He drove the first school bus commissioned in Itawamba County. While still a student at the county's agricultural high school in Fulton, Travis drove a contraption that brings new meaning to the term "custom model."

> My first truck was a 1926 Chevy. I had a shop man to build it. Built for $50. Didn't have a windshield, just a chassis. Dual wheels hadn't been invented. Just single wheels. No front brakes. The rear brakes was just a band around the hub. Open for the weather and mud to splash it, so you can imagine they didn't last very long. (Moore Gray, personal interview, April 1995)

With a wooden top and oiled canvas sides, Travis's bus was not without its amenities, but safety and comfort were definitely not among them. Travis and his father offered bus service for approximately 20 children in rural Itawamba County for $50 a month. While the elder Gray purchased the vehicle and petitioned for the county route, sixteen-year-old Travis drove the bulk of the time. Because, after arriving at his last stop, Fulton's Agricultural High School, Travis Gray the bus driver became Travis Gray the student, it made sense for the younger Gray to drive the route. Additionally, the elder Gray was fifty years old when he first learned to drive an automobile, and, according to his son, "Really nobody that never learned to drive until they were fifty years old really learned to drive good" (Moore Gray, personal interview, April 1995).

The Grays provided the truck, gas, oil, and were responsible for all repairs and maintenance. This arrangement, as well as financially strapped Itawamba County's penchant for issuing the Grays a warrant in lieu of cash payment, was standard practice throughout Mississippi in the 20s and 30s. Payment in county-backed warrants that were tantamount to I.O.U.'s provided no end of frustration for the Grays and other rural bus operators. Banks rarely paid face value on the county notes, and Travis and his father often had trouble finding financial institutions or individuals even willing to purchase the bonds at less than face value.

During a particularly hard time in the spring of 1927, Travis discovered that the local banks "wouldn't even discount 'em," and the Grays searched for weeks before finding a businessman in Mantachie, Mississippi, who would accept the bonds at a 6 percent discount. Thus, for three months they were paid $47 for their services, which had been originally contracted at $50. From 1931 to 1935, the state of Mississippi failed to pay a million dollars in "outstanding obligations to teachers' salaries and school bus drivers' contracts." The paucity of funds statewide forced teachers in 1935 to continue, in the words of the State Superintendent, "to make the same heroic effort they had been making since the beginning of the depression" (*Biennial Report of the State Superintendent of Public Education, 1933–35*; Moore Gray, personal interview, April 1995).

In addition to the financial uncertainty involved in accepting school contracts from impoverished districts, bus drivers throughout the state faced a constant battle for survival aboard Mississippi's notoriously poor rural roads. Many schools such as Humphreys County's consolidated school employed "rainy day schedules" to ensure safe transportation of its students across sodden roads. In cases of heavy rainfall, the school board deemed the area's roads impassable and extremely dangerous, especially at night. Thus, school officials released school early when wet conditions prevailed to ensure that the "busses [could] get safely home before dark." Dorothy Gregg recalled with a sense of nostalgia the delight she and her classmates enjoyed during such holidays, which occurred frequently during the 1920s. What in remembrance seems somewhat quaint and romantic, in reality constituted a nearly constant state of roadside peril for thousands of the state's pupils and bus drivers.[3]

Travis Gray encountered more than his share of rough roads along his route in the hills of eastern Mississippi. He always carried chains and relied on the labor of one of his passengers regularly on his daily trek. Together Gray and his erstwhile assistant worked out a system.

> There was no improved roads, none. Wasn't a rock on any of 'em around here. And when the road was pretty wet we had to have chains on the truck. I picked up one boy in Greenwood. He helped me a lot. When we'd get up to the highway, we'd stop and take those chains off, wash our hands in a mud puddle, and go on to school. (Moore Gray, personal interview, April 1995)

This was the Itawamba's bus driver's *normal* routine. When regularly presented with extremely poor road conditions, Gray and other early Mississippi bus drivers improvised, adapted to the situation, and overcame the obstacles, arriving safely to school almost without exception.

> Sometimes the roads got pretty bad. I remember we got stuck one time, had the chains on. I had a log chain in the truck, probably 12–15 feet long. I just laced that through my chain back and forth 'til I got it all in there—just a knot. Whenever it hit, it come over. The truck would move. Whenever it hit, the truck would move. We got out. I bumped on up to the highway which wasn't more than a quarter of a mile. Took our chains off. (Moore Gray, personal interview, April 1995)

Throughout Mississippi in the 1920s, most indicators of educational progress "bumped on up" along with increased access to and use of motorized pupil transportation. The standard school term increased from 115 to 165 days by 1930. Attendance at all educational levels increased, with the most dramatic increase in upper-level high school enrollment. High school enrollment rocketed from 10,000 students in 1915 to 45,000 by the 1931 term. From 1920 to 1925 the number of high schools in the state doubled. At all levels, enrollment and daily attendance figures rose steadily. From 1901 to 1935 black school enrollment increased 152 percent, white 188 percent. Average daily attendance, a greater indicator of improvements in pupil transportation, increased 208 percent for black and 250 percent for white Mississippi children (*Biennial Report of the State Superintendent of Education, 1933–35; Biennial Report of the State Superintendent of Public Education, 1901–02 and 1902–03,* 1904).

A number of factors explain the growth in both black and white enrollment and daily attendance. Pupil transportation contributed not only to the increase in average daily attendance figures but helped explain the disparity between the rate of improvement enjoyed by black and white Mississippi schools. In observing the truly "unequal" status of Mississippi's and other southern states' educational systems, T. J. Woofter (1934) concluded, "The transportation of pupils to consolidated schools which has progressed so rapidly in white districts has been extended to a negligible number of colored districts." Thus, in the Deep South in 1930, 350,000 white pupils rode busses daily, but only 2,000 blacks were similarly transported. Native Mississippian Richard Wright succinctly summarized the plight for the state's African American population, "Busses are furnished for many white children, but rarely for ours" (Wright, 1941).

During the era of Reconstruction, Mississippi created a system of public schools. From its inception the system had been both separate and unequal. Mississippi chronically underfunded and understaffed schools designated for its black citizens. Black Mississippians continued to struggle for a more equal educational footing into the twentieth century.

Overall, educational indices indicate that the state's black schools improved in the decades preceding World War II. More black children attended at least a few years of school. Yet, for the overwhelming majority of the state's rural black population, that educational experience remained rudimentary at best. In *Twelve Million Black Voices*, Richard Wright powerfully depicted the plight of education among Mississippi's destitute agrarian class.

> Sometimes there is a weather-worn, pine-built schoolhouse for our children, but even if the school were open for the full term our children would not have the time to go. We cannot let them leave the fields when cotton is waiting to be picked. When the time comes to break the sod, the sod must be broken; when the time comes to plant the seeds, the seeds must be planted;

and when the time comes to loosen the red clay from about the bright green stalks of the cotton plants, that, too, must be done even if it is September and school is open. Hunger is the punishment if we violate the laws of Queen Cotton. The seasons of the year form the mold that shapes our lives, and who can change the seasons? (Wright, 1941)

Even when the seasons and white landlords permitted black children to attend school, the physical hardship entailed in reaching that battered one-room schoolhouse proved more than a little daunting. According to Wright, "The distances walked are so legendary that often the measure of a black man's desire to obtain an education is gauged by the number of miles he declares he walked to school when a child" (Wright, 1941).

Hundreds of African American boys and girls made the daily trek across rain-swollen creeks and through muddy fields to school. Sadie Randolph walked 4 miles each way to attend her Bolivar County school. Maggie Reed covered 12 miles round trip from home to school. Compounding the hardship of distance was the rain and chill which accompanied the limited school term. Mississippi's rural black schools convened only during the agricultural off-season, usually 3 to 5 months from late fall to early spring, when black farm labor was not essential. Seventeen-year-old Charles Webster expressed the frustration felt by many black farm youths.

I'm just getting tired of trying to go to school. When it's warm enough to walk, you got to stay out and work on the farm, and when all the farm work is done, it starts being cold and rainy. (Johnson, 1941, pp. 8, 113–114)

During the 1933–34 school year, 118,441 white children rode to school daily. This represented 51 percent of the daily attendance among white children and a huge commitment to pupil transportation. Four thousand seven hundred seventy-eight bus routes covering 38,212 miles of road took each child an average of 8 miles daily to and from school. This enormous undertaking cost an average of $1.87 per pupil, per month, accounting for nearly one-fifth of school expenditures (O'Shea, 1925).

Despite the Department of Education's reports to the contrary, the majority of Mississippi children traveled to school in the traditional manner; they either walked or rode in mule and horse-drawn carts. Even in the mid-thirties, horses and mules continued to service nearly one-tenth of the state's "bus" routes. Second, and more importantly, the state superintendent's office kept no record of black children transported to school. The state's actual percentage of bus-riding children stood at 26 percent when *all* the state's children were considered. In 1924, the *O'Shea Report* on Mississippi educational progress authorized by governor Henry Whitfield found that only "some" of the state's consolidated black schools in 1924 had even the most basic "transportation facilities." Little changed in the decade following O'Shea's study (*Biennial Report of the State Superintendent of Public Education, 1935–37*, p. 32).

The disparity inherent in Mississippi's apartheid educational system manifested itself in the paucity of transportation allotments for the state's black children. Further, financial constraints clearly played a role in determining the extent to which a school district, white or black, implemented a comprehensive transportation schedule. Per-capita spending for white pupils always exceeded that for black students. The beginning of consolidation exaggerated that injustice.

Taking just one county as an example reveals the gap between Mississippi's commitment to black and white education. The 1909 annual report issued by State Superintendent J. N. Powers sounded the initial call for a statewide program of rural school consolidation. That same year Sharkey County residents spent $16 per white and $10 per black pupil. White teachers in the county system made $42 per month on average versus $30 a month for their black counterparts. A racial gap existed in 1909; consolidation turned the gap into a crevasse (*Biennial Report of the State Superintendent of Education, 1907–09; Biennial Report of the State Superintendent of Education, 1923–25*).

Sharkey County heeded the state superintendent's call for consolidation. In the 15 years following the start of the movement to consolidate the number of schools in the county, the number dropped from 56 to 24. The number of white schools diminished precipitously from 24 to 7. The number of black schools fell less sharply from 32 to 17. The most striking change in the first 15 years of Sharkey's school consolidation, however, came in the expanding chasm between the monetary support allotted to black and white schools. By 1924 the county deemed the education of each white student worth $116, a 625 percent increase over 1909. Meanwhile Sharkey County spent a paltry $6.70 monthly for the education of each black student, just two-thirds what the county spent per black pupil 15 years previously (*Biennial Report of the State Superintendent of Education, 1907–09; Biennial Report of the State Superintendent of Education, 1923–25*).

Sharkey County teacher salaries further demonstrate not only the county's history of neglect of black educators but the relative widening of the salary gap between white and black instructors. Sharkey County white teachers saw their monthly compensation increase from $42 to $131. Black teachers' pay increased from 1909's $30 a month to $49 monthly in 1924. Black teachers went from an average salary approximately three-fourths of the white scale to an incredible one-third of a white salary. Instead of ameliorating the disparity between the quality of black and white schools, education reforms, foremost among them the school consolidation movement, increased the chasm between white and black access to quality education (*Biennial Report of the State Superintendent of Education, 1907–09; Biennial Report of the State Superintendent of Education, 1923–25*).

The state of black education in Mississippi showed little improvement over the next ten years, and in many respects, the conditions under which black Mississippians attempted to learn deteriorated. During the next decade, black districts often found themselves unable to manage the financial burdens of consolidation and transportation. The State Department of Public Education estimated that, on average, transportation costs accounted for 18 percent of school costs during the 1933–34 term. Black children paid dearly to support this new slice from the tax-base pie. The neglect of the state's black institutions reached new levels of criminality during the Depression. In 1937 the state superintendent's report contained a table comparing teachers' salaries from 1890 and 1937. The superintendent found it "interesting to note that the salaries of Negro teachers are practically the same today in Mississippi as they were 47 years ago." In fact, the average salary for black teachers in the

21 counties providing statistics increased only 61 cents from 1890 to 1937. The average white teacher's salary doubled during the same half-century of "progressive" educational reform (*Biennial Report of the Superintendent of Public Education, 1935–37*).

Poor white districts stretched across the state's rural hinterland faced similarly daunting fiduciary obstacles when they attempted to transport pupils to new consolidated schools. The previous biennial report warned of the prohibitive cost of transportation for the state's rising tide of white consolidated schools. The state superintendent's warning that "the cost [of transportation] is frequently so great as to interfere seriously with the financing of the teaching" certainly did bode ill for those undertaking efforts to initiate bus transportation in chronically impoverished black and white rural school districts. Thus, black school districts operated along the thin line between the twin confines of local poverty and state-level neglect, but both races faced the new demands of the consolidation movement woefully underfunded (*Biennial Report of the State Superintendent of Education, 1933–35*).

What role did relative prosperity of counties play in determining access to school transportation? Which was a stronger determinant, race or wealth? School transportation and attendance figures offer a window onto the interplay in Mississippi of the historical trinity of race-class-gender. The percentage of white students transported varied considerably from county to county and in the different subregions of the state.

According to the 1930 United States Census, Tunica County and Itawamba County resembled one another in numerous ways. Both counties contained no urban centers. They each supported nearly identical populations, 18,225 in Itawamba and 21,233 in Tunica, in areas roughly the same size. The racial composition of each of these mid-sized, rural counties, however, differed markedly. Tunica County schools were 80 percent black, Itawamba's nearly 95 percent white. Tunica lay in the state's wealthiest agricultural region, the Yazoo-Mississippi Delta region. Located in the rolling hills of the state's agriculturally poorer, northeastern section, Itawamba County in the words of a longtime resident, "never had any money" (Moore Gray, personal interview, April 1995).

During the 1933–34 school year Itawamba County transported 1,995 students daily, or 49 percent of its daily average attendance for white children. In Tunica, two-thirds of all white children rode busses daily. Tunica County employed no motor vehicles for the transportation of its 2,500 daily black attendees, so in fact less than 13 percent of the county's total school population arrived via bus. Itawamba likewise provided no public-sponsored transportation for its black children, yet they comprised only 5 percent of the county's daily attendance. Forty-six percent of Itawamba's school children arrived by bus (*Biennial Report of the State Superintendent of Education, 1933–35*).

Throughout the richest and blackest single section of the state, the Delta, white children enjoyed greater access to public school transportation than in any other of the state's regional divisions. Sixty-eight percent of Bolivar County's white children and 66 percent of all white kids in Sunflower County rode to school daily. Both were well in excess of the overall state average of 50 percent and exceeded transportation rates in counties in the state's Hill, Piney Wood, and Central Black Belt regions (*Biennial Report of the State Superintendent of Education, 1933–35*).

In the Mississippi Hill Counties identified earlier for the sake of this study as Alcorn, Itawamba, Prentiss, Tippah, and Tishomingo, only Prentiss County, with 51 percent of its white children transported daily, and Itawamba with 49 percent transported came close to reaching the state average. Between 35 to 38 percent of Alcorn, Tippah, and Tishomingo's white children rode the bus daily. Taken as a whole, 42 percent of the Hill Counties' white children traveled to school by bus (*Biennial Report of the State Superintendent of Education, 1933–35*).

White children in the Piney Wood and Central Regions of Mississippi were more likely than Hill whites to ride school buses daily but still less likely than Delta whites. Fifty-six percent of the white children attending school in the Piney Wood counties of Forrest, Jefferson Davis, Lamar, Perry, and Stone arrived daily aboard motor bus. Fifty-nine percent of white children in Leake, Neshoba, Newton, Rankin, and Scott counties located in the state's Central section rode public school busses. A clear distinction lay in the taxable value of land in these two regions when compared to the value of Hill Counties land (*Biennial Report of the State Superintendent of Education, 1933–35*).

American schools have traditionally been supported by property taxes. Higher property values means greater revenue potential for area schools. Pre-World War II Mississippi was one of the nation's most rural, agricultural states. Mississippi's richest agricultural lands lay in the Yazoo-Mississippi Delta region. Therefore, Delta counties were the wealthiest counties in the state. The taxable value of Delta lands dwarfed the tax base present in the rest of the state. A decade of depressed cotton prices did little to alter the economic superiority of the Delta. The State Tax Commission valued Leflore County's 379,474 acres at $14,244,780, or $37.54 per acre in its 1923 assessment. In east central Mississippi, Neshoba County residents farmed lands worth $7.15 an acre, and in the hills of Prentiss County, average land value stood at $11.11 an acre. Leflore's valuation may seem gaudy in comparison to non-Delta counties, yet the value of Leflore County land seems modest when compared to Delta land in Coahoma County assessed on average by the State Tax Commission at $56.51 per acre (*Biennial Report of the State Tax Commission, 1923–25*).

Under Mississippi's educational apartheid, Delta blacks witnessed in mute horror as the sweat of their brows made their lands some of the most valuable in the nation. The state then devoted the tax revenues garnered from the rich Delta lands not toward the education of the children of black laborers, but to the children of their oppressors. In the Delta, more dollars cared for fewer white children and thus provided the whites of the region with the best educational opportunities in the entire state. Mississippi's criminal neglect of black educational needs magnified the financial advantage residents of the richest section of the state already enjoyed (*Biennial Report of the State Tax Commission, 1923–25*).

State law additionally reinforced the financial advantages afforded to white Delta schools. Counties divided the annual state educational apportionment on the basis of the census of school-aged children. The state legislature doled out the per-capita fund in semiannual disbursements coinciding with the fall and spring school terms. Each county received in the October 1923 allotment, for example, $0.92 per educable child residing within its jurisdiction. In February 1924, each county or district received an additional $1.79 per child from the state's "common school fund" (*Biennial Report of the State Superintendent of Education, 1923–25*).

Coupled with the state's commitment to separate and unequal appropriations for black and white education, the common school system of per-capita allotment greatly favored white Delta children. The state appropriated approximately $2.44 per pupil during the 1933–34 school term. Bolivar County's 35,526 students rated an outlay of over $86,000. Each black child warranted a grant equal to that awarded for each white child. The state made the appropriation in a block grant that the county then dispensed in the manner it deemed best. One might rationally assume that some of this sum went toward educating Bolivar County's 27,000 black children. One might just as correctly assume, however, that the county's leaders spent the lion's share on Bolivar's 8,000 white children. Much like the three-fifths clause in the federal Constitution allocating an inequitable number of congressional representatives to the slave South throughout the antebellum era, the per-capita disbursement of state funds skewed educational opportunity and equity in twentieth-century Mississippi (*Biennial Report of the State Superintendent of Public Education, 1933–35*).

The assessed value of a county's land and the numerical size and racial composition of its student body affected the amount of money any particular Mississippi county provided for education. Pupil transportation and school consolidation required an increased financial commitment for county school boards and citizens. The combination of these factors, valuable lands, and large numbers of black school-aged children favored Delta whites. Delta school boards could count on a more substantial tax base and a large allocation from the state common school fund, which the county could then dispense toward the benefit of its white schools.

Did the number of privately owned motor vehicles or the extent and condition of a county's road and bridge system influence the number of children transported daily to a county's schools? Mississippi's roads varied little from county to county, generally changing only from bad to worse. Private vehicle registrations did vary widely between counties. The relationship between private vehicle registrations and percentage of pupils transported by bus remains unclear. However, it seems that private ownership of vehicles may have impeded both the need and commitment to public pupil transportation at the county level. Hinds County residents registered over 14,000 passenger vehicles in 1930, far and away the highest figure in the state. However, only 26 percent of the county's white pupils traveled to school aboard public transportation, a figure well below the state average. Jackson's city schools contributed 40 percent of the county's total pupil population. While only 50,000 people lived in Jackson, it nevertheless stood as an island of urbanism in a state where over 8 out of 10 residents resided in rural areas. Additionally, many Jackson children lived within two miles of school and thus did not require transportation according to state law. Thus, Hinds County is less than representative of statewide trends (*Fifteenth Census of the United States: 1930 Population, Vol. III, Part 2,* 1932).

Delta counties contained the next highest levels of automobile ownership. The racial composition of Delta counties, on average between 65 to 85 percent black, also presents problems for statewide postulations. Counties in the state's midsection, Rankin, Scott, Leake, Neshoba, and Newton, however, represent a middle ground conducive for intrastate comparisons. These five counties occupied both Mississippi's geographic and demographic middle ground. According to the 1930 Census, Neshoba was the most populous of the five with just over 26,000 residents. Just over 20,000 men and women resided in the least populous of the central counties, Rankin. The demographic profile of the central region's population closely approximated state levels with regard to urban-rural distribution and racial characteristics (*Fifteenth Census of the United States: 1930 Population, Vol. III, Part 2,* 1932).

Residents in each of the five counties enjoyed the same level of automobile ownership, with approximately one automobile for every nine people in each county. Statewide automobile registrations reveal a ratio of one vehicle per eleven people; thus the central region ran slightly higher than the state average.

The state superintendent of education's 1933–35 biennial report reveals a number of interesting shifts, transformations, and changes at play in Mississippi's two-tiered educational puzzle after 25 years of school consolidation and transportation. The 1933–34 school year marked the first term in which the number of white children enrolled (301,552) in school outnumbered the number of black children enrolled (299,160). That same year the number of school-aged black children enumerated in the school census outnumbered whites by nearly 90,000. Eighty percent of eligible white children were enrolled in school, only 65 percent of the state's black children. The final statewide number of note with regard to the school census, daily attendance, represents the truest benchmark for educational access. Forty-seven percent of the state's black children who by law, reason, and right should have been attending school did so on a daily basis. Sixty-two percent of all eligible white children attended the state's schools. On an average day during the 1933–34 term, one would expect to find well over half of all the state's school-age students truant (*Biennial Report of the State Superintendent of Public Education, 1933–35*).

The state supervisor of "Negro Education" concluded his 1935 assessment on the harsh realities of black educational opportunity by announcing these poor daily attendance figures. "Less than half of those who are supposed to be in school are in regular attendance." He continued, however, on an even darker and telling note when he remarked on the low rate of retention among African American children. "By the time the sixth or seventh grades are reached, pupils begin to leave school in large numbers." In fact, 40 percent of all black children enrolled in Mississippi schools for the 1933–34 term were in the first grade. The state classified 19 percent of whites during the same year as first graders. Taken as a whole, the primary grades 1–3 accounted for two-thirds of black enrollment (*Biennial Report of the State Superintendent of Public Education, 1933–35*).

Whites enjoyed not only greater access to education, they were permitted to reach a much higher level of education. Although the Department of Education's 1933 *Handbook of Information* applauded its own efforts in boosting high school attendance an impressive 872 percent from 1910 to 1931, the state did not make its first effort to accredit black high schools until 1932. The State Board accepted three. By 1934, some apparent "progress" had been made. Fifteen black high schools received state accreditation, and 2 percent of black school children attended the 9th through 12th grades. Placed in comparison to the gains in the number of white high schoolers, these numbers demonstrate not progress but a state-sanctioned program of racially biased neglect. An almost equal number of black and white Mississippians enrolled in the state's public schools in 1933–34. Yet, whites at the 12th grade level outnumbered blacks 15 to 1 (*Biennial Report of the State Superintendent of Public Education, 1933–35;* Mississippi Department of Education, 1933).[4]

Education reforms in the form of school consolidation and its reliance on pupil transportation increased the quality and quantity of Mississippi's educational system. During the first two decades of consolidation, reformers lengthened the average school term for black and white students from 115 to 165 days. White students were still much more likely to attend all of the prescribed days and urban whites even more so. Economic necessity pressured rural Southerners of both races to continue to employ their children in the field, but the number of agricultural child laborers dropped dramatically in the first decades of the twentieth century (Mississippi Department of Education, 1933).

Across the South, farm families became willing and, more importantly, able to send their children to school instead to the fields. In 1900, nearly half of all black boys and a third of all black girls aged ten to fifteen toiled in southern agriculture or industry. Most, 4 out of 5, found employment in agriculture. Meanwhile, one-fifth of rural white boys and only 7 percent of white girls of the same age were similarly members of the labor force. The increase in school enrollments and attendance precipitated a steady decline in these figures so that by 1920 only 21.8% of black children under the age of fifteen labored instead of learned, and 10 years later 16 percent of African American youths were in the southern labor force. A similar reduction in the number of working children occurred in Mississippi during this era. The 1940 Census enumerated only 15,213 Mississippians under the age of fifteen as members of the state's full-time labor force. Racial disparity continued, however, for well over

7 out of 10 of those working children were African American boys and girls (Anderson, 1988).

Perhaps more telling than the rise in school enrollments and the subsequent decline in laboring children in considering the merits of post-World War I educational reform is the success of the crusade against illiteracy. Southern reformers clearly envisioned compulsory attendance and school consolidation as means of attacking the shameful state of adult literacy. When consolidation and pupil transportation began in 1910, 20 percent of all Mississippians over the age of ten could not read or write. Over a quarter of a million black Mississippians, fully 35 percent of the African American adult population, was illiterate. For generations a higher rate of adult illiteracy reigned across the South, and Mississippi, in particular, than in the rest of the nation. In 1910, 35 percent of illiterates paled in comparison to the 49 percent figure for Mississippi blacks in 1900 or the 60 percent rate of illiteracy among the state's African American majority in 1890. Mississippi educational, civic, and religious leaders worked tirelessly for literacy in the years before World War I. Post-war reformers continued the struggle by enacting compulsory attendance laws and engaging in consolidation plans. Literacy advocates envisioned motor vehicle transportation as playing an integral part in their campaign (Bureau of the Census, 1918).

In each of the next two decades of the twentieth century, Mississippians made great inroads in conquering the dark cloud of illiteracy which had hung over the state for generations. In 1920, the illiteracy rate stood at 17.2 percent, and by 1930 the number of illiterate Mississippians fell to just 13 percent of the adult population. Clearly, increases in daily attendance, school retention, and the number of students advancing to secondary grade levels affected the drop in illiteracy.

A pupil's race clearly influenced his or her access to motor vehicle student transportation and, thus, the positive effect of bussing and consolidation on rural education. Inequity existed among the state's regions according to the assessed property value. Other factors such as the amount of personal automobile ownership among county residents and the extent and condition of the county's road and bridge infrastructure played either an ambiguous or ineffectual role in determining a county's commitment to consolidation and pupil transportation. It is clear, however, that those counties employing motor vehicle transportation for their student populations earlier and more extensively enjoyed higher enrollment, attendance, and retention rates. Overall, after a decade of widespread use of motor bus transportation to consolidated rural and urban schools, more Mississippians of both races attended school and learned at least the rudimentary skills of literacy.

Educational "modernization" came unevenly to the Magnolia State. Black teachers taught more children for less pay in facilities equipped well below the level of the average white school. Far fewer black Mississippi children advanced to high school than their white peers did, while far more adult African American Mississippians remained illiterate than adult whites. In many respects, the racial gap widened during the first decades of the consolidation movement. The blessings of the automobile age remained mixed for Jim Crow's Mississippi.

Endnotes

[1] The principal of East Lincoln Consolidated School, A. K. Watkins, was shot and killed shortly after the opening of the school. His successor, Ike Russell, was stabbed the next year and nearly died.

[2] Link claims that not until the 1920s did pupil transportation in rural Virginia begin to become feasible with the arrival of "hard-surfaced highways and the rumbling presence of school buses."

[3] Dorothy Elizabeth Thornton Hamberlin Gregg, in *Memories of Mississippi Collection*, Special Collections, J.D. Williams Library, University of Mississippi.

[4] The school census identified 299,160 black and 301,552 white students for the 1933–34 school term. That same year 10,252 white students enrolled in the twelfth grade while only 687 black students were members of 1934's Senior Class.

References

Anderson, J. D. (1988). *The education of blacks in the south, 1860–1935*. Chapel Hill, NC: University of North Carolina Press.

Biennial report and recommendations of the state superintendent of public education, 1909–10 and 1910–11. (1911). Jackson.

Biennial report of the state superintendent of public education, 1901–02 and 1902–03. (1904). Nashville, TN: Brandon.

Biennial report of the state superintendent of public education, 1923–25.

Biennial report of the state superintendent of public education, 1933–35.

Biennial report of the state superintendent of public education, 1935–37.

Bond, W. F. (1958). *I had a friend: An autobiography* (pp. 95–97). Kansas City, MO: E.L. Mendenhall.

Brownwell, B. A. (1975). *The urban ethos in the south* (pp. 1–38). Baton Rouge: Louisiana State University Press.

Bureau of the Census. (1918). *Negro Population, 1790–1915.* Washington, DC: Government Printing Office.

Danbom, D. B. (1979). *The resisted revolution: Urban America and the industrialization of agriculture, 1900–1930.* Ames, IA: The Iowa State University Press.

Fifteenth census of the United States: 1930 population, vol. III, part 2. (1932). Washington, DC: Government Printing Office.

Johnson, C. S. (1941). *Growing up in the black belt: Negro youth in the rural south.* Washington, DC: The American Council on Education.

Keith, J. (1995). *Country people in the new south: Tennessee's upper Cumberland* (p. 108). Chapel Hill: University of North Carolina Press.

Link, W. A. (1986). *A hard country and a lonely place: Schooling, society, and reform in rural Virginia, 1870–1920* (pp. 139–144). Chapel Hill, NC: University of North Carolina Press.

Mississippi Department of Education. (1933). *Handbook of information.*

O'Shea, M. V. (1925a). *Public education in Mississippi.* Jackson, MS: Jackson.

——— (1925b). *School Laws of the State of Mississippi, 1924.*

Tindall, G. B. (1967). *The emergence of the new south, 1913–1945* (pp. 254–284). Baton Rouge: Louisiana State University Press.

Woofter, T. J. Jr. (1934). The status of racial and ethnic groups. In President's Research Committee on Social Trends, *Recent social trends in the United States* (p. 588). New York: Whittelsey House, McGraw-Hill.

Wright, R. (1941). *Twelve million black voices: A folk history of the Negro in the United States.* New York: Viking.

Epilogue

David M. Callejo Pérez,
Stephen M. Fain, Judith J. Slater

So far as we know, the tiny fragments of the universe embodied in man are the only centers of thought and responsibility in the visible world. If that be so, the appearance of the human mind has been so far the ultimate stage in the awakening of the world, and all that has gone before, the striving of a myriad centres that have taken the risks of living and believing, seem to have all been pursuing, along rival lines the aim now achieved by us up to this point. They are all akin to us. For all these centres-those which led up to our own existence and the far more numerous others which produced different lines for which many are extinct-may be seen engaged in the same endeavor towards ultimate liberation. (Polanyi, 1962, p. 405)

The curriculum field and the modern school are very much products of the twentieth century. The origins can be found in mechanical work, influenced greatly by science. Science was the basis of the efficiency movements that propelled the development of modern industry, and this movement was revered by many who saw it as the appropriate model for the development of the public school and the public school system of a nation which was growing in wealth and power. The centrality of science in the modern educational mind-set controlled the schools even beyond the challenge posed by Joseph Schwab in 1970. More than 30 years later we are confronting the dilemma resulting from the collision of forces advocating efficiency and those championing the cause of the individual.

This collection of essays advocates for the individual by making the case that ultimately school is a place shaped more by the designs of persons than of buildings. The essays, when taken together, demonstrate that the structural elements that define the dimensions of any given space go beyond the physical and the temporal. The space seen as school by the teacher and the learner is supported by tensions resulting from personal and collective experiences, and shaped by opportunities provided for voices to be heard and voices to be silent, for choices to be made by individuals and groups and from the synergy resulting from all of these factors at a particular time in the lives of all participants. This space is powerful in that it is fueled by human potential and defined by the perception of the individual.

The purpose which drew the authors of the various chapters in this text together will be met when the reader understands that this collection is not against the forces of science in curriculum making, teaching, or any other aspect of school and schooling. Rather, the purpose of this collection is to open conversations with persons interested in curriculum making and teaching and learning, which includes the issue of working at the act of creating the spaces and places which release human potential and nurture the human spirit.

Reference

Polanyi, M. (1962). *Personal knowledge: Towards a post-critical philosophy*. Chicago: The University of Chicago Press.

Contributors

DONNA L. ADAIR BREAULT is an assistant professor of graduate curriculum studies at Illinois State University. Her research primarily focuses on Deweyan inquiry and its implications for public intellectualism. Donna is co-editor of the journal, *The Sophist's Bane* and co-editor for an upcoming Kappa Delta Pi book, *The Educative Experience: Teachers Reflect on the Writings of John Dewey*. Donna's recent publications include *"Brutal Compassion: A Requiem,"* an Educational Studies article responding to 9-11 and *"Flesh and Stone: The Aesthetics of Public Space and Its Implications for Professional Artistry"* (in press) for *Educational Theory*.

MICHAEL W. APPLE is John Bascom Professor of Curriculum and Instruction and Educational Policy Studies at the University of Wisconsin, Madison. The recipient of both the UCLA Medal for Outstanding Academic Achievement and a Lifetime Achievement Award from the American Educational Research Association, he has written extensively on the relationship between education and power. Among his recent books are *Official Knowledge* (2000), *Educating the "Right" Way: Markets, Standards, God, and Inequality* (2001), and *The State and the Policy of Knowledge* (2003).

DAVID M. CALLEJO PÉREZ is an assistant professor of Curriculum Studies and Culture at the University of Nebraska-Lincoln. His work addresses the role of culture, politics, history, and identity in schools and curriculum. He is the author of *Southern Hospitality* (2001) and is working on *The Story of a School* (2004). Callejo Pérez has also written several articles on identity and education in Cuba and rural America.

CHERYL J. CRAIG is an Associate Professor in the Department of Curriculum and Instruction at the University of Houston where she coordinates the Instructional Studies and Teacher Education Program. Craig's research interests are in teachers' knowledge, the shaping effects of contexts, and narrative inquiry as a research method. She is the author of *Narrative Inquiries of School Reform: Storied Lives, Storied Landscapes, Storied Metaphors* (Information Age Publishing, 2003).

STEPHEN M. FAIN teaches courses in curriculum history and theory at Florida International University where he is also a Fellow in the Honors College. His interests include school improvement and curriculum development. Professor Fain is co-editor of *The Freirean Legacy: Education for Social Justice*. He is a past president of the American Association for Teaching and Curriculum.

COREY LESSEIG has been on the faculty at Waycross College since 1997, where he currently serves as an Associate Professor of History and Minority Advising Program Coordinator. He received his Ph.D. in History from the University of Mississippi. His dissertation explored the role of automobile technology in shaping early twentieth century southern society. *Automobility: Social Change in the American South, 1909-1939* was published by Routledge Press in 2001. Corey, his wife, Lisa, and daughters Camille, Catherine, and Carolyn reside in Blackshear, Georgia.

MARGARET MACINTYRE LATTA is currently an assistant professor at the University of Nebraska-Lincoln. She completed her Ph.D. at the University of Calgary, Alberta, Canada in 2000. Publications include *The Possibilities of Play in the Classroom: On the Power of Aesthetic Experience in Teaching, Learning, and Researching* (2001), New York: Peter Lang, and *Seeking Fragility's Presence, Philosophy of Education Yearbook* (2002), Urban: University of Illinois.

WILLIAM H. SCHUBERT is Professor of Education and Coordinator of Graduate Curriculum Studies at the University of Illinois at Chicago, where he has been for over 25 years. Former vice-president of the American Educational Research Association and president of the Society of Education, he has published 200 articles and chapters and 9 books, including *Curriculum: Perspective, Paradigm and Possibility; Reflections from the Heart of Educational Inquiry; Teacher Lore; The*

American Curriculum; Turning Points in Curriculum; and *Curriculum Books: The First Hundred Years.*

JUDITH J. SLATER is Professor of Education at Florida International University where she teaches courses in curriculum theory evaluation and organizational culture. She is internationally recognized for her work in staff development. Dr. Slater is the author of *Anatomy of a Collaboration: A College of Education—Public School Partnership,* by Garland Press, as well as co-author and editor of four other books.

P. BRUCE UHRMACHER is an associate professor of education and division director of Educational Leadership: School and Community at the College of Education, University of Denver. Uhrmacher is the book review editor of the *International Journal of Leadership in Education,* past president of the American Association of Teaching and Curriculum, and a writer about Waldorf schools since the late 1980s.

Studies in the Postmodern Theory of Education

General Editors
Joe L. Kincheloe & Shirley R. Steinberg

Counterpoints publishes the most compelling and imaginative books being written in education today. Grounded on the theoretical advances in criticalism, feminism, and postmodernism in the last two decades of the twentieth century, Counterpoints engages the meaning of these innovations in various forms of educational expression. Committed to the proposition that theoretical literature should be accessible to a variety of audiences, the series insists that its authors avoid esoteric and jargonistic languages that transform educational scholarship into an elite discourse for the initiated. Scholarly work matters only to the degree it affects consciousness and practice at multiple sites. Counterpoints' editorial policy is based on these principles and the ability of scholars to break new ground, to open new conversations, to go where educators have never gone before.

For additional information about this series or for the submission of manuscripts, please contact:

> Joe L. Kincheloe & Shirley R. Steinberg
> c/o Peter Lang Publishing, Inc.
> 275 Seventh Avenue, 28th floor
> New York, New York 10001

To order other books in this series, please contact our Customer Service Department:

> (800) 770-LANG (within the U.S.)
> (212) 647-7706 (outside the U.S.)
> (212) 647-7707 FAX

Or browse online by series:

> www.peterlangusa.com